D0852827

Greenhill
Books

Heydrich

'An impressive mix of psychological analysis, biography and historical reporting . . . Dederichs descends into Heydrich's personal abyss and describes it in a captivating and intelligible manner while not rejecting the scientific approach.'

Die Rheinische

'With his comprehensive biography, Mario R Dederichs lays bare for the first time the life of the man who symbolizes the evil of the Third Reich. He has relied not only on written sources, but has done his own research, interviewed eye-witnesses and visited the various venues. The result is a fascinating mix of biography, psychological analysis and historical reporting.'

Stern

'The central question of the biography is how this man came to be an embodiment of evil. Dederichs approaches the person of Reinhard Heydrich through meticulous research and eye-witness interviews. His journalist's pen has made the life of the Gestapo-chief into a gripping story. At the same time, the text withstands scientific scrutiny thanks to its detailed evaluation of sources.'

Main Echo

'This well-researched book . . . captivates the reader by its perceptive content and the clarity of the language. As conclusive as it all is, the most shocking chapter is the last, in which the author shows how Heydrich remains, or has become again, a hero to be honoured in the German Federal Republic.'

Recklinghaeuser Zeitung

'Heydrich . . . who was this man? A question which journalist Mario R Dederichs has investigated thoroughly in this factual popular biography, tracing out an historical picture of the Third Reich to make one shudder.'

Buecherschau, Vienna

'Dederichs has shed light on previously poorly researched areas of Heydrich's life.'

Das Parlament

Heydrich

The Face of Evil

Mario R. Dederichs

Translated by Geoffrey Brooks

Greenhill Books, London
MBI Publishing, St Paul

Greenhill
Books

Heydrich
The Face of Evil

First published in 2006 by Greenhill Books/Lionel Leventhal Ltd
Park House, 1 Russell Gardens, London NW11 9NN
and
MBI Publishing Co.
Galtier Plaza, Suite 200, 380 Jackson Street, St Paul, MN 55101-3885, USA

Copyright © Piper Verlag GmbH, München 2005
Translation © Lionel Leventhal Ltd 2006
Preface © Teja Fiedler 2006

All rights reserved. No part of this publication may be reproduced, stored in or introduced into
a retrieval system, or transmitted, in any form, or by any means (electronic, mechanical, photo-
copying, recording or otherwise), without the prior written permission of the publisher. Any
person who does any unauthorised act in relation to this publication may be liable to criminal
prosecution and civil claims for damages.

British Library Cataloguing-in Publication Data

Dederichs, Mario R., 1949–
Heydrich : the face of evil
1. Heydrich, Reinhard, 1904–1942
2. Nazis – Germany – Biography
3. Germany – Politics and government – 1933–1945
I.Title
943'.086'092

ISBN-13: 978-1-85367-686-4
ISBN-10: 1-85367-686-1

Library of Congress Cataloging-in Publication Data available

For more information on our books, please visit www.greenhillbooks.com,
email sales@greenhillbooks.com, or telephone us within the UK on 020 8458 6314. You can
also write to us at the above London address.

Edited and typeset by Chris Harris
Printed and bound in Great Britain by
Creative Print and Design Group, Ebbw Vale, Wales

Contents

Preface		7
Foreword		9
Introduction		11
1	The Naval Officer and the Nazis 1904–1932	21
2	Reinhard Heydrich's Seizure of Power 1933–1940	59
3	Planning to Exterminate the Jews 1938–1942	85
4	The Military Governor 1941–1942	121
5	The Assassination 1942	141
6	The Man with the Iron Heart and the Unregenerates 1942 to the Present	161
Notes		191
Appendix A: Chronology of Genocide		207
Appendix B: Biographical Notes		215
Bibliography		221
Index		229

Preface

The *Frankfurter Allgemeine Zeitung* called it a 'very convincing biography'. Eberhard Jäckel, one of Germany's foremost scholars in contemporary history, declared himself 'deeply impressed by this most thorough research' and stated, 'This is the best Heydrich biography until now.' As the colleague and friend of Mario Dederichs who had the bittersweet honour of completing this book, I felt of course very rewarded by and grateful for these and other positive reviews. I also felt proud for Mario that the American physician and professor Ray J. Defalque from Birmingham, Alabama, went out of his way to get hold of the German edition. Professor Defalque found in the chapter about Heydrich's death 'the medical details fascinating, especially the interview of Doctor Honek, who administered Heydrich's anaesthesia', and he used them to plug some gaps in his own research about surgery during World War II. But most moving was the reaction of the Haus der Wannsee-Konferenz in Berlin. This institution runs the museum and memorial site at the place where in 1942 at the infamous 'Wannsee meeting' Heydrich initiated the methodical extermination of the Jewish people. 'We all read with great enthusiasm and interest the biography your husband has composed,' wrote the director of the Haus der Wannsee-Konferenz to Mario's widow, who had sent him her husband's research papers and a handwritten note together with a copy of the book. Now *Heydrich: The Face of Evil,* together with the other materials, is on display in its own case at the museum as an important contribution to the understanding of one of the darkest chapters in German history.

Given the great admiration and sympathy Mario Dederichs always had for the Anglo-Saxon world – as a former correspondent in London and Washington he spoke and wrote English perfectly – I am sure that my late colleague would truly appreciate seeing his book published in the language he loved so dearly.

Teja Fiedler, 2006

Foreword

Mario R. Dederichs (1949–2003) was a correspondent for *Stern* magazine in Washington, Moscow and Bonn. He spent much of his life investigating the phenomenon of the Third Reich in the attempt to understand how such a barbarity was possible in central Europe in the enlightened twentieth century. It was his deep conviction that personalities such as Heydrich can surface in any society at any time, and his aim was to combat the drift in Germany towards forgetting and repressing that epoch. As a consequence of his interest, he embarked upon a series for *Stern* magazine entitled *Heydrich – Die Macht des Bösen* (The Power of Evil) which appeared in the autumn of 2002 and was hailed as a great success. This led to his manuscript *Heydrich – Das Gesicht des Bösen* (The Face of Evil) published in 2005 by Piper Verlag of Munich, and of which this present volume is the English-language translation. A substantial part of the work had been drafted when Dederichs died in November 2003. Teja Fiedler, a colleague and friend of long standing, undertook the completion of the work with the help of Dr Angelika Franz.

Heydrich's son Heider and his daughter Marte Beyer were firmly opposed to holding any extensive conversations about their father. They considered themselves 'not competent' to speak. The archive offices of his home town, Halle (Saale), and Dresden also showed little understanding of the need to declassify all historically relevant documents about Heydrich. Until this is achieved universally, the search for truth about The Man with the Iron Heart will go on.

Piper Verlag, 2005

Introduction

The Face of Evil
1904–1942

It lasted just a moment, but the flickering monochrome celluloid has retained its sharpness over half a century, and a glance from those eyes can still send a chill through the observer. On his way into Prague castle, the tall man in the black uniform of an SS-Obergruppenführer, the peak of his service cap with its silvery death's head pulled low over the forehead, passed a cameraman apparently standing too close to his path. The long oval face remained expressionless, but briefly as he passed the camera he looked into the lens and it captured his look: icy, angry, evil, the eyes of a wolf, unexpectedly hostile. If looks could kill . . .[1]

That short scene from the autumn of 1941, included in the 1985 Czech documentary film *Opus pro smrtihlava* (Opus for the Death's Head), allows one to understand why most contemporaries of Reinhard Tristan Eugen Heydrich feared him. He was distant, contemptuous, cunning and cruel, like 'a young, evil god of death', a 'blond beast' or even 'a devil in

11

human form'. From Adolf Hitler's dark Reich, the Face of Evil stares into our century, and continues to exert its eerie fascination upon us. What lies behind its hostility? Into which bottomless abyss do we peer when we make contact with those eyes? What drove this man to commit his crimes?

The search for the answers began inevitably with a visit to the German Bundesarchiv, the former Berlin Document Centre at an old barracks in the suburb Lichterfelde.[2] Most SS files are kept here. Under the main heading 'Der Reichsführer-SS' and 'SS-Personalhauptamt', one finds a brown cardboard box marked *Personalakte* [Personal Files], and a search therein yields a brown sheet of paper, completed on both sides, headed 'Heydrich, Reinhard' and 'SS No. 10120'. The entries are penned in painstaking small script, barely copiable, and this document contains almost everything which the SS State considered worth knowing about the man Heydrich:

> Entry into NSDAP: 1 June 1931.
> Membership No: 544916
> Joined SS: 14 July 1931 number 10120.
> Date of birth: 7.3.1904
> Place of birth: Halle/Saale
> Promotions and Offices Held: (From) Untersturmführer (10.8.1931) to Obergruppenführer (24.9.1941): Fhr Abt 1c Oberstab RFSS (10.8.1931) (head of department 1c at RFSS Staff): Leiter SD (19.7.1932), Chef SD Hauptamt (undated).

His final positions as head of the Reichssicherheitshauptamt (RSHA) and as acting Reichs-Protektor of Bohemia and Moravia are not listed. In the wrong place, one finds the laconic epitaph: 'Died 4.6.1942. Murdered.' Further details follow:

> Marital Status: m'd 26.12.1931.

> Wife: Lina von Osten (b.) 14.6.1911, Auendorf/Fehmarn.

> Party Member: 1201380. Activity in Party: NSV.

Religion: Cath, believer in God. (Customary declarations for Nazis after leaving the Church).
Offspring: Klaus (b.1933), Heider (b.1934), Silke (b.1939). [The second daughter Marte, born in 1942 after Heydrich's death, is not included.]
Profession or Trade Training: Naval officer.
Military Rank: Ob.Leutn.z.See a.D.
Current Occupation: Chef d. SD-Hauptamtes and SS-Führer.

Employer: ——

Civilian Punishments: ——

SS Punishments: ——

Education Higher Schools: *O-I Abitur*

Knowledge of Languages: English, French, Russian. English and Russian to Interpreter Examination Stage.

Licences: I u 3b, pilot licence A2 and licence for sea navigation.

Ancestry check: Lebensborn.

Party Activities: RFSS and Chief of German Police Inspector of Body Exercises/(Aerobics): Leader Reichs Sports Office – Fencing.

State Positions: Appointed to act for Baron von Neurath handling affairs of the Reichs-Protektor: head of Pruss. Gestapo, head of Bav. Political Police, Pruss. Minister. head Sipo, Pres. IKPK (International Criminal Police Commission). Member of Reichstag (22/Düsseldorf Ost V/36 and VI/38). General of Police (24.9.1941).

Awards: NSDAP Badge in Gold (awarded 30.1.1939). SS-Totenkopf ring, SS honour dagger and Julleuchter: SA Sports Badge in Gold: Olympia Insignia First-Class: Equestrian Sports Badge in Silver: Reichs Sports Badge in Silver.

Military Service: Freikorps, Maercker 1919/1920, three months each year Halle (Orgesch). Reichswehr 91/4 year, telegraphy and signals branch Reichsmarine 30.3.1922 – 31.5.1931.

Rank: Oberleutn.z.S.

Decorations and Awards: Iron Cross, I and II (1940): Front Flights Clasp in Bronze and Silver. Grand Officer Cross of the Order of the Crown of Italy. German Order in Gold (1942).

Other: Award by HM King of Italy with the Grand Officer Cross of the Order of the Crown of Italy on occasion of visit by German police delegation to Italy.

Activities Overseas: Foreign voyages as member of Reichsmarine and other foreign journeys.

All other columns (Reich Army, German Colonies, SA, Hitler Youth, SS schools and especial sporting achievements are blank.)

In academic histories of the Third Reich, Heydrich has largely avoided the spotlight, escaping the attentions of even those who have understood how significant he was in the Nazi apparatus of power and the genocide machinery. His early death contributed greatly to this oversight. Heydrich died in June 1942 as the result of an assassination attempt in Prague. Hailed as a hero of the Nazi movement in the Third Reich for his 'blood sacrifice', when the reckoning came for the major war criminals after 1945, being dead he was forgotten. Plenty has been written about other senior Nazi figures who avoided the gallows: Hitler, Goebbels, Goering, Himmler, the latter being Heydrich's immediate superior and partner in the greatest mass-murders of German history, but fifty years after Heydrich's death, the only generally quoted biography was the 1969 doctorate of Israeli historian Shlomo Aronson, a partial account which tails off in 1935.[3]

Heydrich was passed over until recently by German and American historians. Encouraged by the opening of archives in the east, however, a closer look has been taken at the apparatus he erected: the system of surveillance and informers of the SS-Sicherheitsdienst (SD) and Geheime Staatspolizei (Gestapo), the bureaucracy of discrimination, terror, persecution, deportation and finally extermination, which were grouped up to form the Reichssicherheitshauptamt (RSHA) from existing security organs in 1939. Even if the orders originated from Hitler, often only verbally or in evasively worded documentation, and even if, as head of the SS, Himmler bore the ultimate responsibility for what was done, the research has recognised everywhere the hand and mind of Heydrich.

Heydrich worked best behind the scenes, as befits a secret police or secret service chief, but his manipulation of the strings was such that his orders sometimes extended to those more powerful than himself: forging ahead with 'the wishes of the Führer', he ran roughshod over the waverers and doubters towards the uncompromising, merciless execution of decisions concerning the life and death of millions.

It was Heydrich who planned the integration of a political police force into the Hitler dictatorship as its decisive organ of power. *Schutzhaft*, protective custody in concentration camps, was designed to remove opponents of the regime from circulation. Once war broke out, between September 1939 and November 1941, Heydrich's RSHA [Reich Security Main Office] appointed and ran, first in Poland and then in the USSR, liquidation squads, known as Einsatzgruppen, whose relatively small numbers resulted in a disproportionately enormous toll of victims. The policy of genocide was confirmed in writing at the notorious Wannsee Conference of January 1942, and effective industrial mass-extermination methods at fixed concentration camps replaced the Einsatzgruppen.

Always there was Heydrich, the man of tireless industry and unparalleled zeal, reaping unto himself ever more power which was intended ultimately to bring about a more perfect Third Reich with a better Führer.

And that Führer would be Reinhard Heydrich. The State terrorist Heydrich was active everywhere as motivator, planner and organiser. Hitler praised him for his reputation as 'The Man with the Iron Heart', and never found another who was Heydrich's equal. 'He was always the most active executioner,' the Stuttgart historian Eberhard Jäckel concluded, 'he acted when others wavered.'[4]

British author Alan Burgess, whose history of the Prague assassination appeared in German under the title *Sieben Männer im Morgengrauen* (Seven Men at Daybreak) and was later made into a film in Czechoslovakia, suggested that something was not ticking over correctly in the mind of the Nazi superman:

> Reinhard Heydrich was not what you would call a normal person. Somewhere in the jigsaw a piece was missing, somewhere in the labyrinth of his cerebrum a channel was blocked, some tiny fungus in the yeast added to the basic dough of the personality had not done its job properly, and it was from that yeast that the humanity of the person was supposed to come. He was a man without compassion, without goodness, without mercy, motivated by unscrupulous ambition, a man who had included torture and repression in his daily routine. He sent millions of his fellow humans in utter misery to their deaths and kept a ledger of it all without ever once questioning the rightness of what he was doing.[5]

The Kiel historian Michael Freund was invited to tender an expert opinion to a tribunal hearing the matter of an application by Heydrich's widow, Lina, née von Osten, for a widow's and orphans' pension. Freund was opposed to the grant of the pension on the grounds that Heydrich had been a monster, and in his deposition he attempted to reconcile the assassination victim Heydrich with the mass-murderer Heydrich in the following terms:

> The accusations against Heydrich are determined by the nature, activities and the personality of Heydrich himself. In

natural justice, the event of 27 May 1942 is of the greatest possible significance, for the murdered man was directly responsible for one of the greatest crimes of the 20th century, the murder of millions of Jews and other persons. As to methodology, the crime was thought out and put into gear by a grandiose criminal mind possessed of great talent for organisation. Heydrich was the first person in Old Europe to have knowingly conceived the idea of cleansing Central and Eastern Europe racially by the exterminations of whole peoples, by genocide. He is one of the greatest criminal figures of the Third Reich. Nowhere in the histories of the Third Reich has he been awarded his rightful place. He is a man of outstanding significance, a criminal mind of Luciferic grandeur ... if Heydrich had survived the Third Reich we can say with almost absolute certainty that he would have been hanged at Nuremberg. His death sentence would have belonged among the more convincing judgments of the Nuremberg military tribunal. For a conviction by a German court, there would have been no necessity to draft new statutes under which to try him, for even under the German penal code of the Third Reich he was a murderer. The liquidation of the Jews was neither law, nor was it ever set down in a Führer-Order. What Heydrich did was therefore contrary to the criminal law in force in the Third Reich, murder in the worst sense of the legal definition.[6]

Although the tribunal decided ultimately that this opinion had no bearing on whether Lina Heydrich should receive a widow's pension, it remains as true today as when it was written. The American SS-expert Charles Sydnor confirmed the unique role Heydrich played in Hitler's Reich, and made some striking deductions:

Heydrich was the most capable and energetic of the Nazi exponents of radical racial theory. One could rely on him absolutely to carry out the most brutal orders and most inhuman measures

17

towards achieving Hitler's racial and ideological objectives. An early and accurate assessment describes Heydrich as a figure of average intelligence with a colourless personality lacking originality, whose social abilities and gift of communication were scarcely adequate for a person who exercised comprehensive authority within a major Power.

Although this is true, one must remember that in the Nazi cosmos even a dwarf star – if he was determined enough – could shine brightly, and Heydrich had other characteristics which turned him into an important figure in world history. He shone and, if not outstanding, stood apart from all other figures of the National Socialist era because he used certain abilities which made him appear indispensable and irreplaceable to Hitler and Himmler.

Heydrich had a peculiar combination of administrative acumen, a gift for organisation, pragmatic tenacity and a unique ruthless streak. His phenomenal motivation and industry were powered by unlimited physical and psychic energy. Nobody else in the Nazi hierarchy could keep up with him. If he needed a rest from the burdens of high office for a while, he would indulge his passion for chamber music or the cello, or engage in strenuous activities either on horseback, as a world-class fencer, as an enthusiastic sports aviator or patrol the coast in an Me 109 fighter. All in all, Reinhard Heydrich had the appearance of the many-sided, athletic, prototype Führer of the Nordic New Order. He was Hitler's ideal National Socialist.[7]

Not everybody saw his personality as so clear-cut, however. Eyewitnesses describe his inner conflicts: an ideological hard-liner but cynical of National Socialist practices: a mean-hearted chief but jovial drinking mate: an enemy of humanity but friend of little children: a cold-hearted murderer but musical virtuoso.

The widow of his last chauffeur, SS-Oberscharführer Johannes Klein is Lotte Klein, whom Heydrich met only on official social occasions. She closes her mind even today to all negative influences: 'Heydrich was a very nice, a wonderful person – polite, friendly, obliging.'[8]

His nephew Peter Thomas Heydrich knew two Heydrichs: the shining sports idol dressed in white fencing attire, tearing the mask from his face in triumph after winning a bout at a Berlin tournament, and the shadowy host in black SS uniform, oblivious to the world, playing a violin in his back garden. The significance of the black uniform was lost on the small boy although he thought even then that it meant something unhealthy and so was not suited to a 'dear Uncle' who gave so generously within his family circle at birthdays. 'Black and white,' Peter Thomas Heydrich said, 'this man was both by nature. I knew him, and whenever I think of my uncle I see a dual personality.'[9]

Black and white – the man between the opposites remains a tantalising mystery.

Chapter One

The Naval Officer and the Nazis 1904–1932

Even today, the old city of Halle on the River Saale in Saxony celebrates with undisguised pride its most famous son. A monument to him stands in the historic market-place: the house where he was born has been converted into a museum: a festival hall and thoroughfare have been named after him: the city holds yearly festivals, seminars and other conventions in his honour: his works are presented regularly and can be bought everywhere.

Georg Friedrich Händel, composer of the *Messiah*, was born in February 1685 in a baroque city house close to the cathedral. In its prospectus the university city praises itself for having put the great musician on the path to success by its 'stimulating spiritual and musical atmosphere'. A few Halle inhabitants even go so far as to wonder whether Händel might actually have been thinking of his native city when he penned his most famous composition, the '*Halle*-lujah Chorus'.

On the other hand, however, the people of Halle have completely disowned the most notorious son of their city. Even veteran taxi drivers confess they have 'never heard the name before'. No plaque or memorial recalls the man born at 10.30 a.m. on 7 March 1904 at Marienstrasse 21 near the Leipziger Tower. Three days later there appeared in the local newspaper, the *Hallescher Central-Anzeiger*,[1] a small announcement almost hidden in the lower right-hand corner of a page between publicity for a work-out of the Jahn Gymnastic Society on the Rossplatz and a book about a new treatment for syphilis:

In Place of a Special Announcement!

Bruno Heydrich and his wife Elisabeth née Krantz
are delighted to announce
the happy birth of a completely strong and healthy
boy
Halle/Saale, 7 March 1904

The child was not identified by name. On 12 March 1904 the birth was registered by the father at the City Hall civil registry. The entry appears in Main Register 'A' under running number 669: 'Reinhard Tristan Eugen'.[2] These names reflect the musical interests of the parents: Bruno Heydrich was director of the Halle Conservatory, founded by himself: his wife, Elisabeth, worked there teaching the piano and as a seminar inspector. 'Reinhard' was the hero of the opera *Amen* composed by Heydrich senior, 'Tristan' gave the nod to highly honoured composer Richard Wagner and 'Eugen' remembered the father of wife, Elisabeth, the Dresden music professor and ministerial adviser Georg Eugen Krantz. Reinhard Heydrich was the second child of the family: sister Maria was born in 1901 and brother Siegfried Heinz would follow in 1905.

As if to spite the proclamation in the newspaper announcement, Reinhard Tristan Eugen fell gravely ill at the age of six months with an inflammation of the brain. The Evangelical father and strongly Catholic mother had not agreed until then on the religion of their son, but now it appeared urgent to arrange an emergency baptism, in the Catholic rite.

On 6 October 1904 the baby was duly baptised at the Propstei Church of St Franziskus and Elisabeth. Between the names of two children born in September and October that year, priest Schwermer entered in the baptismal register under No. 154 the incorrect forename 'Richard', crossed it through and replaced it with 'Reinhard'.[3] The church had direct links to the Catholic Children's Hospital of St Barbara, and gynaecologist Julius Hermann Lüdicke, who had attended the delivery, was present as godfather. Bruno Heydrich knew him as a brother of the freemasonic lodge Zu den 3 Degen im Orient von Halle. The godmother also demonstrated the circles in which the Conservatory director moved locally: Elise, Baroness von Eberstein belonged to a noble lineage of Halle that went back generations. She and her husband were Wagner fanatics and had met the Heydrichs socially through concert attendances. Later she would play a decisive role at a crossroads in the life of Reinhard Heydrich.

To what extent the encephalitis damaged the mind and soul of the young Heydrich it is impossible to know. In any case, the medical records of St Barbara's have not survived. What is certain is that as a child he was an outsider: attention-seeking, rebellious, irascible, from early on a lone wolf whom his classmates picked on and bullied. At home he craved love and recognition, but his academically inclined parents had little time for their children. His father scarcely bothered himself about their progress in education, and Mama, always the Great Lady, remained distant and strict. Discipline was the byword in a house always full of teachers and pupils, where music was taught continually and a timetable had to be kept.

> She was busy as a bee teaching young ladies to play the piano [a house-guest said later of Elisabeth Heydrich] but you could never get close to her. She lacked womanly and motherly warmth for young people. She always made a rather regal impression. She was always very self-possessed, and would pick you up on the least error. Reinhard inherited the arrogance in her make-up.[4]

At the time of Reinhard Heydrich's birth, his father was working with grim resolution to become a central figure in the cultural life of Halle. He brought to the quiet mining and garrison town the flair of the central European music scene, on the stages of which the man of Saxon birth had already demonstrated his talent. Never one to miss the opportunity of saying a few things about himself, he left little unsaid in praise of his own qualities in a handwritten curriculum vitae in 1903:

> My name is Richard Bruno Heydrich and I was born on 23 February 1863 at Leuben in Lommatzsch. My father was a piano maker. I went to the High School at Meissen where I distinguished myself by winning prizes on a number of occasions. I studied music from age 12, initially violin, cello and tenor horn, later the contrabass and tuba. By age 13 I was already performing in public concerts of the Meissen Youth Orchestra as a soloist and my compositions (songs and marches) were also staged. After my confirmation I was accepted as a music student with the Anders' Music Orchestra at Meissen and won for myself after two years' study a scholarship to the Royal Dresden Conservatory, being accepted immediately after a successful audition (violin, contrabass, tuba) as a contrabass player with minor fields of study. My studies at Dresden lasted three years and in July 1882 I received my qualifying certificate – with the highest possible grade – and a recommendation that I be excused the compulsory military conscription period of one year.
>
> Hans von Bülow engaged me at once for his orchestra in which I spent a year (1882/1883) as a court musician, and was then summoned to the former Royal Orchestra at Dresden. As a member of the Royal Band I satisfied my military obligation and was listed with Ersatzreserve Second Class. During my four-year activity with the Dresden Orchestra I spent time at the Royal Conservatory studying musical scores and composition, playing under Professor Dr Wüllner. It was he who discovered my tenor voice and won me a scholarship as a student chorister. After completing my studies with Professors Scharfe, Eichberger and Krantz, instructors in

court opera singing, I embarked upon my first theatrical attempt as Lionel in *Martha* at the baronial theatre, Sandershausen, on 11 March 1887. I was so successful as a singer that the directors of the Weimar Court Theatre invited me to be a guest performer on an engagement basis. I performed as Lohengrin and Faust, and was then awarded a two-year contract (1887–1889) as an opera singer (lyrical tenor) at Court. Here I continued my studies with Herr Kammersänger of Milde and developed into an heroic tenor. I was given my first appointment in this role after guest performances as Tannhäuser and Faust in 1890 in Magdeburg.

Next I studied under Professor Hey in Berlin, who steered me primarily towards a Wagner career, and later with Professor Schulz-Dornburg in Cologne. First-class engagements followed in Stettin, Aachen and Cologne (where I was the successor to Emil Götze's four years with brilliant success), at Brunswick (three years as leading heroic tenor at the Court Theatre) and two years as guest at Halle (1899).

From Cologne and Brunswick I accepted guest appointments elsewhere, especially in Wagnerian roles and as Jose, Joseph, Bajazzo, Fra Diavolo, Zampa etc. in many large theatres, among others Frankfurt am Main, Antwerp, Mainz, Geneva etc., and sang frequently in very large concert halls. I encountered great success in Cologne as composer and lyricist with my very first opera *Amen* (22 September 1895). The Rhineland Press praised my work *Amen*, which was performed very regularly with my collaboration either as bandmaster or lead singer. *Amen* also experienced acclaim at other stages such as Bonn, Aachen, Brunswick, Halle, Coburg, etc.

Through my marriage (December 1897) into a family of pedagogues (my wife is the daughter of Professor Krantz, director of the Royal Conservatory at Dresden) I became a teacher at the wish of the latter and through his instruction. I was active as a teacher at the time of my engagement in Brunswick and in 1899 I founded at Halle a choral school which I made into a Conservatory in 1901. I have been successful as a teacher and found recognition as a performing artist. Several of my students are already active as performers and teachers, and the results of the last two years are in every respect very pleasing.

My most recent work, a four-act opera, *Frieden*, has just been completed after twelve months' work and it is expected to have its premier during the winter on a large Berlin stage. Many of my compositions have been published: pieces for piano, songs, choral presentations, lyrical triplets and the opera *Amen*, in all, 43 works. Every year, many of my compositions appear on the programmes of outstanding artists, several important song and music societies have nominated me to be an honorary member, to name but a few the Cologne Men's Choral Society Liederkrantz, the Richard Wagner Society of Halle, and so on.

I now exercise my calling as a singer only as a guest artist, and since May 1901 I have devoted myself entirely to teaching and the directorship of my Institute.[5]

Oddly, the fan of Wagner failed to mention a summer in Bayreuth which came to light after his death in 1938: he got to know Cosima Wagner there and sang at soirées pieces from the works of the Master, from *Lohengrin, Parsifal*, the *Meistersinger, Tristan* and in particular *Rienzi*. Perhaps he could not bring himself to admit that no engagement was forthcoming in consequence. Similarly, foreign concerts in Brussels, Vienna, Prague and Marienbad were deemed not worthy of mention, nor was the name of his wife.

In the autumn of 1904, Heydrich's 'Conservatory for Music and Theatre' moved from two separate buildings at Nos 10 and 21 Marienstrasse to one of the more salubrious districts of Halle, at Poststrasse 2, where the citizens of the city enjoyed walking in the park beside the ruins of the old wall. At this time, the *Saale-Zeitung* praised the Institute for having a reached a standard of singing which 'many pessimistic Halle connoisseurs had considered impossible.'[6] In his own prospectus, director Heydrich promised to put an end to 'widespread sloppiness' in musical education at Halle and 'to consolidate, in all areas of our art, the truly good, noble and fine.'[7] On the wall of the Great Music Room at Poststrasse 2 stood Heydrich's motto: 'Talent is important, Diligent Application more so!' Son 'Reini' appears to have had this slogan branded into his mind.

The number of students at the Conservatory grew rapidly, from twenty in the year 1901 to 132 in 1904, rising to four hundred by 1912, the high point. The number of teachers in Bruno Heydrich's employ rose correspondingly from six in 1902 to twenty-six permanent teachers and nine relief teachers by the outbreak of war in 1914.

On 1 April 1908, the Conservatory moved again, this time into an altogether much larger, many-roomed edifice at Gütchenstrasse 20. In the period of the DDR, an anonymous schoolfriend of Reinhard Heydrich described his recollections of the musical family's home:

> The rooms were furbished in classic style. One felt very comfortable there. The place gave the impression of prosperity. Finely wood-panelled rooms, the finest porcelain, a lot of silver and valuable cutlery. In the courtyard building was a fine room with decorated stage. Here I listened on several occasions to rehearsals by the young male and female debutantes. Director Bruno Heydrich would always be seated in the wings.

He was apparently an imposing figure 'round about 250 pounds' but his bulk did not interfere with his activities – he was a member of a number of societies and founder of the 'Schlaraffia Choir' – still the joy of his life. 'He was always a real joker,' the schoolfriend recalled. 'I can still remember some of the stage tales he used to tell us boys. One involved play on the word *weich*. This has a number of meanings, one of which is 'soft'. In the *Valkyries* when Erda came up from the deep, Wotan would call to her in a low voice, 'Erda, how do you like your eggs, hard-boiled or soft?' And the heroine's next line, which she had to sing trying not to laugh, was '*Weich*, Wotan, *weich!*'[8]

Reinhard Heydrich venerated his father even though by character he took after his mother. Once when the father, in the presence of 'Reini' and some of his schoolfriends parodied his talents on the piano, the young Reinhard beamed with pride and whispered to his friends, 'See, my father is first-class!' If he had taken after his father, Reinhard might have followed in the footsteps of great musicians: perhaps he could have become 'a second Mozart'. He had learnt the violin and piano at an early age at the Gütchenstrasse Conservatory, yet nothing came of the career envisaged for him by his father.

All his life, 'Reini' had a peculiar voice which, with his bleating laugh, earned him the nickname *Hebbe* – 'goat'. While a teenager he once sang in a crib scene in high key the role of the Virgin Mary, cuddling a doll as 'baby Jesus'. On the other hand, he had such virtuosity with the violin that he had been known to reduce listeners to tears, but he preferred to perform lighter pieces. The more isolated he became, the more the instrument became 'his only friend'.[9]

The passion for music that he had inherited from his parents remained with him always. Similarly his interest in sport was to leave its mark on him. Because he was a sickly child his parents encouraged him to take up every kind of physical exercise, especially, since 'Reini' was attending the Halle Royal Reform High School in the autumn of 1914, swimming, running, football, sailing, horseriding and fencing. One of his father's many club roles was as an honorary member of the Halle branch of the Reich Fencing School, founded in 1896. His son's fencing career began there, and eventually led to his becoming one of the best épée and sabre fighters of Europe.

Before World War I there reigned among the German bourgeoisie a kind of smug pride in the Fatherland, coupled with a fierce loyalty to the Kaiser, and the Heydrich household was no exception. The father's opera *Frieden* had its debut in Mainz to honour the 48th birthday of Kaiser Wilhelm II on 27 February 1907. The Conservatory director saw this moment as the high point of his career and he conducted a performance as a 'festival concert to celebrate the 25th Silver Jubilee of the German Kaiser and King of Prussia' at Bad Wittekind on 13 June 1913. On this occasion, as the programme stated, 'the public is respectfully requested, at the closing hymn, to rise and join in the singing of the Overture to Joy *Heil Dir im Siegeskranz* (Hail to Thee who wears the Victor's wreath).'[10]

The father's enthusiasm for Wagner and his Nordic-Germanic mythical operas, supercharged with the ideas of honour, heroism, war, readiness to die for an ideal and racial integrity, cannot have been lost on the son. In this spiritual climate, Heydrich junior developed early in life a weakness for the military life. He admired the soldiers of the Mansfelder Feldartillerie-Regiment No. 75 stationed at Halle when they towed out their horse-drawn field guns for manoeuvres. They were joined in 1914 by Friedrich Karl von Oberstein, the son of his godmother. But Heydrich's heart beat fastest during the summer vacation when the family usually holidayed in the Baltic resort of Swinemünde and he could watch the cruisers of the Imperial Navy glide past offshore. He would listen enthralled to the famous 'sea devil' Felix Graf von Luckner whenever he visted the Heydrich household as a guest and reminisced his adventures on the high seas.

Von Luckner is probably Germany's most romantic naval warrior, having become famous after the story of his exploits, *Seeteufel* ('Sea Devil'), became a bestseller in 1921. It was one of the few non-fiction books for which Reinhard Heydrich had a special preference. Von Luckner (b. Dresden 1881, d. Malmo, Sweden, 1966) had circumnavigated the globe as an able-bodied seaman before the mast in his teens, and upon joining the Imperial Navy in 1911 was one of the few German officers with experience in sailing. After the Battle of Jutland, in which he saw action aboard a battleship, he was appointed to command a commerce raider, the three-masted barque *Pass of Balmaha* (1,571 tons) armed with a couple of deck guns and an auxiliary motor which rarely worked. *Seeadler* (Sea Eagle), as he called the ship unofficially, was manned by six officers and fifty-seven men, the majority of them Norwegian-speakers. The barque sailed from Copenhagen on 21 December 1916, and after convincing the Northern Patrol that he was Norwegian, Luckner broke out into the Atlantic. During a voyage lasting eight months, he sank seventeen Allied vessels, sail and steam, a remarkable achievement, for the loss of only one Allied life, before his ship was wrecked, probably through crew negligence, in the Tahiti group on 8 July 1917.

Germany's collapse and defeat in 1918 came as a fearful blow to the pro-nationalist monarchist Heydrich, as it did for millions of his countrymen. The Reich was humiliated, the Kaiser sent into exile, a republic established. The plush existence of the Heydrich family disappeared. The Conservatory went downhill, the necessities of survival left little money spare for evening songs and house music. In the 'turnip winter' of 1916/1917, the Heydrichs had gone hungry for the first time. After the request for an Armistice on 11 November 1918, they gave credence to the 'stab in the back' sworn to as fact by military men and the radical Right whereby 'traitors within' had delivered the 'undefeated in the field German armed forces' to the enemy, to the forefront of these traitors being the Reds, the Jews and the freemasons. In the confusion of the immediate postwar period the young Heydrich elected to take part in political agitation.

Direct involvement offered itself to the fifteen-year-old schoolboy, still attending the Royal Reform High School, in the spring of 1919, a few months after the capitulation, when Communist insurgents occupied Halle. Heydrich rallied to the flag of the Rightist Freikorps despite being two years under age. Recruiting publicity in the local Press advertised for 'young, healthy people without Service experience' of at least seventeen years of age. Das Freiwillige Landesjägerkorps (Voluntary Provincial Rifle Corps) advertised in May 1919 for 'young men without Service experience who are over 17 years of age, 1.56 metres tall or over, with 80 cm chest measurement.'[11] Because of the age limitations, apologists for Heydrich, whose purpose is to portray him as politically naive and disinterested, have attempted to cast doubt on these activities. The fact is that Heydrich himself supplied the information on SS questionnaires that he had served in various Freikorps: in 1937 he identified these as Freikorps Maercker and Freikorps Halle for 1919/1920 and later, from 1920 to 1922, the Deutschvölkischer Schutz-und Trutzebund.

This author has found documentary evidence of the fact at the Washington National Archive in the form of a handwritten identity document signed by a Major Lucius on 6 March 1919 stating: 'Student Heydrich is in the service of III.Abtlg. of the Freiw. Landesjäger-Regt.'

The second document is dated 15 March 1920 and is a typed form completed by hand. It originates from the same 'III Abtlg. 1.Landesjäger-Regt., Abschnitt Mitte' at Halle: 'Senior Student Reinhard Heydrich of Halle,

Gutchenstr 20 [*sic*] is a member of the Civilian Volunteer Group of "Mitte" section. (For the Regiment) Kunstein 1.Lt and acting adjutant of detachment (signature). This document is endorsed with the Imperial eagle and the legend "Freiwilliges Landes-Jäger-Korps/III Abtlg".[12]

At the beginning of 1919, a Leftist workers' and soldiers' council seized power in Halle, supported by a company of disaffected naval ratings and a so-called security regiment. Heavily armed militia patrolled the streets and in January 1919 put down demonstrations by the local population using arrests and terror tactics. A Red general strike which was called for central German industry and the mining community at the end of February was staged with such violence that it provoked a counter-strike by the local population: businessmen, postal services, police, doctors, teachers and other civil servants.

In order to control the unrest, the Social Democrat Defence Minister Gustav Noske ordered a Freikorps unit from Gotha to Halle. (This unit was composed of demobilised German soldiers and was formed into a Landesjägerkorps later.) Its commanding officer was Major General Georg Maercker, a staunch conservative of the Imperial school who served the new Republic as 'a liberator of cities' from Red chaos.

On his entry into Halle on 1 March 1919 he encountered stiff resistance from the Spartacists (Communists). Maercker and his staff were bottled up for a whole day in the main post office building and the Hotel Stadt Hamburg opposite until his machine-gun troops arrive and scythed a way through to relieve him.

It was not until the morning of 3 March that the Government troops drove out the insurgents from their headquarters in the city theatre, and put an end to the street fighting during which the local Spartacist leader was killed: during the night looters plundered about thirty shops in the city centre: fashion, jewellery, food and cigar stores.

Maercker issued an order threatening armed insurgents, looters and arsonists 'with the death penalty' and imposed a curfew from 7 p.m. to 7 a.m. When Spartacists recognised one of Maercker's officers, Oberstleutnant von Klüver, reconnoitring the district in civilian clothing, he was set upon by a mob, beaten half to death and thrown into the River Saale. In reprisal the General had five hundred insurgents arrested and put on trial, and sent an armed column into neighbouring Merseburg in pursuit of the revolutionary sailors who had fled Halle. By 5 March 1919 all red flags had disappeared from Halle. The fighting had left thirty insurgents and seven soldiers killed, more than a hundred wounded. 'I have never known a town then or since where the mob was so grimly entrenched as here,' Maercker stated in an interview with the *Halleschen Nachrichten.*[13]

The sporting Heydrich entered the service of the corps as a despatch runner when the fighting ended. Some of it tailed off just a few hundred metres from the Conservatory in the Gütchenstrasse. Before leaving Halle on 5 March, Maercker ordered the setting up of a salaried Volunteer Information Office, Freikorps Halle and an unpaid citizens' defence force (Bürgerwehr).[14] Heydrich's handwritten identity paper is dated 6 March and is signed by the commander, Mitte section, Major Lucius, who had his command post in the main post office administration office, not far from the Heydrich house.[15]

Another of Heydrich's membership cards from the archive is undated but bears the stamp 'Einwohnerwehr (Residents' Defence Force) Halle, District 21, Friedrichsplatz', and the number '101'. Beneath this it reads: 'The holder of this identity document, Herr Reinhard Heydrich, is a Member of the Einwohnerwehr Halle.' Along the edge of the card is printed: 'Important document. Strictly secret and is to be kept carefully, serves as a licence to bear arms.'[16]

Wearing an old steel helmet, Heydrich served one year as a volunteer despatch messenger. Apparently his parents raised no objections. When a schoolfriend was surprised by Heydrich's mother while trying on the steel helmet in her son's bedroom, she scolded him, 'Ei, who is this adorning himself with strange feathers?'[17] After the failed Berlin putsch by reactionaries supporting the self-appointed 'Reichs Chancellor' Wolfgang Kapp on 18 March 1920, insurgents of the Marxist USPD dealt another blow to Halle in a day-long siege. Troops loyal to Kapp fought the Leftists, who declared that they were one 'with the masses of the revolutionary proletariat' and would continue the struggle 'with constantly increasing energy until the proletarian seizure of socialist power'.

At this time Heydrich was serving with the Technical Emergency Help set up by the Interior Ministry to maintain and repair the supplies of gas, electricity and water. Much blood flowed: hundreds died in street fighting in the inner city, and on 'Bloody Sunday', 21 March 1920, the Händel Memorial in the market-place was damaged by rifle fire, while the Galgenberg Height to the north of the town was brought under artillery bombardment. On 23 March Government troops recaptured Halle and extinguished once again 'the blood-red heart of Central Germany'.[18]

The identity document that confirms Heydrich as a 'Member of the Technical Emergency Help' (Technische Nothilfe) bears No. 2348 and allowed him 'to pass without hindrance all road blocks in exercise of his duty as *Nothilfe*'. On its reverse is a photograph showing a determined-looking young man with light wavy hair on a high forehead. He wore a dark jacket and white shirt with winged collar. Below the photograph Heydrich had signed his name in normal script without embellishment.[19]

Whereas Heydrich's family later played down his Freikorps activity, Friedrich Karl von Eberstein, son of Reinhard's godmother, who took part in the Kapp putsch attempt as a reactionary Freikorps officer, stated in a letter to the Israeli Heydrich-biographer Shlomo Aronson that Heydrich had been extremely '*völkisch*' (racially nationalist) and had attempted to join various *völkisch* organisations. Heydrich mentioned in one of his SS questionnaires that he had been a member of the Völkischer Schutz-und Trutzebund [Defensive and Offensive League]. This racist league of a quarter of a million members had links to the mystical racist and secret Thule Gesellschaft [Thule Society] and was heavily influenced by its guiding light, Dietrich Eckart, Hitler's mentor. It had a swastika for its logo and saw in the 'depressing and destructive influence of Jewry . . . the principal cause of the collapse'. Heydrich, Eberstein continued, had developed into a 'pure-race fanatic'. It is beyond doubt that his contact with the 'stab in the back' Freikorps propagandists had left its mark on his character.[20]

Shortly before Easter 1922, 'Reini' obtained his *Abitur* at the Reform-Real Gymnasium with very good marks and entered the Reichsmarine on 30 March at Kiel, his beloved violin in his luggage: his ambition was to become an admiral. The 'new Navy' was composed of a fleet limited by the Treaty of Versailles to fifteen thousand men, four thousand of them officers, six old battleships, six small cruisers, sixteen destroyers under

800 tonnes and sixteen torpedo-boats under 200 tonnes. A strong motivating factor in his career decision was his hope to play a part in redressing the enforced terms of the 'Diktat of Versailles' and so redeem Germany's honour.

During house visits after the war, as echoed in his book *Seeteufel*, Graf von Luckner had urged:

> Let us keep faith with the sea, precisely now, as its waves, empty and desolate, roll against the German coast! Your clarion call to us resounds, and when in keeping with the old legend . . . Gorch Fock and his companions hold their roll call over the steel coffin of the *Wiesbaden* on the sea bed, while around them lie the fallen victors and the dead of old Hansa, then we hear the North Sea Valhalla sigh to us and our children as if in a German prayer: Seafaring is Necessity! The welfare of our people we shall recover one day, when we are united. Nobody should hope for help or kindness from outsiders, but all must believe in the future German Will and the future German Way. Once the people have found themselves again, then, young eagles of land and sea, shall your wings grow![21]

The cadet training for Heydrich's intake, 'Crew 22', began with a harsh six-month shipboard stint aboard the old battleship *Brandenburg*, followed by three months on the sail training ship *Niobe*, and ended between July 1923 and March 1924 with foreign service on the cruiser *Berlin*. On 1 April 1924 Heydrich was promoted to senior midshipman and sent for officer training to the Mürwik Naval College near Flensburg.

His first years in the Reichsmarine gave little joy to the arrogant outsider with the fiddle. He was picked on by his contemporaries, ridiculed for his long hook nose, the oblique 'wolf's eyes' and the almost squeaky high voice. They made fun of him, called him 'goat' or simply greeted him with a bleat and found it amusing when his face 'grew purple with rage', as Hans Heinrich Lebram recalled: 'He had no friends in the Crew.' Another midshipman of his year, Heinrich Beucke, belittled Heydrich's technical knowledge and intelligence as 'average' and had very little favourable to say about his character: 'In his personality one saw vanity, smugness, a desire for approval, softness and over-sensitivity. In total, he was a contradiction. He very quickly became a figure of fun for nearly all his colleagues. And he always took it the wrong way.'

Nevertheless, the question of leaving the Navy was never an option: to run away from the barracking would have been considered a dishonour.[22] Despite all the ridicule, several crew-members have confirmed to historian Shlomo Aronson that the midshipman never made anybody his enemy, and made every effort to be conciliatory. When he became too miserable, he would take himself to the foredeck and play sad tunes on his violin.

It was this violin-playing aboard the cruiser *Berlin* that brought him to the attention of Korvettenkapitän Wilhelm Canaris one day: from 1924 he invited Heydrich regularly to his house at Kiel to entertain his wife Erika with music.[23] Canaris, whose marriage was on the rocks, disregarded the difference in rank for the chance to make his wife happy. He had no interest in music himself and preferred to cook when he was free. For the senior midshipman the house concerts meant that he was given a social rehabilitation from other Crew-members, and later, when stationed at Wilhelmshaven with the North Sea fleet, he won much appreciation for his musical abilities at parties and in the officers' barracks.

Canaris impressed the young Heydrich with his experience – he had been a navigating lieutenant aboard the small cruiser *Dresden* at the Battle of the Falklands in 1914 and had escaped to Europe from Chile after internment there in 1915 – and politically both were on the same wavelength. The Freikorps despatch runner and World War I officer, who had been involved in the 1920 Kapp putsch, discussed the reasons for Germany's defeat, the means for the rebirth of a powerful Germany, about important territorial ambitions (Germany a *Volk* without *Raum* – space) and their mutual hatred of the French, occupying the Ruhr. 'Once we finally get a decent Government,' Canaris used to say, 'then we can work wonders.' Canaris, according to Heydrich's acquaintance Günther Gerecke, subjected Heydrich to regular indoctrination. On visits to Berlin he spoke about a *Grossraumpolitik* (expansionist policy) and 'the achievements of German technology' as the key to future military strength. Heydrich was especially fascinated by aviation and its future application in warfare. His decision to join the signals officer branch and learn the new techniques of wireless communication, monitoring and encryption was attributable to some degree to Canaris's encouragement: Canaris rose later to be head of the Abwehr, military counter-intelligence.[24]

Although he was considered physically 'ugly', according to Lebram, Heydrich was apparently 'irresistible' to women. As a youth at the parental Conservatory at Halle, he sought and found sexual contacts with the house staff. He was always hungry for sex, constantly on the lookout for women, and proved fascinating to older women.

During a Fleet visit to Barcelona in the spring of 1926, Heydrich as a 24-year-old senior midshipman on the flagship *Schleswig-Holstein* earned himself a disciplinary reprimand from his superior for making his interest in a young lady of the German colony too obvious. A few weeks later his conduct caused a commotion at Reid's Hotel in Funchal, Madeira, where he gave offence by issuing repeated invitations to dance to the wives of British officers. His colleagues of the *Schleswig-Holstein* felt 'very embarrassed' about it. Heydrich did not understand the problem: he considered the reserve of the English ladies to be an insult.[25]

Heydrich was promoted to Leutnant zur See on 1 October 1926 and in the first quarter of 1927 passed a course for signals technical officer, it being remarked that he was 'fairly good in transmitting and receiving.'[26] From then until October 1928 he served as a No. 2 telegraphy officer in the rank of Oberleutnant zur See, the highest grade he achieved in the Navy, and continued until his discharge in the signals branch attached to Naval Station Baltic at Kiel. 'His knowledge and ability were above average,' was the opinion of the later Vice Admiral Gustav Kleikamp, his instructor at the Naval Signals School, in a letter in 1950 to *Der Spiegel* magazine. 'On the other hand, Heydrich had already shown that he was very convinced of his abilities, ambitious and could make a very persuasive argument.'[27] Yet two years later, he came only twenty-third among the full lieutenants of his intake.

In the Navy, as at high school, he was an active sportsman, participating in fencing, riding, sailing, pistol shooting, swimming, long-distance running: in his degree of commitment his desire to be the best at every-thing was obvious: 'He sailed so close to the wind that he would either capsize or win first prize,' a young lady remembered.[28] While horse-riding at the Army Sports School at Wünsdorf he broke his nose. He confided to a friend that he wanted to take part in the Olympic Games one day, naturally in a solo discipline, for he was not the kind of person who could give himself to the full in team games.

Since the beginning of his naval days – and perhaps earlier – Heydrich had been much unsettled by a persistent rumour that he had Jewish blood and his father's name was really 'Isidor Süss'. On a home visit to Halle one day, somebody called out, 'Look there! Young Itzig Süss in naval uni-form!' Such insults were not new to him. In 1916 his father took action regarding an entry in the eighth edition of Hugo Riemann's *Musik-Lexikon*, wherein his potted biography began with the line: 'Heydrich, Bruno (actually Süss), b. 23 Feb. 1863 at Leuben (Saxony), son of a piano maker . . . ' The suffix 'actually Süss' was deleted from the following edi-tion.[29]

In a letter of July 1922 to the Halle city magistrate in which a desper-ate Bruno Heydrich begged financial help and two hundredweight of coke for his Conservatory, having fallen on hard times through inflation and a diminishing intake of pupils, he wrote: 'Due to the erroneous assumption that the director and proprietor is a Jew and has been raking it in at the school, which is emphatically denied, I also declare that even in the best of times before the war no undue purchases were ever made.'[30]

Somebody had noticed that Conservatory Director Heydrich occasionally sent money to a Frau Süss at Meissen from the Halle main post office. The 'assumptions' were based primarily on the fact that Bruno Heydrich's mother, Ernestine Wilhelmine Lindner (1840–1923) married locksmith's assistant Gustav Robert Süss (1853–1931) three years after the death of her husband Carl Julius Reinhold Heydrich (1837–1874). The parents of Gustav Süss, landowner Ehregott Süss and Marie Rosine Stegedly were Evangelical-Lutheran and not of the Jewish religion, according to the ancestral list.

'A lot was spoken – even among ourselves – about her Jewish ances-try,' Friedrich Karl von Eberstein said later about the Heydrichs. 'I'm no racial fanatic, but the old Heydrich really did look Jewish.'[31] Many Halle music lovers recalled how the faithful Bruno parodied 'the Jews' at carnival time.

Bruno Heydrich had no strong feelings about the Jews. He rented out the cellar of his house at Gütchenstrasse to a Jewish salesman named Lewin. Occasionally before the war Bruno Heydrich had conversations with the cantor of the Halle Jewish community, Abraham Lichtenstein. Quite often Lichtenstein would bring his son along, and while the two parents talked about music, the boy would play with little 'Reini'.[32]

Even when his naval colleagues called him 'the white Jew', Heydrich defended himself, mostly unsuccessfully, by adopting an anti-semitic stance, according to fellow midshipman Lebram. He told a Crew-member that his father had grown up with gypsies and been adopted by Carl Heydrich on account of his musical talents.

At about this time, together with his mentor Canaris, Heydrich was seeking contacts to those other exponents of the *Völkisch*, the supporters of the Munich agitator Adolf Hitler. He had caused a furore with his book *Mein Kampf* written at Landsberg Prison, where he had been incarcerated following the attempted Beerhall putsch in Bavaria on 9 November 1923.

Hitler was a dangerous mixture of hate-monger and Messiah, as his book demonstrates:

> If the Jew, with the help of his Marxist dogma, triumphs over the people of this world, then his crown will be the wreath of death for humanity, and this planet will drift, as it once did millions of years ago, uninhabited through the ether. Eternal Nature avenges remorselessly the infringement of her rules. Thus I believe myself to be acting as the Mind of the Creator: in fighting the Jew, I do the work of the Lord.[33]

In the confusion of the Weimar Republic, in which order had collapsed under the persistent attacks of Left and Right-wing extremists, Hitler's National Socialistische Deutsche Arbeiter Partei (NSDAP) appeared to many Germans as the alternative to an inherently weak democracy and economy, and grew eventually into a power that was impossible to restrain internally. From the end of the 1920s, the Austrian private first-class – never a corporal – of World War I, a despatch runner of a Bavarian regiment, decorated with the Iron Cross First and Second Class, stood increasingly in the centre stage of German politics even though his toothbrush moustache, his wild gestures and hoarse roar at the speaker's dais seemed to many ridiculous or repulsive.

While sailing, the young naval officer Heydrich had made the acquaintance in Kiel of a law student named Werner Mohr. In the autumn of 1925 in his home town of Eutin, Mohr had helped found the NSDAP local branch and its paramilitary strongarm SA detachment after meeting Hitler in the Munich Bürgerbräukeller following the reconstitution of the banned Party.[34] Mohr also took part in at least one political naval training exercise of the 'Black Reichsmarine' (Germany's secret navy set up in defiance of the Versailles Treaty) at the Hanseatic Yachting School, Neustadt, Holstein, where Hitler was often a guest. At this school the old discipline and ways of thought held sway. 'We are all German men, bound by a common idea, to work together for the regeneration of our people,' a 1925 pamphlet proclaimed. The Hanseatic Yachting School was run by the Deutscher Hochseesportverband Hansa, whose senior administrator Heydrich must have known at Halle: he was former chief of staff of the Imperial High Seas Fleet and later Chief of the Admiralty, Adolf von Trotha (1868–1940), who had retired in 1919 and taken part in the failed Kapp putsch the following year. He also dreamed that the 'Hanseatic spirit in the struggle with storm and seas of the ocean will again carry the name of Germany over all the oceans, earning it respect.'[35]

This quest for revenge and the restoration of national pride following the ignominious defeat were imbued in Heydrich from the beginning of his service in the Navy of the Weimar Republic. On 3 June 1923, for example, he took part with other cadets at Mürwik in a ceremony to commemorate the 1916 Battle of Jutland in which the Imperial Navy had been superior in tactics to the Royal Navy but gained no strategic advantage since the German High Seas Fleet, apart from a few desultory minor sorties, remained on its home anchorages until the war's end. At the ceremony a plaque had been unveiled bearing the inscription – still extant today – 'Never complain, dare again! Seafaring is Necessity!' and beside it: *Exoriare aliquis nostris ex ossibus ultor:* (May an avenger arise from our bones).[36]

During his military career, Heydrich also kept contact with Friedrich Karl von Eberstein, the son of his godmother. As a member of the Stahlhelm veterans' organisation, he had joined the Notbund (Emergency League) Halle, a forerunner of the NSDAP in Central Germany, in November 1922. In 1924 at a Party parade celebrating Deutscher Tag (German Day) he put on his steel helmet painted with a white swastika and stood beside World War heroes and Hitler-promoter and World War I General Erich Ludendorff on the Halle athletics track. In 1928 he joined the SS and by the end of the 1920s with the rank of Untersturmführer was adjutant to the SS leadership in Thuringia and the NSDAP city council at Gotha. In the service of the Party, Eberstein felt himself to be a 'dyed-in-the-wool political soldier'.[37]

At Wilhelmshaven Heydrich got to know a young Nazi, Hermann Behrends. The innkeeper's son was one of the few people whom the ever-mistrustful and reserved Heydrich called his 'friend'. Later he took him into his service. However, it was an enthusiastic Hitler-supporter of the other sex who finally changed Heydrich's life fundamentally.

On 6 December 1930 at a rowing-club ball held at the Kiel concert hall he met the daughter of a schoolteacher. Lina von Osten was a nineteen-year-old blonde who came from impoverished Holstein landed nobility.[38] Born on Fehmarn Island, she had grown up after the war in Lütjenbrode, 'on the other side of the Sound', which was not connected at that time by bridge to the mainland. Her father, Jürgen von Osten, headed the political 'Old School' there. The whole family were committed Nazis. Her cousin Peter Wiepert had coined the local motto: 'On Fehmarn there are no snakes, moles or Jews.'

Lina von Osten and her friends had become bored at the ball. There was a large turnout of college girls and a shortage of male dance partners. Her escort, farmer's son Wulf, excused himself and left. Just as she was about to go, however, as she describes in her memoir, two naval officers arrived, 'one small and dark, the other tall and blond.' Using a deceitful ploy', which she does not explain further, the two men steered the teacher's daughter and her friend to their table where the 'small, dark one' introduced himself as 'von Manstein' while 'the tall, blond one' stated with a brief military bow, 'Heydrich, Reinhard Heydrich'.

Once the ball was over, the lieutenant escorted Lina von Osten to the Henriettenhaus, the campus living quarters of the Berufsfachschule Kiel. He asked her for a date, and they met again a couple of days later. While strolling through the Hohenzollernpark (today Schewenpark) Heydrich told her about himself and his family and asked the young lady for her origins and ambitions. 'I felt sympathy for the ambitious yet reserved man,' she wrote later, 'he was not so much a lover as a comrade, a friend – and was really much more.'

Three days after the first date, Heydrich invited her to the theatre and afterwards, something to which the college girl was unaccustomed, for a glass of wine at Wicht's Weinkeller, known for its 'stimulating atmosphere and good music'. After a long pause he asked her suddenly, 'Fräulein von Osten, will you be my wife?' Taken aback she replied, '*Mein Gott,* Herr Heydrich, you haven't even met my parents and know nothing about my father's reputation. You are a naval officer, have your rules, your marriage regulations . . .'

He interrupted: 'That will all sort itself out. I am not interested in marrying your father, but would not mind having you as my wife.' She raised a few more objections, but finally said yes. On 18 December they became engaged secretly. At Christmas, Lina brought her cavalier to the family house in the village school, a red brick building in Lütjenbrode. Her father had announced that he wanted to 'look the man over carefully' and had a long conversation with the usually taciturn lieutenant, the result being that the village schoolmaster found his own tongue and did most of the talking. He told Heydrich about his family and his wife Mathilde von Osten, née Hiss, whose ancestors had been seafarers and had panned for gold 'on the banks of Sacramento'.

Heydrich's response was brief and to the point. He was quite candid that nothing much remained of the once-flourishing music conservatory at Halle, and no rich dowry was to be expected from his parents. 'He will fit into our landscape,' Lina's father said. A smart, nationalist-thinking naval officer with his sights set on higher things suited his image as a prospective son-in-law. But the dream bubble would soon burst.

Without further comment Heydrich published the announcement of his engagement 'to a college student at the Rendsburg Kolonial Frauenschule whom I have been courting for some time'.[39] There was close link between this private school overlooking the Kiel Canal, which provided young ladies with a two-year course in 'family and home economy for settling purposes at home and abroad' – including firearms training – and 'the boys in navy blue'. Whenever a warship returned from distant parts, the girls would run down to the canal bank to wave to the crew, and would receive soon afterwards an invitation to a homecoming celebrated in Kiel. If making the passage by night, as they cruised below the school the ratings would illuminate the building with the ship's searchlights and call out through loudhailers, 'Good night, sweeties!'

This was the way that Heydrich had become friendly with another female student at the college some time previously. They had met on a number of occasions until the 'Kolo' course finished and the young lady returned to her parents in Potsdam. When she saw the announcement of Heydrich's engagement, the girl, said to be the daughter of an influential officer at Naval Command, although nobody knows for sure, reacted with horror, for since she had spent a night at a pension in Kiel with him, at his insistence, she considered herself 'engaged' to him even if they had not actually shared the same bed. Her father was of the same opinion and lodged a complaint against the officer with Admiral Erich Raeder, head of Naval Command, whom he knew. Heydrich was summoned to appear before an honour court headed by Admiral Gottfried Hansen, Commander-in-Chief Naval Station, Baltic.

Now everything would have ended in a reprimand for a 'girl's story' lacking proof, had not Heydrich's attitude got him into difficulties with the court. In a high-handed manner, he informed the court that it was irrelevant to him what they thought a German officer should or should not do. He disavowed the engagement because he had not been contemplating marriage to the girl. The girl had more or less pestered him to admit her to his room.

According to Admiral Kleikamp later, 'his proven insincerity, aimed at white-washing himself' displeased the court, which concluded by asking whether it was 'possible for an officer guilty of such unforgiveable behaviour to remain in the Reichsmarine' although it avoided making any recommendation itself. In the spring, Admiral Raeder gave the answer: 'Simple discharge for conduct unbefitting an officer.' Kleikamp added emphatically: 'It was a decision which – if harsh – was recognised by all as impartial and correct and to which there was no alternative for anybody who knew the facts closely.'[40]

Even those of Heydrich's Crew 22 colleagues who were initially inclined to protest the decision stepped down once they were apprised of the events at the honour court. No papers relevant to the proceedings, held in camera, have been found, which has fuelled speculation that Heydrich was railroaded out for political reasons because of his association with Rightist groups. This allegation would certainly have its origins in Nazi propaganda. Once the facts surrounding this 'girl's story' became known, however, it seems clear that the 'political discharge' angle does not hold water, except for the interesting fact that the identity of the young lady from the Rendsburg Kolonial Frauenschule, and that of her father, never became public knowledge. Yet almost everybody who has written about Heydrich has managed to ferret out 'the correct version'.

The girl was the daughter of 'an influential naval architect' (Aronson/Deschner): of 'a shipyard director' (Crankshaw): of 'a senior officer at the Hamburg arsenal' (Delarue/Paillard/Rougerie): of 'an IG Farben director working at a Kiel shipyard' (Brissaud): of 'a man responsible for Kiel Dockyard Supply' (Sydnor), while 'her family had no connection at all to the Reichsmarine' (Kleikamp).

A comparison undertaken by this author between the names of girl students at the Kolonial Frauenschule and the military and political higher-ups of the Reichsmarine between 1929 and 1931 gives no clue. It is noteworthy that Heydrich, at the height of his power in the Third Reich, as Kleikamp confirmed in 1950, 'never undertook any action against the honour court panel' (although he continued to snipe at Raeder).

On 1 May 1931 there appeared in the *Marineverordnungsblatt* [41] the brief notice:

Discharged: Oberleutnant zur See Heydrich, v.d.N.A.d.St.O.
[A short while later there appeared a fuller report in the

journal *Marine-Offizier-Zeitung* under 'dismissals' explaining the abbreviations:] As of 30 April 1931, Oberleutnant zur See Heydrich of the Signals Branch, Naval Station Baltic, departs naval service under the lawful provisions applicable thereto and receives for the remainder of his three-month period of notice, and for the month of May 1931, those monies referred to at Chapter VIII B2, title 1a of the Naval Budget.[42]

In the certificate of discharge, the reason for his dismissal is not stated, but he received a good reference:

All superior officers state that Heydrich is a conscientious and reliable officer with a serious approach to duty and has undertaken zealously all duties required of him. Towards his superiors he is open and conducts himself in a military manner. He is well liked by fellow officers. He has a good understanding of handling men. Heydrich has a good sporting abilities, and is a good sailor and fencer.[43]

So ended a promising naval career. Lina Heydrich was not alone later in posing the question of what would have become of her husband if he had not been suddenly confronted by the abyss in 1931, in the midst of the economic crisis. Ejected from naval service, it was eleven months before he obtained his pension rights and so, from June 1931 onwards, he was practically without income. The ex-Oberleutnant went home to Halle, locked himself in his room and cried for days in rage and self-pity.[44]

His parents were horrified and perplexed, unable to help him. The Conservatory was undergoing an official inspection which would lead in the autumn to loss of State recognition. Elisabeth Heydrich, who until recently had been able to afford a maid, had to do the housework herself when not teaching the piano. Besides her husband she was having to feed her daughter Maria, also a teacher at the Conservatory, and her unemployed son-in-law Wolfgang Heindorf, her younger son Siegfried Heinz and his new bride Gertrud Werther. In desperation she argued endlessly with her brothers Hans and Kurt about the takings of the

Dresden Conservatory, which court adviser Krantz had bequeathed to his three offspring. Bruno Heydrich was barely fit to work after a heart attack and Siegfried Heinz had abandoned his studies at Dresden. When Lina von Osten visted Reinhard at Halle, they found the home atmosphere so depressing that they would flee the misery and spend hours beside the new lions' enclosure at the zoo wondering where it would all end.

Heydrich rejected an offer from his friend Mohr to teach sailing at Neustadt even though it would have brought in 380 Reichsmarks a month: he did not fancy the idea of being 'a sailing domestic for rich kids'. Besides, he wanted nothing more to do with the Reichsmarine and he could not have avoided coming into contact with naval officers at the Hanseatic Yachting School. Nothing could recompense the loss of his beautiful uniform or his broken dreams of becoming an admiral. At her wits' end, his mother appealed to Heydrich's godmother, Elise, Baroness von Eberstein. Her son Friedrich Karl had been promoted recently to SS-Sturmführer and was serving at Munich, 'Capital City of the NSDAP Movement', and on the staff of the most senior SA leader, Ernst Röhm. 'Little Karl' knew that the new SA-elite troops were looking for a 'Nachrichtenmann'. The word *Nachricht* can mean 'signal' in the military sense but to the SA and SS it meant something else. What this other meaning was he would discover in due course. The SS would have a smart black uniform for 'Reini' – that was important.

On 1 June 1931 in Hamburg, Heydrich joined the NSDAP, membership number 544916.[45] That was the precondition for the job with the SS. On 14 June he arrived in Munich by train to present himself to the Reichsführer-SS Heinrich Himmler. Lina recorded that it was this day, her twentieth birthday, that there occurred 'the starriest hour of my life, of our life'.[46]

Although Eberstein had advised him before departure to postpone his visit because Himmler was at home trying to shake off a bout of influenza, Heydrich went to the little poultry smallholding at Waldtrudering. The SS leader had studied agriculture but experienced no success before joining the SS as a bodyguard for Hitler.

With some annoyance Himmler received the applicant, but was immediately delighted by his 'Nordic appearance', 'tall and blond with honest, sharp and good-natured eyes', as he was to say later. Himmler explained that he was looking for a 'reporting officer', a man who could design and set up a system of informers and stool-pigeons for the Nazi Party 'in order to draw up a picture of its Communist, Jewish, freemasonic and reactionary opponents'.

'Yes, Reichsführer, but I am not the man you want,' Heydrich responded at once, 'I was a signals officer.' Himmler replied, 'It makes no difference to me. Take a seat, I'll be back in fifteen minutes. Write down how you imagine the intelligence service of the NSDAP should work.' Heydrich racked his brains for all he knew about military organisation and intelligence, coupling it up with material from the English detective novels of which he was so fond. Himmler was satisfied with the result: 'Yes, I concur.' While the poultry clucked in the farmyard outside, the pact which would bring upon Germany the powers of evil was sealed between the two young men (Himmler was only four years older than Heydrich).

The SS chief said curtly, 'Good, I'll take you on.' A starting wage of 120 Reichsmarks was agreed upon, enough to keep the leader of the newly-to-be-created security service from starving.[47]

Himmler was very pale in complexion, aloof and reserved, and was not the kind of man one might envisage to be the leader of an organisation of Nordic giants following Hitler's ideals of racial beauty. Heydrich was much more the type. Himmler was small and unimpressive, particularly out of uniform. His blue eyes were cold behind rimless pince-nez, his moustache and hair clipped short in military fashion, his chin weak. There was something of the schoolmaster about him, which was not surprising, for in 1900, the year of his birth, his father Gebhard Himmler had been tutor at Munich to the Wittelsbach prince Heinrich von Bayern, and worked from 1913 to 1919 as co-rector at Landshut high school. 'He was a model of pedantic correctness,' his biographers Heinrich Fraenkel and Roger Manvell said of the father in their book *Himmler, Kleinbürger und Massenmörder*[48] (*Himmler, a Mass-Murderer from the Petty-Bourgeoisie*).

Although the pro-nationalist Heinrich Himmler was keen to fight at the front in World War I, he was not called up until 1917 and experienced the capitulation the following year as an officer candidate at a barracks at

Regensburg. He joined a Freikorps to oppose the 'Republic' of Leftist councils and was indoctrinated with copious Rightist literature in which a 'world conspiracy' of Jews, freemasons and Jesuits was spoken of. He received his *Abitur* school-leaving certificate and between 1919 and 1922 studied at Munich University, obtaining a diploma in agriculture. He worked for a year at a factory at Schleissheim producing fertiliser from dung but was obsessed by politics: through old Freikorps contacts he came to the NSDAP, which he entered in August 1923 and in whose ranks on 9 November that year he took part in the attempted Hitler Beerhall putsch wearing a steel helmet several sizes too big for him as a standard bearer for the Reich War Flag paramilitary group. In the summer of 1924 he became secretary of Gregor Strasser's Greater German Freedom Movement from where he rejoined the NSDAP in 1925 after it was reconstituted following the lifting of its proscription. While acting as Strasser's propaganda chief, he travelled by motor-cycle from place to place throughout Bavaria electioneering to the idealised 'folk of the land' on behalf of the Nazis. Himmler himself turned again to 'holy Mother Earth'. His marriage in July 1928 to nursing sister Margarete Boden, born in 1893 in Goncercevo near Posen in Prussian-occupied Poland, enabled him to purchase a smallholding at Wasserburger Landstrasse 109 in Waldtrudering, where he later met Heydrich for the first time. Marga sold a nursing home which she ran in Berlin and put the proceeds into a poultry enterprise with about fifty hens. It was not a financial success, for Himmler was soon in Nazi service full-time.

On 6 January 1929 Hitler nominated him Reichsführer-SS in place of Erhard Heiden. Himmler, SS number 168 since 1925, had been Heiden's deputy. At that time, the SS numbered 280, but under Himmler's aegis, it grew from what had been envisaged originally as a bodyguard troop for Hitler, a body of thugs known as Stosstrupp Adolf Hitler, into a hand-picked and well-drilled guard unit inside the SA. Himmler devised for them the motto *Meine Ehre heisst Treue* – 'Loyalty is My Honour' and had it engraved on their belt-buckles and 'honour daggers'.

As he stated in 1940 in retrospect, Himmler saw in Adolf Hitler 'one of those great figures of Light who always arise from among the *Germanen* when the deepest physical, mental and spiritual need for him demands it'.[49] He had been a fervent admirer of Hitler since reading *Mein Kampf* and Hitler used the absolute loyalty of 'loyal Heinrich' for his own purposes. Himmler was never so close to the Führer personally as Goering or Goebbels, with whom Hitler would take supper and invite to sleep over, and although he visited Himmler's house at Waldtrudering and later at Gmund as well, he never stayed there very long.

Although one would not have thought so on first impression, Himmler was as great a tactician as Hitler, and pursued his aims with great patience and perseverance. 'It is a basic error to underestimate Himmler,' biographers Fraenkel and Manvell wrote: 'he was a man of passionate convictions' for whom Might was the means 'to turn into reality a self-imposed Messianic mission in the service of the Germanic race'.[50]

Himmler knew how to put people to their best use, and the value of a well-oiled organisation. At the forefront of the latter an outstanding intelligence system to monitor friend and foe would be essential, and in Heydrich he recognised the man who could engineer this favourable situation for the SS.

Before Heydrich began work at the Party headquarters in Munich, Das Braune Haus, in 1931, ahead of him lay the time of his consecration to Nazism: the *Kampfzeit*, the time of struggle. In *Gau* Hamburg on 14 July, the retired naval lieutenant joined the SS as Untersturmführer (membership number 10120). He combined his small SS troop with hooligans of the newly formed SA-Marinesturm to fight the district elections of 27 September. In street-fighting with Communists, deaths and serious injuries occurred. Within the ranks of the KPD (German Communist Party) rumours were soon circulating of a 'blond beast from Dovenhof' with the Nazi commandos, 'trained militarily', who struck like lightning and then withdrew before the police could intervene.[51] Lina Heydrich states in her memoir that her husband had experienced 'at the Dovernhof [*sic*] and in other parts of the city . . . political fighting in which, so to speak, man fought against man, stabbing, clubbing or even shooting'.[52]

In the local elections, the National Socialists won 43 of the 160 seats. The Hamburg Senate had an SPD (German Socialist Party)-led minority government which could only retain power with the tacit support of the thirty-five KPD deputies. The Nazis smelt the fresh winds of change. SA man Pidder Lüng composed a poem ending with the line:

> The swastika our symbol of victory calls us forward
> To hammer on the door of the New Age![53]

It can scarcely have escaped the astute Heydrich what kind of political party he was serving, for the Nazis were not only taking on the Reds and the Jews with utter viciousness: Hitler wanted to destroy the 'State of the November Treason' of 1918, the Weimar Democracy. 'Give the system the knock-out!' Goebbels cried to an electioneering meeting in Hamburg: 'We want to carry through our idea, no more and no less. To do it we need power, and we will get it whether you like it or not!'[54]

Their opponents understood the dark intentions of the Nazis. 'The real goal of fascism', Chairman of the SPD-deputies Rudolf Breitscheid told a Party convention at Leipzig in June 1931, 'is to abolish democracy.' The Nazis were turning their backs on every agreement and treaty, and through anti-semitism were 'creating a new lure for the downtrodden middle-classes suffering from the power of the capitalist banks and high interest rates': 'the only way to defend the national interest is by force'.[55]

There were 5.7 million unemployed in Germany in the autumn of 1931 and very few Nazis were optimistic. The NSDAP was distracted by internal party power struggles between Hitler and Strasser; morale in both SA and SS was at a low ebb. The great election victories were still in the future: before that there would be more bloody fighting. For Heydrich there was no turning back.

On 10 August 1931 Heydrich set his surveillance service on its feet. Following the example of military intelligence units he gave it the title 'Ic'. This was the birth hour of the SD Sicherheitsdienst, which awoke like the kraken over all Germany and later overshadowed half of Europe and much further afield. 'From the outset, Heydrich owed his SS career to Himmler,' US historian Charles Sydnor emphasises, 'and he in turn as head of the SS relied on the dynamic, unscrupulous but utterly reliable Heydrich. In the history of the Third Reich there is no other relationship of similar significance.'[56]

On 11 August Heydrich wrote to his 'parents-in-law' at Lütjenbrode that he had 'manoeuvred himself in', had been made Sturmführer and would receive his first pay packet on 1 September. At that time he would be 'in a position to work off my debts, if at all possible in large instalments, by careful monthly budgeting.' Among these debts was money lent to him by the von Ostens when he was unemployed. He worked long hours every day 'so that even in the evenings I am to be found bent over my work desk if the Reichsführer, Prince Waldeck or von Eberstein don't fetch me from the building'.[57]

Heydrich's instinct for people and power impressed Himmler from early on. Heydrich denounced a Party member called Horninger, whom Himmler was also considering for the position of Ic head, as an informer for the Munich police. This allegation stuck and cost Horninger his life in Nazi custody in 1933.[58] Based on the Munich police files, from November 1931 they had considerably less information about the SS leadership and the Ic service than in previous months, and so Heydrich was probably right. 'He had an unerring nose for people,' Himmler said in praise of his new giant. 'With amazing foresight he saw the paths which friend and foe would follow. His men would scarcely dare to lie to him.'[59] The ever-suspicious Heydrich saw it as his primary duty to root out enemy informers, from the police to the KPD. Soon SS colleagues were calling him the 'Great Creator of Suspicion', and he took that as a compliment. Shortly after taking office, on 26 August 1931, a Party member for only three months, he convened his first lecture at Das Braune Haus in Munich, 'Tactics of the Opposition'.

The Government had the intention 'of damaging the NSDAP by every means possible', he said, according to a file note. Nobody should fall into their trap, everybody had to await the orders of the Party leadership in all respects. Opponents of various hues were watching the NSDAP and manipulated even the most minor negative occurrences to discredit the Hitler Party in the Press. At least as dangerous as the snooping was the attempt to incite National Socialist and SS leaders, and 'sow discord in the organisation'. In conclusion Heydrich announced the formation of 'a small department of SS people' whose task it was to 'identify the informers within the Party', and he warned the assembled SS leaders against loose talk regarding internal Party affairs: 'There must be no distrust among colleagues: one never knows who the traitors are.'[60]

Therefore he began to assemble, initially in a cigar chest, a card-index system in which he filed all the information he could obtain about members and enemies of the Party, and especially anything which might be useful later to use against a person. At first he was allocated at Das Braune Haus only half an office and one typewriter which he shared with the much-travelled SS-Stabsführer Richard Hildebrandt. On 4 September 1931 in a 'secret SS order' Himmler decided that every SS section and Standarten-troop had to create an Ic post to report to Munich, for 'the offensive, snooping and demoralisation activities, especially those of our Marxist opponents, demands a monitoring and counter-intelligence service.' The activities of the latter would be 'absolutely legal' and were aimed only at 'non-State organisations'.[61] These guidelines were purely for external show, for Heydrich's spies were active at Munich Police headquarters and in the Bavarian Interior Ministry. Heydrich's work was pursued with such zeal that even Nazi bosses such as Gauleiter Karl Kaufmann of Hamburg were reporting whisperings in the ranks. Himmler protected his man and on 1 December 1931 rewarded him with promotion to SS-Hauptsturmführer (captain).

Whoever would see Heydrich merely as a 'Nazi by opportunity' has only to look at his marriage ceremony to know that it went much deeper. On Boxing Day 1931 during Christmas leave he married Lina von Osten at the Evangelical Church of St Katherine at Grossenbrode on Fehmarn. He wore a tuxedo, since SA and SS uniforms were illegal at the time. Above the altar was a swastika of fir-tree branches. The approach to the Church door was lined on either side by uniformed Nazis with right arms extended in the Hitler salute. At the dedication mass Bruno Heydrich sang a prayer composed by himself especially for the occasion. As the married couple and the congregation left the church, the organ played the *Horst Wessel*, battle hymn of the Nazi Party. Those 'gathered together in the sight of God' – mainly SA, SS and NSDAP men – made the most of the opportunity because the police had no jurisdiction on hallowed ground. The Church authorities later gave the priest a compulsory transfer as a punishment.[62] To celebrate the happy day, Himmler promoted

Heydrich to SS-Sturmbannführer (major) so that he was now two ranks higher than when he was discharged after nine years naval service. Himmler also authorised a pay rise to 290 Reichsmarks.

By the previous autumn, Heydrich's Ic office, consisting of himself and three assistants, had moved into its own independent premises, two rooms sub-let by a widow loyal to the Nazis, Viktoria Edrich, on the fourth floor of Türkenstrasse 23, Munich. Heydrich also lived in one of these rooms, being joined there by his wife at New Year 1932. Shortly afterwards, however, the couple found a dilapidated flat at Lochhausen, which Lina managed to furnish with her father's dowry. She considered the surrounding area to be 'rural Bavarian' and they moved again after a few months to a pretty white villa at Zaccalistrasse 4 close by the Nymphenburger Schlosspark. The villa was a discreetly hidden property well-suited to the 'secret intelligence service' of the SS leader. During the period between April and June 1932 when the SA and SS were banned, it housed Ic under the guise of the Press and Information service (PI) of Reichstag deputy Himmler. At this time Ic had seven full-time workers.

'Everything was done to make it look like a private dwelling,' Lina Heydrich explained, 'the house, a little set back into the garden, gave us the chance to hide anything incriminating if unexpected callers arrived. Our dogs gave us good warning.' She saw herself as 'protectress of the alarm system' and 'maid of all work', the 'PI woman'. She cooked for everyone, usually a soup of dried vegetables since 'it was the cheapest'. [63]

Heydrich beavered away tirelessly. While travelling across Germany to recruit qualified personnel he would revise his espionage material, poring over the secret files and NSDAP and SA membership cards. Fed by informers everywhere, including the police, the 'opposition cards' were already spilling out of the cigar chest.

In July 1932 Heydrich was formally named 'Chief of the SD at Reichsführer-SS'. This SD was so poorly financed, however, that initially its allocation of funds did not extend to covering the office supplies and mostly unpaid volunteers had to be resorted to. Sufficient cash only became available once Hitler had taken power. Heydrich preferred for his unit young academics, officials and businessmen such as lawyer Dr

Herbert Mehlhorn, Dr Johannes Schmidt, or the Hamburg businessman Carl Oberg, who despaired of the 'Weimar System' and the economic crisis, and sought a radical alternative. Heydrich, who could be charming and enthusiastic if he chose to be, convinced them that this path led through the NSDAP, SS and SD. Himmler wanted to develop the SS as a 'Black Order', an elite of Aryan warriors blindly loyal to Hitler and his doctrine by a sworn oath. With the SD, Heydrich was aiming to create the spiritual leadership-elite of the SS, the 'cream of the cream of the NSDAP'.

At first the SD was just one of several informer services of the Party which was obliged to compete for the favour and attention of the leadership. Heydrich identified the head of the SA intelligence service, the Munich lawyer Karl Graf du Moulin Eckart, as the main rival whose ace he needed to trump. Heydrich was looking well ahead. He made a study of the far larger and more powerful State espionage services such as the Soviet GPU and the French Deuxième Bureau, but he tended to favour British Intelligence, where Gentlemen made deals based on personal honour, and for this reason, copying the British head of MI6, he liked to be called 'C', and often signed his correspondence with this initial.[64]

When the Oldenburg police arrested an Ic agent in February 1932 and obtained a confession that he was spying at the Wilhelmshaven naval shipyard for the 'SS intelligence service', Heydrich decided to tighten up his organisation. In principle he required his workers in Germany, about thirty-strong at the time, not to report to individual SS sections, but to himself directly.

The SD grew slowly within the SS to be an independent organisation, since the SS itself was actually a component of the SA. This was why the SA leader Röhm had made a joint tour with Himmler of the SD centre at the Zuccalistrasse address in the spring of 1932 and had had the secret card-index files explained to him, resulting finally in approval for additional money for Heydrich's work.

At the beginning of June 1932, the spectre of the old trauma revived to haunt Heydrich once more. The NSDAP Gauleiter of Halle/Merseburg, Rudolf Jordan, had written to NSDAP organisational leader Gregor Strasser at Das Braune Haus:

It has come to my ears that there is a person in the Reich leadership called Heydrich whose father lives in Halle. There is reason to believe that this father, Bruno Heydrich of Halle, is a Jew. I enclose herewith an extract from Hugo Riemann's *Musik-Lexikon 1916* from which you can see the thing for yourself. Perhaps it might be an idea if the Personnel Department could look into this matter.[65]

The extract referred to was the fatal entry 'Heydrich, Bruno, (actually Süss)'. Strasser passed the matter at once to the ancestry expert Dr Achim Gercke, head of NS-Auskunft. Where others often had to wait months, the result came surprisingly quickly, scarcely two weeks later, obviously the fruit of earlier research, and bearing an unequivocal opinion.

It is evident from the attached list of ancestors that Oberleutnant zur See a. D. Reinhardt [*sic*] Heydrich is of German origin and free from any admixture of coloured or Jewish blood. This damaging rumour for the family, that they were formerly called Süss, led to the father of Oberleutnant Heydrich being given the nickname 'Isidor Süss' which in turn gave rise to the assumption that the family was indeed Jewish in origin. The following background is pertinent: One sees from the ancestral tree that Oberleutnant Heydrich's grandmother Ernestine Wilhelmine Heydrich, née Lindner . . . contracted a second marriage with assistant locksmith Gustav Robert Süss. As the mother of a large number of children from the first marriage with her husband Reinhold Heydrich, she was often known by the surname Heydrich-Süss. It is worth mentioning in this regard that assistant locksmith Süss was himself not of Jewish ancestry.[66]

The annexed ancestral list was very superficial for an organisation such as the SS, whose leader Himmler required his senior people to produce a certificate of 'Aryan origins' going back to 1648, marking the end of the Thirty Years War. It was perhaps a portentous omission that the birthdates of Heydrich's mother and grandfather, as well as those of three of the four maternal great-grandparents, were absent. Nevertheless Gercke wrote on the document: 'I take full responsibility for the accuracy of this opinion and declare myself prepared to testify to it before a court should the need arise.'

Although the Party was happy that 'all questions open to debate had been answered', Heydrich continued his private search for Jewish ancestors. As Felix Kersten, Himmler's masseur and confidant, and continually in his presence during the war, wrote subsequently, the SS chief and Hitler both played on Heydrich's fears. After a long talk with the SD head, Hitler observed to Himmler, 'This Heydrich is a very dangerous man whose talents the Movement needs to hold on to. One can only keep such people working if one has them in one's hand. His non-Aryan origins will suit us admirably. He will be eternally grateful to us for having retained him, and will obey us blindly.'[67] Some historians consider the Balt Kersten (actually a Finnish national born in the Baltic province of Livland, then in Tsarist Russia), 'unworthy of belief'.

Everybody who saw the broad picture of the Heydrich–Himmler relationship noticed how curiously subordinate was Heydrich's demeanour in the presence of his chief: '*Jawohl,* Herr Reichsführer! As ordered, Herr Reichsführer!' And that from a man who was accustomed to giving orders and came down hard on every minor error of his own subordinates. Did he perhaps live in fear that his Nazi career could end as abruptly as his naval career had?

Heydrich engaged the genealogist Ernst Hoffmann privately and had himself kept regularly informed about the specialist's research over several years.

> To judge by the way he looked at me whenever I arrived at his office, his doubts were evident, [Hoffmann wrote,] yet before I had spoken a word his tension would evaporate. He knew by just looking at me that 'everything was in order' so far. Once doubts befell him when he saw the name Birnbaum. It was understandable but without foundation.'[68]

Heydrich's ancestry has remained puzzling, even though historians Aronson and Karin Flachowsky have dismissed all speculation about a 'Jewish grandmother' after comprehensive research. However, they have not explained the following. In Heydrich's files, his great-great-grandmother, married in 1810 to innkeeper Johann Gottfried *Heidrich*, bears the name Johanna Birnbaum. She was born at Reichenbach in 1773, died at Arnsdorf (Saxony) in 1841. Her husband died at Arnsdorf four years previously. In an ancestral search prepared for Heydrich's brother Siegfried Heinz, the great-great-grandmother Birnbaum, no further details being supplied, was Maria Rosine Lichner. The name Birnbaum, which is not necessarily Jewish in origin, does not appear anywhere in the documentation.[69]

Heydrich had more familiar problems at this time through the continuing financial distress of his parents. They had fallen heavily into debt because the income from the Dresden Conservatory had dried up. Even though poorly paid by the SS, Heydrich offered them a covenant 'for the necessities of life through their son'. In it he agreed to pay his parents' rent up to sixty-five Reichsmarks plus heating costs and fifty Reichsmarks assistance monthly. In return, they had to 'take upon themselves no fresh debt' and 'avoid conversing with known business peoples, shops etc. which might endanger the reputation and the existence of their children.'[70] Was this the affair of the Jewish ancestors again?

Heydrich now concentrated at Himmler's side on the major political problems. On 30 January 1933 the Nazis achieved their goal. The power of Government fell into their laps from the hands of middle-class political administrators, and this they called 'the seizure of power'. At 11.40 that morning, old Reich President Paul von Hindenburg, manipulated by his advisers, summoned Hitler to accept the Chancellorship. Afterwards, as he drove in an open Mercedes through cheering crowds to his room in the nearby Kaiserhof Hotel, Hitler rejoiced sobbing: 'We have done it! We have done it!'[71]

The conservatives, who had helped him come to power, led by the former centrist-politician and Chancellor Franz von Papen, hoped that they had the Brown leader firmly reined in. In Hitler's first Cabinet, apart from himself, there were only two Nazis: Goering as Reichs Minister without Portfolio, Reichs Commissioner for Aviation and Prussian Minister of the Interior, and Wilhelm Frick, Reichs Interior Minister. Most of the other twelve were representatives of the Deutsch-Nationale Volkspartei (DNVP), the Stahlhelm veterans' organisation, or without affiliation at the insistence of Papen and Hindenburg. The new man bided his time. On taking office, Hitler had prophesied, 'No power in the world will drag me out of here alive'.[72]

In Unter den Linden and in the Wilhelmstrasse that evening, twenty-five thousand Berlin SA and SS men celebrated with a triumphal torchlight procession. Hitler watched the parade from a window on the first floor of the Reich Chancellery. 'The endless chanting of *Heil! Heil! Sieg Heil!* sounded in my ears like a storm bell,'[73] Vice-Chancellor von Papen reported. Did he suspect that he had opened the gates to the Devil in human form?

Chapter Two

Reinhard Heydrich's Seizure of Power 1933–1940

Towards eleven o'clock on the morning of 27 March 1933, Lina Heydrich received a telephone call in the service flat on the Nymphenburger Schloss. Her husband, Reinhard, head of the SD, told her, 'Send my pistol to the Braunes Haus right now.'[1] The Bavarian provincial administration, whose seat was at Munich, was proposing to mount an armed attack against the SA, he alleged. Lina Heydrich was appalled, but had the pistol taken to NSDAP headquarters. The Nazi 'seizure of power' in Bavaria was about to begin.

A little later, SA chief, Ernst Röhm, Himmler and Heydrich held a con-ference in the State Chancellery with Minister-President Held of the Bavarian Volkspartei. Held was refusing to nominate Franz Ritter von Epp, an old Nazi from the earliest days of the Movement, as Reichs-Kommissar unless he had the order from Hitler in black-and-white. Röhm telephoned Berlin and received the promise of a telegram which had failed to arrive. The hours went by: a second telegram was promised but this too never came: it appeared that officials at the Munich Telegraph Office loyal to the existing State Government were withholding delivery. Heydrich took matters into his own hands and soon the 1.85-metre-tall military officer arrived at the Telegraph Office, pistol drawn. The telegram authorising the appointment of von Epp was handed over and the coup went off as planned.

That same afternoon, black SA cars raced to the offices of the Munich Police Steering Committee in the Wittelsbach Palace. Two SS officers in black uniform and wearing red swastika armbands stormed inside: Himmler, new police chief of Munich, and Heydrich, leader of the political administration office, Referat 6, had arrived.

The SS chief and his prodigy seized in Munich what had escaped them on 30 January 1933 in Berlin. In the first photos of Hitler as Reichs Chancellor, Himmler is present as the only man in uniform. Himmler left empty-handed after the distribution of ministerial offices and went back to Bavaria, sending Heydrich to Berlin as liaison officer *zur besonderen Verwendung* (for special purposes). Heydrich was held in such low regard there, however, that SS-Führer Kurt Daluege, later head of the uniformed non-political police, conspired with Himmler's rival Goering to give him the cold shoulder. On headed notepaper from the Savoy Hotel near the Bahnhof Zoo, the SD chief complained that never once had Daluege deigned to receive him before his return to Munich. He had been bounced off Daluege's rubber wall: 'I must have phoned him six times without success.'[2]

The 'seizure of power' in Munich came on the very day that Heydrich was intending to move to Berlin. Now he remained where he was, together with Himmler, as the head of the newly founded Political Police of All-Bavaria. As he told his wife, his intention was to 'stir up the shit' before dedicating himself again to the SD fully.[3]

The two SS heads began their work by rounding up hundreds of Communists using the emergency legislation 'For the Protection of the German People' that had become law on 27 February barely twenty-four hours after the Reichstag fire apparently set by Communists. This was the new legal device to underpin the Nazi dictatorship: Injustice By Force of

Law. Hitler made it perfectly clear at this early stage the way things would be going henceforth: 'There will now be no more mercy, whoever blocks our path will be put down.'[4] Even before this, by the end of the first fortnight in power, Himmler and Heydrich had the jails overflowing. On 22 March Himmler reopened an abandoned factory just outside the town of Dachau as a camp for up to five thousand people in *Schutzhaft* – protective custody. Heydrich referred to it simply as 'the KL' – *Konzentrationslager*.

The Nobel Prizewinner for Literature Thomas Mann wrote satirically in July that Heydrich should be sent there as the head of an 'Un-German, pro-Marxist, pro-Jewish and anti-Nationalist Movement'.[5] The author, on vacation in Switzerland, never returned to Germany, and his possessions in Munich were confiscated.

On 11 April 1933 the control of Dachau was transferred to the SS. The next day SS guards shot the first three Jews. A fourth survived seriously wounded and was taken to hospital. The circumstances surrounding the incident are not certain. State attornies investigated and found that the camp was a place where human dignity was trampled underfoot. They were powerless to act, however: Himmler blocked them with denials, delays and threats, and in the end they gave up.

Bereft of all legal controls, Dachau gave birth to the School of Violence, as local historian Hans-Günter Ricardi wrote: it became the blueprint for the concentration camps and death camps which were to follow, the training ground for their administrators, such as Auschwitz commandant Rudolf Hoess and the 'Chargé for Jewish Affairs', Adolf Eichmann: the breeding ground for concentration-camp thugs of the so-called SS-Totenkopfverband units from 1936 onwards. Replacing numerous 'freelance' torture camps, used by SA stormtroops for lodging countless Reds and Jews after the 'seizure of power', the terror was now organised, torture and murder with German thoroughness. Dachau camp commandant was the moronic Theodor Eicke, whose motto was 'Tolerance is Weakness'.

For the least infringement of camp rules, 'Papa' Eicke could have custodees subjected to a series of punishments culminating with a beating with an ox-whip which often resulted in death. As 'Inspector of

Concentration Camps' he used the model of Dachau to design the camps at Sachsenhausen, Buchenwald and Ravensbrück. Of the 206,000 persons who went into Dachau between 1933 and 1945, only 31,591 perished there, and so Dachau did not qualify as a 'death camp'.

In order to fully realise their purpose to 'eliminate the enemies of the State', Himmler and Heydrich decided next to remove to Berlin, the real 'Capital of the Movement', where Hitler was dismantling democracy and the freedoms, where SA chief Röhm was dreaming of a 'second revolution' and Goering had set up a Gestapo office of his own.

Heydrich consulted Police Secretary Heinrich Müller, an expert on the Communist system whom he had had no qualms about transferring into the Bavarian Political Police, and was briefed at length on the structure and methods of Stalin's GPU, the organ of State repression and sabotage in the Soviet Union. A centralised police force in the Reich in place of the provincial police force system presently in force seemed to him a precondition for the consolidation of the National Socialist State which would eventually become the SS State under the Reichsführer-SS. That was Heydrich's idea. Himmler liked it at once, and between the autumn of 1933 and the summer of 1934, the political police headquarters from Lübeck to Schaumburg-Lippe were absorbed step by step under the central umbrella

If Goering felt superior to the small, bespectacled Reichsführer-SS ('Himmler and Heydrich never came to Berlin'),[6] by March 1934 he had caved in to him completely. It was agreed that Himmler would head the political police in Prussia. Hitler had been pressing for this because, in his opinion, Goering was becoming too greedy for power. During his trial at Nuremberg, Goering, former head of the Prussian police, said:

> At that time I did not protest although I considered the manoeuvres unpleasant and wanted to keep the Prussian police in my own hands. But when the Führer himself gave the order and told me that it was for the best, and that there was an urgent necessity to tackle all the enemies of the State within the German Reich in the same manner, I handed over the office at once to Himmler, and he gave the running of it to Heydrich.[7]

His Gestapo chief Rudolf Diels did not fear Himmler, but rather that 'Heydrich will come and have all the police forces under his control.' Goering shouted, 'What would that mean?' and Diels groaned, 'Poor Germany!'[8]

On 20 April 1934 Himmler became head of the Gestapo office, Heydrich, as expected, being his deputy while continuing as SD head. From 6 June the SD functioned as the only secret service organ of the NSDAP. One of Heydrich's most important collaborators was Bavarian police chief Heinrich Müller. By his choice of this man, who had been a loyal and industrious servant of the Weimar Republic, Heydrich showed that he placed more emphasis on efficiency in his staff than the long-term experience of the civil servant. Provided his colleagues were loyal to him, he would take care personally of the ideological organisation of the German security service. Müller did not disappoint his chief in the coming years.

In 1933 Müller had belonged initially to those who opposed a take-over of their offices by the Nazis. His political department at Munich police headquarters was known for its close links to the democratic parties, particularly the Bayrische Volkspartei. 'Just let them come, and we'll sort them out,'[9] Müller is alleged to have said on 9 March 1933, shortly before the SA stood at the door. By 31 May at Himmler's urging, however, he had joined the NSDAP with the high membership number 4,583,199.

It was immaterial to Heydrich that 'Gestapo' Müller, as he was known in Nazi jargon, had kept away from the Party for so long and that as a new Party member showed very little enthusiasm for its affairs. Equally unimportant was the fact that his No. 2 man had completed only eight years' formal education and had had to catch up the missing years much later, the cause of his feelings of inferiority in the presence of intellectuals in the Gestapo. Müller would attempt to conceal his insecurity from his colleague Walter Schellenberg behind statements such as: 'One should put all the intelligentsia in a mineshaft and then blow it up.'[10]

For Heydrich it was important to have an expert like Müller in Berlin who knew his way around the dangerous activities of the Left from his time with the Bavarian Political Police and who was no less ready to serve his new masters and their ideology as conscientiously as he had the Weimar Republic. A colleague from Munich police headquarters described Müller's attitude after the National Sociaist seizure of power in Bavaria: 'After the occupation of the Munich Police Praesidium by the rulers of the Third Reich, Müller busied himself very actively with the tasks National Socialism set him. The close relationship with the then Standartenführer Heydrich led to the recognition of his total reliability and unstinting co-operation with the National Socialist State.'[11]

With zeal verging on obsession, between 1933 and 1938 Müller prepared for his new chief a compendium on the development of the Communist Party. He dictated every last detail of his knowledge to his secretary: from the Spartacist League to the Central Committee, from the aims of the KPD to its underground activities and the methods it adopted, including those of its agents from the East.

The interrogation methods of the Russians fascinated Heydrich as much as Müller himself. Horst Kopkow, who handled Sabotage Counter-Intelligence at RSHA from 1939, recalled:

> Müller told me a couple of times that he was really keen to know how they had got the generals to confess in the Tuchatshevski case. Apparently he was astonished how Tuchatshevski frankly admitted contacts with German officers. He thought the Russians must have had some medicament – he often spoke about the use of drugs which would deprive people completely of their will and move them to make enormous confessions.'[12]

Heydrich's SD and his Communist-expert Müller were possibly involved in the downfall of Mikhail Tuchatshevski – the General was executed in 1937 together with a large portion of the Soviet military leadership in a major Stalinist purge. It is difficult today to reconstruct the extent to which the SD had a finger in the pie but it has been suggested that fake correspondence may have been planted by Heydrich's agents at the instigation of Hitler 'to cripple the Red Army'.[13] The forged signatures of German officers had apparently been copied from bank cheques making official payments at the time of the Weimar Republic when the German 100,000-man army was secretly hosted by the Soviet Union for training purposes. Poor Tuchatshevski's forged signature on the 'correspondence' gave the impression that he was spying for Hitler's Germany.[14] The successful plot, if it was one, turned out to be a fiasco of strategy. In the autumn of 1943 Himmler sighed to high-ranking SS officers:

> When the Bolshevik General Tuchatshevski was shot in Moscow – I think it was 1937 or 1938 – we in Europe, in the Party and SS, were convinced that the Bolshevik system and Stalin had committed their biggest mistake. But in our judgment of the situation we have completely bamboozled ourselves. I believe now that Russia would not have been able to hold out for two years of war if they had kept the Tsarist generals around Tuchatshevski.[15]

To the tireless Bolshevik-expert Müller, Heydrich's office became a second home. Camp commandant Hoess stated: 'Müller made very few service journeys, but you could reach him at any time, day or night, even Sundays and public holidays.'[16] Heydrich rewarded this loyalty by promoting Müller head of Amt II (Internal-Political Affairs), of which he had previously been chief himself. When Amt II and Amt III were merged into Amt IV (Warfare on Opponents) in 1939, Himmler appointed him head of that too. Officially Heydrich had no deputy, but whenever he was absent from office, Müller would take over affairs, possibly in hopes of being first in line of succession. Yet with Heydrich's death the brakes came on for the career of the man who, as Gestapo chief, had been responsible for thousands of acts of torture and murder, and after 4 June 1942 he received no further promotions.

Two years later the true servant of his master was awarded the Knights Cross of the War Service Cross with Swords. This high decoration was actually reserved for those who had fought at the front.

Müller had never seen any fighting. At the award ceremony, Himmler and Heydrich's successor Ernst Kaltenbrunner praised Müller's deeds of heroism on the Home Front:

> SS-Gruppenführer Müller has built up, as the result of great efforts and enormous personal involvement over the years, the Gestapo of today from the few suitable forces available at the seizure of power, including the non-political Kripo. This has enabled the Gestapo, as a political surveillance service, to supply constantly a flow of information relating to illegal activities in the Reich territories. Through lightning intervention in numerous cases he has prevented significant sabotage and espionage successes by the enemies of the Third Reich. The Gestapo, imbued with the political world view of Müller, was responsible for the swift putting down, arrest and extinction of the traitors of 20 July 1944 together with their accomplices.[17]

Few can have served the Reich so well. Müller's eventual fate is unknown. After the war a warrant was issued for his arrest and he was declared officially dead at the same time. Possibly he really did die in early May 1945 in the last street fighting for Berlin, but may have had the techniques and contacts – possibly to Soviet agents – to assist him to quietly disappear.

With capable and unscrupulous helpers like Müller, the clique around Himmler and Heydrich turned Goering's Gestapo inside out. In the Prinz-Albrecht-Strasse, only two blocks from the Reich Chancellery, Himmler occupied a former hotel at No. 9, Heydrich next door at No. 8, a former arts and crafts school where Goering had housed the secret police in 1933 so as to have them in the immediate vicinity of his Ministry and to keep a close eye on them.

The Bavarian squad began the big clear-out at once. The majority of senior men were transferred to the Interior Ministry. Criminal-adviser Arthur Nebe, another of Heydrich's experts, was given the job of choosing those useful enough to retain. All vacant positions were filled at once with SS personnel. In vain Rudolf Diels made a last attempt to discuss matters with the new landlords but they were apparently under orders not to talk and their assistants kept all enquirers at arm's length. 'The reception area looked like an Army camp,' Diels wrote, 'everywhere black uniforms, mixed with girls sporting snail-hairstyles, and all speaking the Bavarian dialect.'

The *Basler Nationalzeitung* saw the signs of the times: 'The nomination of the Reichsführer-SS to replace Diels, who has been on leave of absence for some time, doubtlessly indicates a sharper course for the Gestapo, becoming ever more political,'[18] it commented on the change of hands in Prinz-Albrecht-Strasse. Diels also knew that his hour had struck and left for Prague. From now on the Himmler–Heydrich duo had an open road. Himmler criticised Heydrich for his 'cold, rational censoriousness'[19] and Heydrich made fun of Himmler's 'schoolmasterly' mannerisms,[20] mocked his fascination for giants' tombs and the *Germanen*-cult – nevertheless the two remained close partners as pitch and sulphur. 'Reinhard Heydrich is nothing without Himmler, and Heinrich Himmler is everything with Heydrich,'[21] said the later Resistance conspirator Hans Bernd Gisevius, who knew them both: 'This man in the darkness, with his fanaticism and untiring watchfulness, with his brief, clear reports and the awful consequences which follow them, this technician of terror with his inexhaustible dossiers, this 'believer', he is the true founder, ideologue and organiser of the National Socialist State.'[22]

Also Dr Felix Kersten, chiropractor and Himmler's masseur to the end of the Third Reich, described the noticeable symbiosis of the two most powerful men in the repression-apparatus of the Hitler State. Despite reservations that some historians may have at relying too heavily on his diary entries in general, they make a credible first-hand impression of the Himmler–Heydrich relationship:

> He [Heydrich] has permanent access to Himmler and tends to
> show up in the middle of things to present urgent written
> reports . . . contrary to Himmler, who can be rather detailed
> in the way he expresses himself, Heydrich is like sharpened
> steel. I have often listened to reports in which Heydrich put

forward his suggestions. They were always masterpieces of reporting: a short description of the person or subject matter, then an efficacious argument leading to the decisive trump which he played last, following it all with his recommendation, which Himmler had difficulty in denying. At times I gained the impression that after such a report he seemed raped mentally. Often he would go to the telephone and after a short pause have someone send a message to Heydrich saying that he did not want to authorize the measures just yet, he would have to discuss it first with the Führer. He would inform Heydrich later of his denial in the shape of an alleged Führer-Order.

On the other hand, Himmler always treats Heydrich in the friendliest manner, yet Heydrich is completely servile to him in a manner I fail to comprehend. Instead of 'Reichsführer', he addresses Himmler as 'Herr Reichsführer', which is strongly forbidden in the SS. Conversations between Himmler and Heydrich follow a certain pattern, as follows: *'Jawoll,* Herr Reichsführer, if Herr Reichsführer concurs, I will do the necessary immediately and make my report to the Herr Reichsführer, *jawoll, jawoll, jawoll.'* As a political personality, Heydrich is undoubtedly more dynamic and far superior. He knows this and expresses his superiority in the elegance of his reports, and Himmler is simply unable to match him. Here again, Heydrich always goes on the back foot at once if Himmler challenges him or utters a contrary opinion. Himmler seems to have some secret hold over Heydrich which makes Heydrich submit to him unconditionally.[23]

Was it the already-mentioned 'Jewish strain' in his family, or unconditional belief in the 'Führer Principle' which turned the intellectually superior Heydrich into such a crawler before his chief? Himmler seems to have believed that Jewish blood flowed in the arteries of his No. 2, as his observations to Kersten following Heydrich's death show, and that he used this 'flaw' as a latent threat to keep Heydrich and his ambitions in check can be presumed, but not proved.

Heydrich's unconditional acceptance of the Führer Principle is reflected to some degree in his remarks in Prague in October 1941:

> The SS [and the SD and Sipo are part of the SS] is the assault troop of the Party. The troop of course does nothing which is contrary to the will and plans of the overall leader . . . so we act as executive organs conscious of the mission which follows the path from the Greater German to the Greater Germanic Reich . . . I see my task here as a mission in battle which I have to fulfil as the representative of another in order . . . to be able to report to the Führer, 'Mein Führer, I have completed the mission.'[24]

Heydrich probably transferred this unconditional subordination to Hitler on a one-to-one basis to Himmler as his direct superior.

Not everybody in Himmler's circle valued Heydrich's talents as much as the Reichsführer-SS's doctor. Himmler's sister-in-law Bertha was less convinced of his qualities. She visited the Prinz-Albrecht-Strasse offices frequently and on these occasions tended to speak her mind. Of all her brother-in-law's colleagues it was Heydrich who came off worst: she considered him so incompetent that whenever Himmler was away from Berlin she, Bertha, had to run the office for him. On 19 April 1936 Himmler had had enough of it and sent her a formal letter:

> I hear you have been to our offices again making tactless and pig-stupid remarks. I hereby forbid you, first, to enter my offices and secondly, to ring anybody there apart from myself or Brigadeführer Wolff . . . in future you will refrain from making any remarks about SS affairs and personalities. All heads of section have been made aware of this letter. Heil Hitler.[25]

Himmler and Heydrich delivered their journeyman's piece on the 'Night of the Long Knives', from 30 June to 1 July 1934, when they liberated their leader from the obstinate SA. Hitler had formed this organisation into a private bodyguard in the 1920s from social rejects, the unemployed and other twilight personalities. Sworn to loyalty to the Führer's person, the SA would wade in against all who dared utter criticism of National Socialist ideas at rallies and demonstrations, and it had thus become an instrument of terror for the NSDAP.

The force of ruffians and thugs, which by June 1934 had swollen to a membership of 4.5 million, was developing its own dynamism and demanding reforms. The Brown army of millions had become a millstone for Hitler and, principally because its homosexual chief of staff, Röhm, was planning to take over the Reichswehr and with it the officer corps, which Hitler needed for his military plans later, the time was favourable to allay Hitler's anxieties by a major mopping-up operation under a threat from actual and potential enemies.

In concert with Goebbels, Goering and Himmler, Heydrich convinced Hitler that a putsch was imminent. On Friday 29 June, Hitler lodged at the Dreesen Hotel, Bad Godesberg on the Rhine while SS-Gruppenführer Sepp Dietrich, commanding the Berlin Wachbataillon of two hundred carefully selected men, waited in readiness. Towards one o'clock the next morning the Bavarian Interior Minister, Gauleiter Adolf Wagner, telephoned to report that there had been anti-Hitler and anti-Reichswehr demonstrations on the streets of Munich. This was the last straw. Hitler decided 'to burn out the cancer down to the raw flesh'[26] and with that had himself flown at once to Munich. Always looking to the future, Heydrich had drawn up from his card-index system the list of SA leaders who were to be liquidated. Heydrich specialist Friedrich Karl von Eberstein stated after the war that he had seen orders for the executions brought by courier from Berlin to the Dresden SD; 'They were signed by Heydrich.'[27] Ten SA and National Socialist administrators were shot to start the operation. There was never any kind of judicial process or tribunal. In all between 30 June and 2 July 1934 in the so-called Röhm putsch eighty-nine persons – not all *Stürmer* types – were shot for treason. Heydrich simply removed Hitler's arch-enemies in a bloodbath, leading the operation from the Gestapo basement at the Prinz-Albrecht-Strasse. The first to find himself in Heydrich's subterranean dungeon was the former NSDAP organisational leader, Gregor Strasser, who had broken with Hitler at the end of 1932.

He was deliberately shot in the corridor by an SS man and thrown into a cell. Other prisoners could still hear him gasping for breath long afterwards. Once or twice they heard Heydrich's voice: 'Isn't he dead yet? Let the swine bleed!'[28]

'C' sent his old SD croney Johannes Schmidt to kill off the former Reich Chancellor Kurt von Schleicher at home. About midday on 30 June, Schmidt and five henchmen burst into Schleicher's villa in Neu-Babelsberg and thrust aside his housekeeper, Maria Grünel. General Schleicher was seated in his study. One of the gang asked if he was the general. When he said yes, they shot him three times. At that moment his wife appeared from another room. She was also gunned down and died the next day in hospital.

The anti-Catholic Heydrich gave SS-Hauptsturmführer Kurt Gildisch a pistol and told him, 'You handle the Klausener case. You are to shoot him personally. For the purpose, you are to go at once to the Traffic Ministry.'[29] Erich Klausener, leader of Catholic Action, worked there as a ministerial director. Before the seizure of power in 1933, he had shown himself to be a bitter enemy of the Nazis while head of the police department at the Prussian Interior Ministry. The dust would have settled after Goering had him transferred to the Traffic Ministry, had he kept quiet, but he continued to make public speeches against the National Socialist regime, for his position within the Catholic Church gave him a broad platform. Neither Goering nor Daluege, his successor as head of the police department, were able to find a way to silence Klausener legally, and so the matter was handed to Heydrich.

Since Klausener's outburst on 1 May 1934, in which he had called on the Catholic faithful to attend Church service that day as a 'special recognition of the social doctrine of the Church',[30] a statement which Heydrich considered was intended to sabotage the May Day holiday, he had been watching Klausener closely. Barely two months later, Klausener preached openly against the National Socialists on Catholic Day in Hoppegarten. For Heydrich this was the final provocation and he placed the politician's name on the death list.

At Klausener's office, Gildisch told him that he was under arrest. As the surprised politician went to fetch his jacket, Gildisch shot him in the back of the head, then rang Heydrich from the telephone on the dead man's desk to confirm the execution of the order. He was ordered to put the pistol near the victim's right hand so as to make the murder appear to be suicide. Not until his return to office did Gildisch learn whom he had murdered and why. 'He was a dangerous leader of the Catholics,'[31] Heydrich explained. At the Nuremberg War Crimes Trials Goering stated, 'That was a savage action by Heydrich.'[32]

In the heat of events, the music critic of the *Münchener Neueste Nachrichten*, Willi Schmid, became a tragic victim of mistaken identity. The hunters were either looking for his namesake, SA-Oberführer Wilhelm Schmid, manager of the newspaper, or his journalist colleague Paul Schmitt. Unfortunately the order read merely: 'Schmid, *Münchener Neueste Nachrichten*'[33] and so Dr Willi Schmid was dragged from his flat at Schnakkenstrasse 3 by three SS men and taken to Dachau. His wife shouted to the uniformed men that there surely must be some mistake. On 4 July she received a coffin which she presumed contained the remains of her husband, but she was not permitted to open it.

Ernst Röhm was arrested by Hitler personally. On 30 June the Führer travelled to Bad Wiessee on the west bank of Tegernsee where his old comrade-in-arms was taking the cure for rheumatism. Hitler, well-disposed to his former friend, wanted to pardon him 'in recognition of his services', but Goering, Himmler and Heydrich all urged him to carry out the execution order.

On 1 July the SA-Führer, godfather to Heydrich's first son, Klaus, died in cell 474 at Munich-Stadelheim. In a last effort not to stain his hands with the blood of Röhm, Hitler ordered that the SA leader should be given the opportunity to commit suicide. Theodor Eicke, commandant of Dachau, and Waffen-SS colonel Michael Lippert, who had been given the task of ensuring that the job was finished, left a pistol in Röhm's cell. They waited ten minutes, but when nothing happened, the pair entered the cell, weapons drawn, and fired simultaneously at the man facing them. The Führer had remained in the Reich Chancellery garden awaiting news of the outcome of the Röhm affair, and then held a tea party.

The retroactive *Gesetz über Massnahmen der Staatsnotwehr vom 3.7.1934* (Law respecting State Emergency Defence Measures) prescribed briefly:

'The Reich Government has approved the following Law. Article 1: The measures taken on 30 June, 1 July and 2 July 1934 to put down certain acts of high treason and treason are held legal as State Emergency Defence.'[34]

For public consumption, however, Hitler pointed to Röhm's homosexuality as the reason for the measure. A communiqué from the Reich Press Office explained:

> His [Röhm's] known unfortunate predilection led to such unpleasant implications that the Führer of the Movement and the Supreme Führer of the SA suffered the most difficult conflict of conscience . . . the circumstances of the arrest provided such a sorry picture morally that one could have no sympathy for the perpetrators. Some of these SA-Führern had taken up with male prostitutes. One was flushed out and arrested in the most disgusting situation. The Führer then gave the order for the ruthless removal of this cancer. He is determined never to tolerate in future having millions of decent people offended or compromised by individual sick perverts.[35]

As a result of the Nazis' 'St Bartholomew's Night Massacre', the SS emerged victorious over the SA. On 20 July 1934, the SS became an autonomous organisation, the SA played no further significant role from then on. Heydrich was promoted to SS-Gruppenführer, to be feared in future as one of the blackest demons of the Third Reich. He was just thirty years old.

To the eyes of Swiss envoy Carl Jacob Burckhardt, in his black uniform he looked like 'a young evil god of death'.[36] to Goering's cousin Ilse 'exactly like the devil'.[37] At a reception in Berlin the columnist Bella Fromm, a Jewess who was later able to emigrate to the United States, had a meeting of the most unpleasant kind: 'A shudder ran through me as Heydrich politely clicked his heels. Not for all the gold in the world would I have offered this mass-murderer my hand.'[38]

Heydrich attempted to justify his policy to Burckhardt, who inspected the newly set-up concentration camps on behalf of the International Red

Cross in 1935: 'Abroad we are considered bloodhounds, are we not?' he said. 'It is almost too much for the individual, but we must be hard as granite for fear that otherwise our Führer's work will be lost.'[39] He argued similarly in the Party pamphlet *Wandlungen unseres Kampfes* (Transforming our Struggles) 'In order to preserve our people, we must be hard with our enemies even at the risk of over-reacting against individual opponents, and even though we may be denounced in future by well-meaning people as being uncouth ruffians.'[40] In order to 'annihilate' the enemy, 'years of bloody struggle' lay ahead. The SS and Gestapo built to Heydrich's concept would be an 'inner-political protection corps for the National Socialist State'.[41]

In 1936, Himmler and Heydrich had the police apparatus completely under their control. Hitler nominated his 'Reichs-Heini'[42] to be chief of the German police on 17 June: nine days later he made Heydrich chief of the security police, Sicherheitspolizei (Sipo), which embraced the Gestapo and Kripo. Heydrich was anxious to fuse the SD with the Gestapo and so consolidate the NSDAP State surveillance system into a single unit, but failing this in an edict of 1 July 1937 he urged them to co-operate 'while avoiding all duplication of work'.[43] 'C' could now command a shadowy army of at least fifty thousand men. He was thirty-three years of age.

His collaborators were also still young – in those early days the average age of the SD leadership squad was around thirty. Their generation had come of age immediately after World War I, most of them were no strangers to poverty and hardship, and all knew the taste of defeat. They were motivated by extreme-Right slogans and the ideological dogma of the early 1920s, when many of them had had their first active experience of politics.

For Heydrich, the eternal enemies of the State were all equally dangerous, whether Jew, freemason or political Churchman.[44] In a sense he was turning against his own origins: the – perhaps only imaginary – Jewish forebears, the freemason father, member of the lodge Zu den 3 Degen in Halle, and the Catholic mother brought up by nuns in Switzerland. When he ordered the arrest of the Catholic bishop of Meissen, this caused a severe altercation with his pious wife, who usually went along with whatever her 'Reini' did. Heydrich's mother never dissuaded her Catholic-baptised Nazi son from his anti-Catholicism.

The cold hatred with which Heydrich attacked Catholicism assumed at times paranoid features. In his pamphlet *Wandlungen* he inveighed against not only the Jews but the Church too:

> It is not enough that they (the priests) have made the effort over the centuries to destroy the blood and spiritual values of our people, deceived them by appearing to maintain outwardly those values, and insisting today that they are guardians of the world. Instead of being true, unselfish mediators, while simulating Church affairs they have conquered one worldly position of power after the other.[45]

Heydrich felt the manoeuvres of the Church to be a serious threat to his own religion, National Socialism.

> In order to broaden their worldly sphere of influence after the seizure of power in Germany they stepped up enormously the indoctrination of the non-priestly laity. They are being exercised, as the name suggests, in hundreds of exercise-houses, i.e. everything must be mechanized if at all possible so that those involved do not notice how all inherited strength of blood and spirit is being systematically distorted or killed off. [He added,] In truth, they are not fighting positively to uphold religious and cultural values (which are not endangered at all) but they are continuing their old, remorseless struggle for the world mastery of Germany.

In 1973, Lina Heydrich commented on the very personal, icy enmity of her husband towards the Catholic Church: 'Of all "enemy groupings" of the interior, he considered the Church the most dangerous'.[46] Political Catholicism was the principal enemy because it could not be harnessed. Heydrich even toyed with the idea of infiltrating the Church of Rome, eviscerating it from within. This would have involved passing convinced young National Socialists through the priestly seminars, gradually permeating the Catholic hierarchy with the concept of the thousand-year Reich.

As for the other two main enemies of his 'world view', the Jews and freemasons, Heydrich believed that here he was looking at both sides of the same coin. At an evening social meeting with Carl Burckhardt during his inspection tour of the concentration camps, Heydrich told the Swiss Red Cross man: 'The freemasons are the instrument of Jewish revenge. At the back wall of their temples stands a scaffold before a black curtain, which conceals the Highest of the High, and only to the highest initiates is it accessible. Behind the curtain is just the single word "Yahve" – Jehovah – a name which says it all.'[47] Should the freemasons get the upper hand in the struggle with National Socialism, they would celebrate 'orgies of cruelty' compared with which 'the severity of Adolf Hitler will appear rather moderate'.[48] With this wild ideological illogic, the fencer Heydrich attempted to rationalise in quite typical style the setting up of the camps.

Two days later he conducted his guest, with apparent enjoyment, through his Freemasons Museum in the Prinz-Albrecht-Strasse basement. In the first room, Heydrich explained to the Swiss historian, were to be found the names of all the world's freemasons. A black-painted, windowless second room was in total darkness.

> Heydrich switched on a violet light and slowly there appeared all kinds of masonic cult objects in the shadows. Ghostly pale in the dimness, Heydrich moved around the room explaining the whys and wherefores of the world conspiracy, the degrees of initiation and, standing occult, naturally, at the head of the hierarchy, the Jews, leading all humanity to its destruction. There were more low-ceilinged, narrow rooms, equally dark, which one could only enter bent double, to be seized by the shoulders by the bony hands of automatically operated skeletons.[49]

So much for Burckhardt's description of the macabre 'spooky passage' in the cellars of Heydrich's headquarters. The mixture of efficiency, twisted ideology and puerility to which this 'museum' bore evidence led the shocked Red Cross man to characterise Heydrich in words as 'the evil young god of death'.

Not a few contemporaries noticed that Heydrich, despite all his powers, was a deeply split personality. Outwardly he could be the snappish, sportive, hard soldier and also the soft, courtly feminine music lover: his penetrating stare and snarling tone were matched with soft hands and narrow hips. A criminologist diagnosed his personality after the war as 'ambivalent schizoid'. Once in a drunken rage he fired at his reflection in a mirror shouting, 'I've finally got you, you swine!'[50]

It was not all roses in the marital home and Heydrich would occasionally confide to Himmler's adjutant Karl Wolff about things that were annoying him. His wife, Lina, who bore him four children by 1942, harped on about his constant absences, alienated as were many Nazi wives such as the careworn Marga Himmler, who flew into a rage if somebody overtook her SS car.

The senior police chief, so Wolff maintained later, was henpecked by the cool blonde from the North: Lina should have been told that something of that nature was interpreted by the Reichsführer-SS as a weakness: 'Whoever can't lead his own brood, cannot lead a troop.'[51] Apparently Wolff, like Heydrich, had hopes of becoming Himmler's successor. The Reichsführer strengthened their rivalry by indicating that he foresaw both as his successor: Wolff for the good times, Heydrich for the bad. In this way he protected his position of strength: for the same reason he never gave Heydrich full control over all 'police affairs': the regular, non-political police remained under Daluege, the administration of the camps went to the SS-Hauptamt under Oswald Pohl, the staffing was the responsibility of 'Papa' Eicke.

When Heydrich required a diversion from his marital problems and affairs of State, he looked for sex, 'anything in a skirt', and Lina knew that there were always 'other women in my marriage'.[52] He often got his closest colleagues such as the young SD-Foreign chief Walter Schellenberg to accompany him on all-night forays through Berlin bars and brothels, where no heterosexual escapade was too bizarre for him. A passionate, long-lasting extra-marital affair, in short a lover, there probably never was. Kersten recalled:

> He was shamelessly brutal and cynical in his attitude towards women. They sensed it and shunned him. That was why such a good-looking man, who should have been attractive to most women, had little success with them. On occasions when he went out with his adjutants in civilian clothes, the latter would make the running with the ladies, which often led next day to major complications and violent reactions from Heydrich against the unfortunate aide who had emerged victor for the lady's favours.[53]

After his nightly cruising, Heydrich would often appear the pale shadow of the man of whom everybody had their fears. In a bar the guests who did not recognise him laughed when he shouted: 'I am head of the Gestapo! I am Heydrich! I can send you all to a camp!'[54]

The aides forced to accompany him on these excursions were never more than drinking companions. Next day at work he would be as distant and reserved as ever. 'Heydrich had no real friend, his friendships were all based on political necessity and he gave them up as soon as they had served their purpose.'[55] Heydrich looked on with disapproval when his departmental leaders crossed the limits to fraternise with one another – he, and he alone, was to be their point of reference. Cross-connections at the lower levels prejudiced his absolute power. Only among his SS sporting comrades in the fencing camp did Heydrich ever resemble a good companion.[56]

The 'smooth, agile animal' could not handle human closeness. Horst Naude, a senior chargé d'affaires in Prague during Heydrich's time as Reichs-Protektor for Bohemia and Moravia, wrote: 'In personal relationships he could be totally loveable, a charming companion, but then again he could exude an icy coldness when those eyes in the long, horse-shaped head narrowed.'[57] Even the official *Völkischer Beobachter* obituary writer found himself compelled, in the edition of 8 June 1942, to mention this shortcoming among the otherwise unstinting praise for a heroic life: 'His personal popularity was scanty', the 'warm-hearted man buried' within the necessary struggle for 'Führer, Volk und Vaterland'.[58]

Lina Heydrich described the human isolation of her husband:

> He did not want friends. He believed he did not need to make friendships . . . probably he was predisposed through personal experiences. The discharge from the Navy, which his comrades worked with such energy to oppose, and the experience with Ernst Röhm, to whom he felt such an affinity that he made him his son's godfather, then later having to obey a service order and take the Führer's side [in Röhm's execution], these all played their part in it . . . the thing went so deep that one day he reported to Himmler and begged him in a very personal statement never to use the familiar form of the noun 'You' to him . . . he had the fear that if Himmler used this intimate form of address to him, he would not be able to put a convincing argument to Himmler if it were necessary.[59]

Nobody dared withhold respect from Heydrich. Not the aides whom he drove constantly to ever greater effort with his endless passion for work: not the prisoners, such as the later Nuremberg witness Robert Kempner, whom he visited in the Gestapo cellars to agitate with 'evil banter', not the Party acquaintances who would have been only too pleased to discover what was said about them and their shortcomings in his card-index system. 'C' had, as Schellenberg wrote of him, 'a feeling for the inadequacies of people and could register that knowledge just as easily in his phenomenal memory banks as in his card indexes, and use it at the appropriate moment, often for the first time years later.'[60] Heydrich knew all the secrets of the Third Reich. He knew Hitler's illnesses and the sins of his youth, knew his acquaintances even in the Vienna flop-house of 1910, knew the details of the suicide of Geli Rabaul, Hitler's 'favourite niece', in 1931. Heydrich also knew the peccadilloes of the other members of the Nazi ruling clique. He knew about Goebbels's dalliances. He probably knew that Goering became a morphine addict as the result of treatment for the wound he sustained in the 1923 putsch attempt. Two years later the police of Stockholm, where he then lived, had even registered Goering as a violent drug addict and had him admitted to the mental asylum at Langbro. He had assaulted a nurse at a private clinic who refused him morphine. The later Reichsmarschall spent about three months in the institution. Shortly after his first release he had to go back because he had still not shaken the habit.

Heydrich knew about Himmler's stomach cramps. The attacks were sometimes so bad that Himmler would pass out. They could last days, during which time he would be scarcely able to work. He feared that they indicated cancer – Himmler's father had died of stomach cancer. His adjutant Wolff recommended him finally to the Finnish chiropractor and doctor Felix Kersten. A fateful association: Kersten rose so high in Himmler's favour that the Reichsführer-SS rarely let him out of his sight and called him 'my magical Buddha'.[61]

Naturally, Kersten was sworn to the strictest secrecy about Himmler's condition in order to preserve the outward appearance of a strong, basically healthy Aryan. The pretence was maintained that Kersten was treating him only for rheumatism. Himmler's faith in the wonder-doctor finally went so far that he used Kersten as a kind of 'espionage secret weapon' against his immediate adversaries. He praised the doctor to Foreign Minister Ribbentrop, and discovered that he suffered from severe headaches, vertigo, partial loss of vision and also stomach cramps. (Himmler and Ribbentrop were in good company; Hitler had been plagued by cramps since taking power). Heydrich's ever-suspicious eye did not overlook the grey eminence at Himmler's court, and he attempted on several occasions to pump Kersten for information.

Parallel with information from the highest circles of power, 'C' had the SD prepare 'Reports from the Reich' for the leadership to provide them with an unembellished picture of morale among the common people. For himself and his office he collated Gestapo reports from all *Gaue* for the daily score on how the suppression was proceeding. The report for 13 October 1936, for example, lists arrests as: Berlin 36, Hamburg 21, Düsseldorf 17, Dortmund 12, Bielfeld 10, Frankfurt/Main 4, Frankfurt/Oder 1.

In 1935 the Jewish publisher Berthold Jacob was kidnapped from exile in Basle and brought to Germany. In the Gestapo dungeon on 11

March he got to know the man in the blue civilian suit who was apparently 'the lord of this house and prison'. At first he heard only the voice: 'So this is where the swine is!' Jacob wrote:

> Heydrich expressed in a jolly manner his satisfaction that he finally 'had me' and advised me 'for my own good' to make 'no difficulties', since these might be very dangerous to health . . . on leaving my cell Heydrich asked the warder if I was eating properly. 'Don't try hunger-striking or similar hokum to impress us,' he concluded, 'that would be very bad for you.'[62]

In September after diplomatic moves 'C' was obliged to allow Jacob to return to Switzerland. Yet Heydrich's long arm grabbed him again later: in 1941 SD agents smuggled him out of Portugal and he died in a Berlin prison in 1944.

Heydrich's career record gained a black mark at the beginning of 1938. Hitler and Goering were looking for ways to rid themselves of leading military figures of the Old Guard. War Minister Werner von Blomberg and Army C-in-C Generaloberst von Fritsch were openly opposed to the Nazi plans for warfare.

Blomberg was discharged on the grounds of 'irregular marriage', to a former prostitute.[63] In Fritsch's case a two-year-old Gestapo dossier was discovered which appeared to place him in a homosexual relationship with a young man by the name of Otto Schmidt. Hitler had ignored the matter in 1936 but Heydrich had kept a copy in his 'poison cabinet' and now it had come in handy. The 'witness' was shown Fritsch in Hitler's presence and exclaimed, 'Yes, that's him!' In a daze, the Army C-in-C said, 'What does this gentleman want of me?' It soon became evident, however, that the overzealous Gestapo Commissioner Josef Meisinger had not done his homework and Schmidt's testimony against von Fritsch had been obtained against a promise that he would have 'an early trip to heaven' if he did not go through with the false allegation. As Fritsch's lawyers discovered, the man's client had not been General von Fritsch but Rittmeister von Fritsch. On 17 March 1938, the Reich War Court acquitted Fritsch 'for proven innocence' although he had actually been released in early February.

Although aware of the true facts, and in order to hide his negligence, Heydrich had attempted unsuccessfully to have the general commit suicide in Gestapo custody. Schmidt was shot. At one point Heydrich was in fear of a putsch by loyal military men. Gulping down aspirin, he waited in a Berlin bar with Schellenberg until he felt sure that 'if the people in Potsdam don't march in half an hour, the danger will probably be over.'[64] The time passed, as did the wrath of Hitler and Himmler over the scandalous error.

Meanwhile Hitler was about to invade Austria, and the Gestapo and SD were being kept busy with Heydrich-compiled lists of opponents to arrest. At lightning speed a police net was thrown over the Bavarian Alps. On 14 March Hitler celebrated in Vienna's Imperial Hotel overcoming the diktat of the victors of 1919 by annexing Austria to the Old Reich. Heydrich praised him: 'You have contributed decisively to the tearing up on the Treaty of St Germain. That is glorious, and I thank you!'[65]

The annexation brought crowds of new victims flocking into the concentration camp machinery of the SS. Soon, close to Hitler's home town of Linz, there was erected Mauthausen concentration camp, in which inmates were worked to death dragging blocks of stone up a stairway, once at the top throwing them back to the bottom to start again. Everywhere in the Third Reich the bloodhounds used 'protective custody' with impunity to keep people as long as they liked behind bars and barbed wire. Protest was pointless once the Prussian Administrative Court had ruled on 2 May 1935 that the Gestapo was not subject to the processes of normal justice. Heydrich, the master of *Schutzhaft*, argued that it was 'idle to wait' for 'degenerate criminals' to offend again, it was more important to prevent 'acts against the people before they happened'.[66]

How such injustice worked in practice is illustrated by the Düsseldorf Gestapo archive in the case of the Jewish businessman Alfred Oppenheim, one of many. Because he had had contacts with the German Communist Party, an illegal organisation, and these contacts had been deemed by the court to be 'preparations for treason', in 1936 at the age of twenty-nine years Oppenheim was sentenced to six years' penal servitude. Upon his release from Siegburg prison on 6 June 1941, he was automatically an 'enemy of the people' since he was Jewish and a Communist. Rearrested at the prison gate, he was put into *Schutzhaft* at Düsseldorf.

His wife Martha wrote begging the Gestapo to release him so that the whole family could emigrate to the United States as previously arranged. Oppenheim drafted a written undertaking that when abroad he would 'never engage in activity against the German Reich'. It was all in vain. On 7 July 1941 a letter arrived from Berlin: 'For the above-mentioned I order herewith protective custody without limit of time . . . Oppenheim is to be taken to the concentration camp at Neuengamme . . . Frau Martha Oppenheim, Düsseldorf, Kreuzstrasse 58: I request you to respond in my name negatively to her request. Signed. Heydrich.'[67]

Oppenheim died in Neuengamme from 'tuberculosis of the lungs' as reported in a telegram from the camp commandant to Stapo-Hauptamt, Düsseldorf on 24 June 1942. It was a lie: he had been killed at Bernburg Hospital during poison-gas experiments where, in the opinion of Dr Fritz Mennecke, they were dealing with 'a fanatical German-hater and an asocial psychopath'[68] – his death sentence. The Gestapo was unable to contact his wife to advise her of her husband's death since she had been 'evacuated' to Minsk, her own death-warrant. At this point in 1942, a great wave of killings was in progress everywhere in the territories under German control, and Heydrich was constantly having to make decisions of life and death, without compassion, without mercy, without regrets.

'He was a man like the crack of a whip,' the historian Joachim Fest said of him, 'in his Luciferic coldness of emotion, his amorality and unquenchable lust for power'.[69]

Heydrich had been promoted to head the International Criminal Police Commission, the forerunner of Interpol, in 1940, and in a speech on German Police Day the following year, alluding to the work of the SD he said, 'We are, I put it jokingly, something between "a maid of all work" and "the rubbish bin of the Reich".' Nobody laughed.[70]

Chapter Three

Planning to Exterminate the Jews 1938–1942

On the evening of the day when Germany finally sank into barbarism, the Heydrichs had gone to bed early in their house at Berlin-Schlachtensee. A tapping on the bedroom door awoke Lina Heydrich while her husband Reinhard, chief of the security police of the Third Reich, slept on. 'Who is there?' she called. Her bodyguard replied, 'This is Schmidt. The Gruppenführer is requested at his office immediately!' She asked what was the problem. 'The synagogues have been set afire!' came back the awful answer. She awoke her husband. He dressed quickly in his black SS uniform and rushed out. It was several hours before he returned. He seemed 'distraught and preoccupied', his wife wrote. Finally he gathered himself together sufficiently to blurt out: 'They have attacked everything, destroyed and plundered all Jewish businesses . . . we can probably no longer talk of a scaling down of the aggression against the Jews.'[1]

This was the role played by Heydrich in the events of Reichskristallnacht on 9 November 1938 according to Lina, his wife, in her memoir, *Leben mit einem Kriegsverbrecher* (Living with a War Criminal). It appears to be pure invention. That particular evening, together with nearly every other member of the Nazi elite, which did not include Lina Heydrich, Reinhard Heydrich was in Munich to help celebrate the fifteenth anniversary of the Feldherrnhalle march. This had been the putsch attempt in 1923 in Bavaria when Adolf Hitler was intending to seize power. After his 'seizure of power' by democratic means ten years later, the Feldherrnhalle affair had been elevated into 'the baptism of fire of the National Socialist movement'.

Whilst the Führer and his paladins were dining in the old City Hall, a message arrived which 'greatly agitated'[2] Hitler, according to an eyewitness: in Paris, the German diplomat Ernst vom Rath had died of his wounds following an assassination attempt. He had fallen victim to the Polish Jew Herschel Grynszpan. The seventeen-year-old emigrant, embittered at the deportation of his parents from Hanover to the border with Poland, had fired two shots into the legation official at the German Embassy. Since 27 October, about seventeen thousand Polish Jews resident in the Reich had been herded together in deplorable conditions prior to their expulsion into Poland. Warsaw was proposing to deprive them of Polish citizenship.

Heydrich's Gestapo organisation led the German operation. He had never contributed to any 'scaling down in the aggression against the Jews' but, on the contrary, used the spreading anti-Jewish feeling in the country to expand his field of competence. While Jews in the Reich suffered boycotts, attacks and the systematic loss of civil rights, Heydrich's Gestapo made arbitrary arrests while his SD kept busy on plans for 'ridding Germany of Jews'. Heydrich had recognised earlier, as Himmler observed later, that for Hitler nothing more important appeared to exist. 'Heydrich intended to excel Himmler in this,' said Stuttgart historian Eberhard Jäckel, 'It was Heydrich's ambitions and lust for power which made it possible for Hitler to do what he had always wanted.'[3]

The SD chief shared this insight into Hitler's world with Joseph Goebbels, whom Heydrich did not like but nevertheless admired because of his 'diabolical manipulation of people', according to Lina Heydrich.[4] The Paris assassination provided the excuse for a leap forward in the anti-Jewish policy from discriminatory laws to physical violence.

In the Munich City Hall, Hitler held a long, whispered conversation with Goebbels and then left without making his customary speech. Goebbels led the tirades instead. The Propaganda Minister inveighed not only against 'the Jewish rabble' as he usually did but referred to 'spontaneous actions' against Jews in Kurhesse at midday: the Führer had decided that the NSDAP 'would not initiate attacks' but if they happened 'he was not going to do anything about them'.[5] The assembled Party leaders made the necessary inference and after eleven o'clock that evening called on Party comrades by telex and telephone to begin the pogrom. Swastika flags were not to be in evidence.

Shortly before midnight, after a discussion with Heydrich, Gestapo chief Heinrich Müller in Berlin instructed the State police: 'Shortly, there will be demonstrations against Jews, and especially their synagogues throughout Germany. No action is to be taken.'[6] The police should be ready for the arrest of '20,000 to 30,000 Jews', mostly the wealthy. Himmler considered the Goebbels-*Aktion* 'empty-headed' and kept the SS out of it, but after being brought into the picture by Hitler at his private flat in the Regentenstrasse Munich, he informed Heydrich at the Vier Jahreszeiten Hotel.

On 10 November 1938 at 1.20 a.m. in a secret telex, Heydrich, chief of Sipo and SD, relayed precise guidelines that 'only such measures are to be taken which do not endanger German life and property [e.g. only set synagogues on fire if there is no danger of the fire spreading to the surrounding area]. Jewish businesses and residences can be destroyed but not looted.'[7] At 3.45 a.m. Heydrich sent a signal adding that the 'Jewish *Aktion*' would not give rise to criminal investigations against the perpetrators.[8]

The Brown mob raged for two days before the pogrom died down. On 12 November at a ministerial conference chaired by Reichsmarschall Goering, the damage was estimated at 7,500 businesses and 177 synagogues destroyed, damage of 'several hundred million Reichsmarks' inflicted, 800 cases of looting and – as an afterthought – 35 Jews killed.

The number of victims rose later to 91. This was not a good bargain, according to Goering, who 'would have preferred 200 Jews killed rather than all this physical damage done to property'.[9]

Now came Heydrich's hour. He was not satisfied that, to expiate their part in this disaster, the German Jews should pay one billion Reichsmarks in compensation, but 'even after removing the Jews from the economy,' he complained, 'in the final analysis we are still left with with basic problem of removing them from Germany.'[10] To that end he recommended the setting up of a Reich Centre for Jewish Emigration in order to empty Germany of all Jews within ten years, preferably to Palestine. Of the 566,000 Jews living in the Reich in 1933, by 1939 half had fled abroad. Heydrich had nothing but praise for the Vienna Emigration Centre, run by his SD under Adolf Eichmann and which, since the annexation of Austria in March 1938 had helped 'at least 50,000 Jews' to emigrate.[11]

Heydrich also wanted every Jew in Germany to wear a distinguishing badge.[12] 'A uniform!' Goering joked. Heydrich repeated: 'A badge.' At the time Hitler thought this was going too far and not until September 1941 were the Jews required to wear the 'yellow star' by edict. The Emigration Centre under Heydrich was established in Germany on 24 January 1939.

Nevertheless in November 1938 the SS weekly journal *Das Schwarze Korps*, controlled by Heydrich, revealed the true intentions of the Nazis: 'with sword and fire' they threatened the Jews with *Restlose Vernichtung* – 'extermination to the last person'. It was in the same sense that on 30 January 1939, the sixth anniversary of his coming to power, Hitler promised to the Reichstag: 'If international financial Jewry succeeds within and outside of Europe in plunging the peoples of the world into another World War, then the result will not be the bolshevization of the Earth and with it the victory of Jewry, but the destruction of the Jewish race in Europe.'[13] When war arrived in late 1939, however, it was due more to Hitler's efforts to reverse the 'dictated peace of Versailles' than to Communists or Jews: against its terms he had rearmed (1935), reoccupied the demilitarised Rhineland (1936): annexed Austria and the Sudetenland (1938) and finally, in breach of the Munich Agreement the previous year, had occupied the remainder of Czechoslovakia and seized Memel (1939).

Heydrich was always involved in the politics. Just as the Gestapo and SD had assisted in establishing Nazi mastery over Austria and the Reichs-Protektorate of Bohemia and Moravia, his agents were responsible for preparing the public excuse for Poland. At the beginning of August 1939, Heydrich arrived at Gleiwitz with a group of high-ranking SS officers and assembled them in the ballroom of the Haus Oberschlesien Hotel. 'The Führer requires a reason to take military action in order to clear the eastern border,' he explained. The plan, worked out by Hitler, Himmler and Heydrich in concert was to pretend that Polish forces had crossed the frontier into the Reich and attacked the Hochlinden Customs House, the Pitschen forestry lodge and the Gleiwitz radio station.

The scheme took shape over the next few weeks and any doubter soon aroused the wrath of Heydrich. Operational leader SS-Oberführer (Brigadier-General) Herbert Mehlhorn was returned to unit forthwith for laughing at Heydrich's insistence on being addressed at all times as 'C'. When Gestapo-Führer Emanuel Schäfer thought the pretence of a raid 'a bit thin', Heydrich retorted: 'When the first panzers roll, we'll hear no more about it'.[14]

To make the operation seem more credible he decided he ought to have some corpses for effect, and for that purpose six inmates from Sachsenhausen concentration camp were brought for the sub-operation *Konserven*. On 31 August 1939 they died at Hochlinden customs house, shot to death wearing Polish Army uniforms. 'C' appointed his top agent Alfred Naujocks to lead the raid on the Gleiwitz radio station. The SD officer said he would need a *Konserve* 'insurrectionist' in civilian clothes, and Gestapo chief Müller concurred. On the afternoon of 31 August 1939, Naujocks and Müller received through a direct telephone connection to Berlin Heydrich's order 'Grandmother dead'.[15] That evening, Naujocks's squad occupied the radio station and broadcast an announcement in Polish. That was sufficient for the headline 'Polish Insurgents Cross the German Border'.[16] At the entrance to the building, Müller dropped off a body sprayed with bullets. This was the pro-Polish Silesian Franz Honiok, arrested on 30 August, the first German death of World War II.

Honiok's murder was the prelude to the invasion of Poland early on 1 September 1939, the conventional forces being followed by SD Einsatzgruppen which Heydrich had been forming since July. Their mission, so he told ministerial heads in Berlin on 7 September, was 'to render the ruling class in Poland as impotent as possible . . . we want to spare the man in the street, but the nobility, the Catholic religious leaders and the Jews will have to be killed off.'[17] From the outbreak of war to the spring of 1940, the SS murdered over sixty thousand people. The massacre outraged even Wehrmacht officers. Wehrmacht C-in-C Wilhelm Keitel rejected their complaints about 'unrestricted brutality' while awarding the perpetrators amnesty, and Hitler observed that the military should be glad it had 'not had to have anything to do with this handiwork of the devil'.[18]

At the same time the SS stepped up its 'anti-Jewish policy' from harassment to embryonic extermination by Heydrich's creation of the Reichssicherheitshauptamt (RSHA) in a document dated 27 September 1939. The RSHA was a super-authority with around sixty thousand staff and with it Heydrich now controlled the SS-Sicherheitshauptamt and the Sicherheitspolizei (Sipo – the security police organisation embracing the Gestapo and Kripo). The criminal police operated the *Schutzhaft*, which was the 'protective custody' measure without specific limit of time, and now extended it against anybody who objected to, or complained about, National Socialism or the war. This was a step on the path by which 'C' was creating the preconditions for all-out war and the creation of the 'Greater Germanic Reich'.[19]

There was no place for Jews. In November and December 1939 the RSHA arranged for the deportation of approximately eighty-seven Jews and Poles from the German-occupied west of Poland into the General-Gouvernement, the part of Poland remaining in German hands after the deal with the Soviet Union to share it between them. It was the intention of Himmler, who had recently been appointed *Reichs-Kommissar für das deutsche Volkstum* – Reich Commissioner for the German People – to 'germanise' the region, naming it 'Warthegau' and forcibly resettling there persons of German stock from the eastern Baltic States and Wohlhynien (a district of western Ukraine around the towns of Kowel, Luzk and Rovno.)

On the basis of plans which he had presented previously to Hitler, Heydrich enlarged on his proposals in a courier letter of 21 September 1939 that the Sipo would group together all Jews into ghettoes at the 'fewest possible number of towns' on the main railway lines and establish 'Jewish councils' as intermediaries so as to 'smooth over the later measures'. The 'End goal' aimed for in the longer term was to be kept 'strictly secret'.[20] In December Heydrich made Adolf Eichmann head of the Special Administrative Branch IV D4 (later B4) at RSHA, the 'chargé d'affaires for Jews'. RSHA expert Michael Wildt argued that: 'In these first steps lay the germ of genocide.'[21]

Initially, even the 'pioneer of extermination' stated that it should be possible to expel the Jews to 'somewhere' where they could be abandoned to their fate. The RSHA considered the possibility of a 'Jewish reservation' at Nisko on the San river or the African island of Madagscar. Hitler liked the Madagascar solution and informed Mussolini on 18 June 1940 of his intention to use the island as a 'Jewish reservation'.[22] After the defeat of France, Hitler believed he would have the French colony at his disposal. With the enthusiastic support of Heydrich, Eichmann drafted a memorandum referring to the files of the French colonial ministry which had considered the question of using Madagascar as a resettlement region for Europeans some years before. He also had before him the plan of the official in charge of Jewish affairs at the German Foreign Office, Franz Rademacher who, like his head of department, Under-Secretary of State Martin Luther, proved himself a strong advocate of the SS State at the Wannsee Conference.

> The Madagascar solution, seen from the German point of view, means the creation of a Great Ghetto. Only the Sipo has the necessary experience in this area: it has the means to prevent escapes from the island, and it also has the experience to take those punitive measures, in a suitable manner, which may become necessary on account of hostile actions against Germany by Jews in the United States.[23]

Eichmann sounded out the two major German shipping lines, Hapag and Norddeutscher Lloyd, for their views on how to solve the transportation problem. The intention was to compel France to make Madagascar available and, at the end of hostilities, to co-opt all European States to join the Jewish resettlement project.[24] The abandonment of the invasion plan for Great Britain caused the Madagascar plan to be dropped because the sea routes from Europe to the Indian Ocean could not be secured.

With the defeat of Poland, the Germans now had 3.5 million Jews, far more than ever before, inhabiting Reich-controlled territory, and no resettlement area away from Europe to where they could be sent. Heydrich's great deportation schemes for the East were in disarray: General-Gouverneur Hans Frank, administrator of the Warthegau, had blocked the departure of trains required by the Wehrmacht for troop movements to the Western Front on the grounds of hunger and disease among the deportees. Already in June 1940 Heydrich was realising that the 'Jewish Question' could 'no longer be solved by emigration': instead, 'a territorial Final Solution is therefore necessary'.[25] Whether by this he meant genocide is not clear.

Himmler, the 'people's floor scrubber', was still opposed to such a proceeding in May 1940 when he drafted a memo to Hitler stating that he 'rejected from inner conviction the Bolshevist method of physical extermination of a people as being un-Germanic and unfeasible'.[26] Heydrich, on the other hand, had no such compunctions. 'His God was might,' his SD colleague Wilhelm Höttl concluded: 'For Heydrich the life of others was not in itself a thing worth protecting: if the purposes of might demanded it, that life would be extinguished.'[27] To Heydrich's confidant Walter Schellenberg he seemed like 'an animal of prey'.[28] His adviser Werner Best, with whom Heydrich parted company in 1940 because of his 'formalistic' attitude, considered him 'the most demonic personality in the National Socialist leadership', having an 'unconscious self-evident inhumanity which took no account of those he mowed down'.[29] On the other hand, his wife reported: 'Often he was unable to sleep, why he could not explain.'[30] Outwardly he remained what Hitler called him: 'The Man with the Iron Heart'.[31]

In the spring of 1941 at the Pretsch military training camp on the Elbe he addressed the heads of the newly formed Sipo and SD Einsatzgruppen to obtain their assent to their greatest murder initiative, 'the war of the world view': the offensive against the Communist-controlled Soviet Union, wherein dwelt five million Jews, was imminent. 'The eastern Jews', Heydrich stated, according to eyewitnesses, 'are the intellectual reserve of Bolshevism and in the view of the Führer must be destroyed.'[32] In a discussion in Berlin afterwards, a Kommando-Führer, wanting to make sure he had understood correctly, asked: 'Are we supposed to shoot the Jews?' Heydrich assured him that that was 'rather obvious'.[33]

The RSHA leader discussed the 'Jewish Question' almost every day with his chief, Himmler, who had the direct line to Hitler, from where the orders came down in the greatest secrecy. Whereas Himmler trembled with horror at 'the most terrible mission an organization could receive',[34] Heydrich accepted it as a challenge to his evil side. He urged the SS leader to appoint some of the most important RSHA departmental chiefs to head the four Einsatzgruppen or their sub-groups 'so as to pour steel into their veins'. They had to 'learn to act without mercy' and 'to give and receive death'.[35] Without protest, lawyer Otto Ohlendorf, police chief Arthur Nebe and sociologist Franz Six left their offices and mutated into murder-squad commanders. This occurred because Heydrich wanted his SD to be the elite of the SS and NSDAP, not 'a load of bureaucratic officials' but 'a fighting line'.

Their colleague Bruno Streckenbach, former head of Hamburg Gestapo and head of personnel at RSHA, had already proved in Poland his capacity for 'action' – euphemism for murder. When as chief of Einsatzgruppe 1 he had led the General Pacification *Aktion* at Cracow, in which, in May and June 1940 at least two thousand men and women, allegedly members of illegal organisations, had been sentenced to death in 'summary special proceedings' and executed.[36] He now announced his willingness to serve the same ends on the Eastern Front, but Heydrich would not let him go – Streckenbach was needed in Berlin to co-ordinate the *Aktionen* of the other divisional heads in Russia.

Ohlendorf, Six and Nebe are good examples of the way in which intelligent men, who under other circumstances would have lived a respectable civilian life, became enraptured of a criminal ideology and fell under the spell of an unscrupulous and fanatical schemer, who turned them into mass-murderers. None of them could stand the abrasive, calculating Heydrich, but none of them would stand up to him. Each of the three carried out Heydrich's orders in his own way, although what they did amounted to the same thing. They killed the innocent.

'Ohlendorf told me that the order to shoot Jews had come from the Reichsführer-SS through Heydrich, and had been received by all Einsatzkommandos. It was a Führer-Order. Ohlendorf never gave me more precise details. He said simply that it was for racial reasons and added that the Jewish children of today would be our enemies of tomorrow,' a member of Einsatzgruppe D told a Munich State Attorney.[37]

That was how the 34-year-old lawyer and economist Otto Ohlendorf saw the world: orders are orders, and the Jew is the arch-enemy. A Wehrmacht medical-corps man witnessed at Kishinyov, Moldavia on 1 August 1941 what the world view of the head of RSHA Principal Division III actually meant:

> These Jewish women and girls lined up at the mass grave site were now to be shot by an execution squad. There were terrible scenes. People crying and wailing. Some were begging the SS leader [of the execution squad] to spare them. All to no avail. Right and left of the mass grave Jewish men stood ready to throw the bodies of the women in once they fell. After all the women and girls had been shot, the men were next. There must have been about 250 who were shot in the same way as the females. But I didn't stay there until the end.[38]

Ohlendorf was born on 4 February 1907, the son of a farmer at Hoheneggelsen near Hanover. In his childhood and youth he worked for his father, which filled him with pride. After his *Abitur* he studied law and economics at Leipzig, then Göttingen. At age sixteen he led a youth group of the German nationalist *Volkspartei*, but he soon found it too bourgeois and in 1925 at age eighteen he transferred into the NSDAP. Ohlendorf soon won for himself the reputation of a capable orator. He built up an SS group in his district. His own membership number was 880.

After his qualifying examinations in law, in 1933 Ohlendorf went to Padua for a few months to study Italian fascism at its source. The 'Defender of the Holy Grail of National Socialism',[39] as Himmler later called him, found the hollow pomp of Mussolini's State repulsive, and he swore that his own Party in Germany would not develop into the same thing. After the Nazi seizure of power, the rising lawyer would always intervene to maintain 'the pure doctrine'. In 1936 he entered Heydrich's SD of the SS as an economics adviser. He found it to be 'chaotic': 'about twenty young people, no typists, no archives, no office helps, no kind of properly organised apparatus in the Reich whatever.'[40] This worried the systematic worker. He rolled up his sleeves and soon won the approval of his superiors for his reports detailing 'Failed Plans and the Political Damage to National Socialism'.[41] This work developed later, when Ohlendorf was Inland-SD chief, into 'Reports from the Reich'. For the internal information of National Socialist heads only, until the end of the Third Reich these reports from his office provided a relatively unvarnished picture of opinion and morale of the population and in the Party.

Ohlendorf took over the Inland-SD section in 1937. Two years later it was merged with the full SD into the RSHA. Although Ohlendorf was 'well in' with Himmler and Heydrich, after a while he manoeuvred himself away from the centre because of his discomfort at seeing that Himmler had no desire for an ordered structure within Heydrich's RSHA and gave tasks not to institutions, but to individuals.[42] Ohlendorf's sober, scientific attitude did not appeal to his superiors, Himmler and Heydrich. 'We had turned against the rejection of the old technical school teachers by the Party and pointed out that opportune young culture knights were certainly not going to be suitable to replace the knowledge of the old teachers. At this Himmler rebuked me sharply.' This was the beginning of the quarrel.[43] He was branded a pessimist, but despite that, Heydrich held on to his most brilliant departmental head and declined to accept his resignation.

For all his rational sobriety, Ohlendorf was and remained at heart a fanatical National Socialist. At the end of the war, when tried with other

Einsatzgruppen leaders, he remained convinced. He criticised the leading exponents of the regime as 'having a split personality' (Himmler); of being 'completely materialistic' (Bormann); of being 'average' (the milieu surrounding Hitler). For Ohlendorf it was not National Socialism that was rotten, but the men who represented it.[44] Thus it is not surprising that Ohlendorf should snap to attention when Heydrich detached him 'for foreign service' in the summer of 1941. It was to be against Jews and Bolshevists, to him the arch-enemy of the German people. Ohlendorf was earmarked for Einsatzgruppe D, to 'work' the southern end of the conquered territory known today as Moldavia, the southern Ukraine and the Black Sea region.

Allegedly, according to Ohlendorf in his statement postwar, he was the victim of a web of intrigue spun by Himmler and Heydrich 'to destroy him morally'.[45] On two previous occasions he had turned down 'missions' in the East. A third refusal would have stamped him as a 'coward'. Therefore he had assented in order to avoid this humiliation and a possible loss of office. In the operational area, however, the street fighter of old did not conduct himself in the least like somebody who obeys only reluctantly or is in fear of moral disintegration.

Apart from the remark to an adjutant regarding a 'most terrible order' which nevertheless had to be carried out,[46] there is nothing to suggest that Ohlendorf was in any way repulsed by the idea of going ahead with the murders which he was now obliged to commit, and it seemed superfluous to him to add anything to his explanation to Einsatzkommando leaders 'that in future all captured Jews are to be shot for racial reasons'.[47]

At mass executions he always found sympathy for the perpetrators. When Austrian Martin Mundschütz could no longer tolerate the hours and hours of endless shootings and suffered a nervous breakdown, Ohlendorf took him off execution duty and put him in charge of catering. This led to Mundschütz being ridiculed by Kommando members as an 'Austrian wimp'. When he requested release home because 'although he would sacrifice himself utterly for Germany's cause' he did not want to spend the rest of his time at the front 'always worrying about whether he was being thought a cissy',[48] Ohlendorf returned him to Innsbruck, where Mundschütz resumed his career with the Kripo.

Another Einsatzgruppe member had a fierce row with the unit catering officer when, after a bloody morning slaving over a hot machine-gun, the midday meal was found to be blood-sausage. 'I shouted at him, what kind of filth was he feeding us . . . in this situation we were refusing to eat such garbage. Ohlendorf didn't speak to him about this personally but he mentioned to Zapp, an Unterführer (sergeant) who came running up, that people had to act like officers.'[49]

The 'blameless' SS officer Ohlendorf returned to his desk at RSHA in July 1942. After Heydrich's assassination in Prague, the office needed capable heads. Resuming his old job preparing 'Reports from the Reich' from then until the capitulation, he was sweetened with the rank of Generalmajor der Polizei. In his year with Einsatzkommando D, Ohlendorf had murdered ninety thousand men, women and children, a fact which he admitted openly to the War Crimes Tribunal.

When prosecuted with twenty-two other Einsatzkommando members one year later at Landsberg, Ohlendorf did not deny the accusation. He merely pointed to the Führer-Order which made it impossible for him to have acted in any other way. Yet even without this binding instruction from the highest level, mass-murder in the East would still have been justified for the Defender of the Holy Grail of National Socialism. In the 'total war for the world view', der Weltanschauungskrieg, one had to ensure that no later generation of 'avengers' could ever arise.[50] The Allied court sentenced Ohlendorf to death by hanging and the sentence was carried out at Landsberg on 7 June 1951.

Franz Alfred Six – The Assiduous One

On trial for his life, Professor Six presented himself as an enlightened spirit:

> My political concept from the point of view of a German was that our task had been to reintroduce into the political administration of that country (i.e. Russia) the basic principles of political, economic and also religious freedom. When I crossed the border into the Soviet Union, I was firmly

convinced that that was the political programme of the
German Reich in the occupied eastern territories, and it came
as a most terrible shock to discover from the documents
which had been kept hidden from me . . . that instead of
correct political administration, only terror was intended.[51]

Michael Musmanno, presiding judge in the Landsberg trial of the
Einsatzkommandos, interjected: 'Are we to understand from what you
say that your efforts were all intended to get the churches reopened, and
to ensure that the civilian population was able to practise religious and
cultural freedom?'[52]

The Landsberg court was more interested in Six as leader of
Vorkommando Moskau, however, whose men, according to Report No.
73 of 4 September 1941, together with other Einsatzgruppen between 22
June and 20 August that year, shot to death 144 people and, operating
independently, another 46 persons, including 38 Jewish intellectuals, who
had been 'sowing discord and unrest in the new Ghetto at Smolensk'.[53]

Before taking over Vorkommando Moskau, Six had been in charge of
Amt VII at RSHA, and from 1940 with the Waffen-SS artillery. Heydrich
had given him the Moscow command. 'I was summoned after evening
roll call one day to make myself available to discuss with him important
events, the most special cases.'[54] Born in 1909 and of lower-middle-class
origins, Six obtained his *Abitur* school-leaving certificate. He joined the
SA in 1932. 'I became a National Socialist, less for reasons of its political
programme than from a recognition of the political strength of National
Socialism. It seemed to promise the solution to social questions not by a
single class, but through the whole German people.'[55]

Even if the often-confused details of National Socialist ideology
escaped him, one thing at least was clear to Six: there was one social
group which did not fit in among the German people, and that was the
German Jews. That the breaking down of the European peoples and
States by the Jews 'were the greatest and most obvious symptoms of
19th-century disease' was one of his basic beliefs.[56]

After the 'Night of the Long Knives' and the emasculation of the SA
in the summer of 1934, the ambitious journalist and academic went over

to Heydrich's SD, taking charge of the Press office and later the broader portfolio of *Gegnerforschung* – 'research into the opposition'.

In parallel with this career work, the 'dogged', 'brooding' and 'enormously industrious' man with the thinning blond hair rose to be Professor of Journalistic Science at Königsberg and – in the face of violent academic opposition – Professor of Political History and the Humanities at Berlin. When Heydrich created the RSHA in 1939, after months-long wrangling with rivals Ohlendorf and Schellenberg, Six was given Amt VII on the basis of his *Gegnerforschung* so that it should become 'the real central archive of the entire Sipo and SD'.[57]

In all his offices, the rising star of National Socialist humanities served the regime faithfully and taught with scientific aplomb its basic values of 'race, the Führer principle, obedience, of German-ness, of the community' in which every German was obliged to believe because they formed for him the self-evident moral orientation of his conduct and life – he cannot and will not act in any other way'.[58]

As did Heydrich, Six identified the main enemies of the Reich as being the freemasonry, the Jews and the Churches. His team of investigators in *Gegnerforschung* busied themselves setting up comprehensive card-index systems containing full details of the enemies of German-ness and National Socialism including all important Jews, 'especially those active in international science'. The 'scientific' aspect of this work was frequently abstruse, but always within recognisable parameters. In a working plan dated 17 July 1939 about possible fields of research, Six suggested that 'such a problem might be, for example, the proposition that the pro-Jewish stance of England is founded in its Puritanism and the belief that the English originated from the lost tribe of Israel.'[59]

During Six's time at SD, Heydrich thought a lot of him, but was anxious for it to become the rule that 'the convinced political SS man should also be the best expert both in the examination room and in practice.' The nearer war came and, with it, out of Heydrich's sight, the beginning of extermination policy, the more did the brooding theoretician get on his nerves. Six was, in his opinion, 'weighed down with inhibitions and doubts'. He made fun of him, as he did of other subordinates and made no secret of his antipathy. Heydrich's representative Werner Best said in

1947: 'Dr Six suffered a lot for Heydrich's maltreatment of him, and his aversion to Heydrich amounted almost to hate.'[60] The parting of the ways came in 1939 when Heydrich allegedly called him 'a pedantic Professor' although this was simply another insult and Heydrich was not thinking of relieving Six of his office.

Six continued to take part in all important conferences at RSHA and, as a member of Heydrich's staff after the German invasion of Poland in 1939, was also fully informed of the activities of the Sipo Einsatzgruppen in that country. He knew what Hitler, Himmler and Heydrich considered necessary for the reorganisation of Poland, that is 'to render the ruling class as harmless as possible' and to convert the rest of the population into 'eternal seasonal and casual workers'.[61] The German Jews were to be shipped in rail cattle trucks to Poland where, in the region east of Warsaw and around Lublin, a 'natural reservation' or 'Reichs-Ghetto'[62] would be set up. Was it scruples about the brutal resettlement policies of the National Socialist leadership which convinced Six in 1940 to volunteer for duty at the front with the Waffen-SS, or was it perhaps the realisation of his dwindling influence which hurt his vanity? The projects in which his colleagues were involved had become increasingly more marginal and removed from reality. One of his assistants was researching the relationship between the European princely houses and freemasonry, another investigating good-humouredly Himmler's allegation that medieval witchcraft trials were actually an attack by Roman Catholicism on German womanhood.

Six trained with an artillery unit at Berlin-Lichterfelde but did not resign as head of Amt VII at RSHA: of his service at the front as a Waffen-SS artilleryman nothing is known. His regimental commander submitted an assessment, however: 'Six is officer material. He is extremely correct in the military sense. His world-view and political outlook have made a great impression on the men at the batteries.'[63]

Shortly before the German attack on the Soviet Union, Heydrich recalled Six to Berlin for the purpose of offering him a job which would enable Six to realise to the full his yearning for a symbiosis of science and action. As leader of Vorkommando Moskau, the scientist was given the allegedly additional task – the first task was never proved in court – of ensuring the safe custody of libraries and archives in the conquered Soviet capital when it fell to the Wehrmacht. For this purpose his motorised troop of about thirty men was attached to Einsatzgruppe B under Arthur Nebe who, like Six, also headed a department at RSHA: Kripo was his responsibility there. Six signalled his obedience.

Was the mission of Professor Six simply to safeguard books and documents or was he present at RSHA, together with other Einsatzgruppen and Einsatzkommando leaders, on 17 June 1941 when Heydrich spoke the words which Einsatzgruppenführer Karl Jäger heard, namely that in the case of war with the Soviet Union, the Jews in the East were all to be shot dead?

In his trial at Landsberg, Six denied having been present at this conference. He had not been given his mission until 22 June, he stated: he had received it from an aide to Heydrich, and not from Heydrich himself, and his only orders were to secure the archives. Six was more vehement when denying that he had ordered the murders near Smolensk as his unit awaited the fall of Moscow. The execution of a total of 190 persons mentioned in Report No. 73 between 22 June and 20 August 1941, if they happened at all, had occurred under the leadership of Nebe at a time when he, Six, had already been allowed to leave his Kommando and was either on his way back to Berlin, or had already arrived there. (Because of chronic disputes over jurisdiction with Nebe, Six had applied to be returned to RSHA, and this was granted in mid-August.)

Beyond the defence argument that he could not have committed this crime because he was not there, Six proceeded to wash his hands of it morally. He was already on record as saying that the destruction of the synagogues on Reichskristallnacht in 1938 was 'a disgrace and a scandal', and if he had ever received an order to execute women and children during operations in the East, Six maintained, he would have committed suicide to avoid compliance.[64]

This was the same man who, in April 1944 as head of the Cultural–Political Department of the German Foreign Office, had candidly admitted at a conference on 'World Jewry' that 'Jewry in Europe is at its end, for the physical removal of the Eastern Jews deprives Jewry of the biological principles.'[65]

The court commented on Six's outpouring with contemptuous irony but, unlike Ohlendorf and fifteen other accused from the Einsatzkommandos who received a sentence of death or life imprisonment, in his case the question of participation in the Einsatzgruppe B murder programme could 'not be proved with scientific certainty', and so he was given a prison term of twenty years, since Six had been 'a member of an organisation which committed deeds of violence, crimes and inhuman acts against civilian populations'.[66]

On 3 November 1952, after serving four years six months, Six was released from Landsberg. Mostly 'undiscovered' by German justice thereafter, he lived comfortably as marketing director at Porsche-Diesel and later as an independent business adviser. Heydrich's erstwhile 'researcher into the opposition' died of heart disease in 1975 aged sixty-five at Bozen in the southern Tyrol.

Arthur Nebe – A Man Rent Asunder

'There are no convictions, there are only circumstances.' This sentence from Honoré de Balzac was a favourite quote of Reichskriminaldirektor Arthur Nebe, head of Amt V at Heydrich's RSHA.[67] It could have been the guiding principle of the life which ended at Plötzensee Prison on 3 March 1945. Two months before the collapse of the German Reich, the erstwhile star of Nazi criminalistics was executed as a traitor, probably by hanging, for his part in the German resistance to Hitler.

In a sparkling career the zealous Nebe had led Einsatzgruppe B in Russia and been responsible for the execution of thousands of people using Himmler's 'efficient' killing methods for Jews, partisans and the mentally afflicted. He was a constant advocate of the proposal that in criminology lay 'not only the eradication of the criminal layers of society but at the same time the purification of the race.'[68]

It was the same Nebe who, as far as can be ascertained, had been conspiring since 1940 at the latest with the circle of military plotters who launched the failed assassination attempt on Hitler on 20 July 1944. He supplied the military resistance with signals material from RSHA, was possibly involved in procuring the explosives for the attempt and, had it succeeded, would have led the arrests of top-level figures of the Third Reich as the controller of a great multitude of reliable civilian police officials.[69]

This most inwardly torn of the office administrators, into whose arteries Heydrich proposed 'to pour steel' by carrying out murders, was born the son of a teacher in 1894. After obtaining an emergency *Abitur* school-leaving certificate in 1914, he volunteered for the armed forces and was eventually decorated with the Iron Cross Second-Class. In 1920 he entered the criminal police in Berlin, joined the SS and NSDAP in 1931 and a year later, thus before the Nazi seizure of power, founded the National Socialist police staff association in Berlin. Once Hitler was Reichs Chancellor, Nebe began his fast ascent through the police apparatus. By 1935 he was head of the Prussian Landeskriminalamt, by 1937 head of the Reichskriminalamt under Heydrich, to whom the detective force as well as the political police were subordinate. This office became Amt V at RSHA after its establishment in 1939.

Nebe proved himself a devoted Party member and gave an impression of servility in the presence of Heydrich and other National Socialist leaders. By this time, however, he had distanced himself inwardly from the Third Reich and its Party bosses, and spoke of them only 'contemptuously', according to Hans Bernd Gisevius in his 1966 book *Wo ist Nebe?*

Criminologist Gisevius was Nebe's colleague and close friend in Berlin during the early years of the Third Reich and, although discharged from police service in 1936, remained close to Nebe. It was through Gisevius that Nebe was put in contact with the Resistance circle around General Ludwig Beck, Oberst Hans Oster and the mayor of Leipzig, Carl-Friedrich Goerdeler.

Gisevius's book is an attempt to whitewash his friend. In view of the known facts, his effort to explain it all away is mostly unsuccessful. It is clear that Nebe ran up the SS career ladder, rose from Sturmbannführer to Oberführer and finally, as an RSHA departmental head, became SS-Brigadeführer and General der Polizei. As a police chief he was 'decent' and, unlike his Gestapo colleague Müller, did not allow suspects to be beaten. Nebe initiated criminal proceedings against a number of police officers against whom such abuses could be proved.[70] 'Hold high the Kripo banner' was his advice to subordinates upon their being transferred to the Gestapo. In Warsaw, after the fall of Poland, he set up an investigation of SS-Brigadeführer Lothar Beutel for a sexual offence committed against the sixteen-year-old daughter of his Polish cook.

Nebe's relationship with 'C' at RSHA was no less tense than that of other *Amt* heads. Heydrich enjoyed playing Nebe, who suffered from an anxiety complex and doubled up with stomach pains in critical situations, against his rival 'Gestapo' Müller. Nebe never dared complain, except to his friend Gisevius, to whom he described the 'gangster tactics' of Heydrich and other Nazi leaders.[71] Heydrich valued Nebe for his efficiency, however. Lina Heydrich recalled: 'I never heard my husband speak of Nebe disparagingly.'[72]

In 1939 the Nazis embarked upon a programme to rid themselves of 'lives unworthy to be lived': the euthanasia of all long-term mental patients incapable of work. The Criminal Technical Institute (KTI), Nebe's pride and joy, played a decisive role in the enterprise and developed a method of killing using pure carbon monoxide in a closed environment which gave the victims a lethal dose of poisonous gas within a few minutes.

In the 1967 prosecution at Stuttgart of Dr Albert Widmann, former departmental head at the Reichskriminalamt, the judgment contained a passage stating:

> At the planning stage, Nebe, who had received orders from the highest level, informed the accused that the euthanasia had been decided upon and that KTI would be involved in an advisory capacity. In response to the accused's enquiry as to whether humans or animals were to be killed, Nebe said that it would be neither humans nor animals but rather 'animals in human form'. In response to another question, Nebe had assured the accused that no criminal responsibility would attach and that the whole thing was being legalized by a law.[73]

Between January 1940 and August 1941, seventy thousand mentally ill or disadvantaged persons were terminated by gassing. Was the 'decent'

Nebe secretly beset by his conscience? Nobody knows. His apologist Gisevius avoids any mention of this unpleasantness, although he justifies with great skill the darkest stage in the life of his friend, as leader of Einsatzgruppe B in Russia between the end of June and the end of October 1941. As far as Gisevius could recall, Nebe had refused 'in no uncertain terms' to fall in with Heydrich's ideas and had submitted his application for a transfer to the International Commission of Criminal Police (the forerunner of Interpol). Nebe had seen, according to Gisevius, 'something approaching which made him apply the brakes'.[74]

Apparently a conversation with Generaloberst Beck, leader of the Resistance, had convinced him to obey Heydrich. According to Gisevius, Beck explained to Nebe that it was one of the most difficult decisions for an army commander to make sacrifices for the tactical leadership in order to bring about a shift in strategy, and if necessary even abandon large troop units to the wolves.[75] Nebe was needed and Beck hoped that he would not leave the conspirators in the lurch.

The 'shift in strategy' was a *coup d'état* against Hitler with the co-operation of his chief of criminal police. The 'tactical sacrifice' was the need to acquiesce in Heydrich's liquidation plans so as not to be unmasked as an opponent of the regime. In this manner Gisevius justifies Nebe's murderous period in the East, this being synonymous with 'abandoning large troop units to the wolves'.

An eyewitness to the scene when Heydrich assembled departmental heads to call for volunteers to lead the Einsatzkommandos was police commissioner Dr Bernhard Wehner. Nebe was the first to step forward with a brisk, 'Gruppenführer, you can count on me'. Wehner: 'His colleagues grinned inwardly. They knew that "their" Arthur always liked to be thought of as the most courageous and bravest of them all. They would often joke about his longing for the Iron Cross First-Class.'[76]

Perfectly disguised as Heydrich's industrious assistant, the man of the Resistance had taken upon himself the liquidation of thousands upon thousands of victims as head of Einsatzgruppe B. According to Event Report USSR No. 113 dated 14 November 1941, by that date he had executed a total of 45,467 persons. So as not to blow his cover, so Gisevius would have us believe, whenever his unit followed the troops into a captured town, Nebe would urge them to energetic involvement against selected civilians, for Heydrich expected no less of him.[77]

Himmler had felt so close to vomiting at Minsk on 15 August 1941, when for the first and last time in his life he witnessed a mass shooting, that he ordered Nebe to look for alternatives. Nebe therefore told his subordinate Dr Widmann of the KTI to bring 400 kilos of explosive and two metal tubes from Germany. Twenty-five mentally afflicted Russians were locked into a wooden bunker wired for explosives, and when Widmann hit the plunger the following happened:

> The wood ceiling fell in partially and the door was blown off but half the patients crawled or ran panic-stricken out of the bunker screaming. While Jewish forced labour had to chase the surviving patients back into the gloomy ruins, Widmann and his assistants discussed what had gone wrong. They decided that the charge had been too small and prepared a bigger one. This second explosion collapsed the wooden bunker completely and there was no more noise from within. A few body parts hung in the trees.[78]

Nebe dismissed the explosives experiment as 'utter rubbish' and turned to the considerations of more 'humane' methods. At a mental asylum at Mogiliov in White Russia he introduced the two metal tubes into a sealed room. One was fitted to the motor of a lorry. Once the patients were locked in the room, the exhaust gases from the engine were pumped in, but had had no apparent ill effects on the patients after several minutes. Next, Nebe ordered the second tube connected up to the vehicle exhaust pipe and this time it was not long before the patients were all motionless.

The results were analysed a few days later. The explosive method was rejected because it required too much work before and after. 'Under these circumstances it is preferable to kill by exhaust gassing because vehicles are available everywhere and can be used wherever desired.'[79]

When Nebe returned to his desk at RSHA in November 1941, he was, as Gisevius writes, 'a mere shadow of his former self, highly strung, miserable'. For his unstinting efforts at the front he was promoted Generalleutnant. Yet his verve was gone. In his office he fell prey increasingly to madcap ideas, such as the one for winning the American mafiosi over to the Nazi cause. 'Sabotage! Arson! Catastrophes! These must decide the war!'[80]

When Heydrich succumbed to the effects of the assassination attempt at the beginning of June 1942, Nebe made no emphatic statement of regret although he did join the SS deathwatch at the coffin side from time to time. To Heydrich's successor at RSHA, Dr Ernst Kaltenbrunner, he continued to be a reliable servant, at least outwardly. Another example of the split in Nebe's personality was the incident in April 1944 when, according to eyewitnesses, he was 'visibly shaken' and 'overcome' when passing to a subordinate Hitler's secret order to execute fifty recaptured British prisoners of war 'while attempting to resist arrest'. This was the aftermath of the famous mass break-out from Stalag Luft III prison camp. Nebe's Reichskriminalamt was obliged to choose the names of the candidates for death. Nebe pacified his colleagues and his own troubled conscience by pointing out that there was no appeal against a Führer-Order, and in any case the Gestapo would do the dirty work. Thus the killings went ahead.[81]

Four months later Nebe was at the RSHA building in Prinz-Albrecht-Strasse when the attempt was made on the life of the Führer. Had all gone off to plan, it would have been the responsibility of Nebe and his Kripo officers to arrest Kaltenbrunner, 'Gestapo' Müller and other National Socialist leaders. But Hitler survived. Nebe remained beyond suspicion initially and moved among his colleagues loyal to the regime until 24 July when during the first wave of arrests and interrogations his name began to crop up in confessions. He now decided it was wisest to go to ground.

For almost six months Nebe was harboured by farming friends in the Teltow area, hoping for an early end to the war and 'discussing seriously whether, as a Resistance fighter, he would be entitled to take over Heydrich's properties in Bohemia or on Fehmarn.'[82] Betrayed by a jilted ex-lover, Nebe was arrested on 16 January 1945, having given up without a fight. He confessed without the need for threats or torture. To the end, the 'decent, ambitious, anxious head of murder'[83] hoped that Himmler might give him the opportunity to prove himself at the front, but in the end a Nazi gallows claimed him.

As regards the major killing operations of his office heads and the other Einsatzgruppe leaders, Heydrich had himself kept continually updated by radio and telex – himself, not Himmler. 'C' had accompanied his operational orders with various additional directions from time to time: 'spontaneous uprisings among a population against its Jews', which he called 'self-cleansing measures', were to be instigated without leaving any traces (29 June 1941); all Communist career politicians as well as Jews in Communist Party and State offices, saboteurs and rabble-rousers were to be executed (1 July); and then 'all Jews' (17 July); political commissars and Jews among prisoners of war were to be shot 'if possible without it being noticed' but 'certainly not in the camp' (17 July); all persons assisting partisans were to be shot and their villages 'razed to the ground' (18 September). Heydrich demanded of his henchmen not only 'ruthless and energetic execution of measures' but also 'smartness of appearance on and off duty'.[84] He constantly demanded 'results'. On 30 June with Himmler he visited Grodno in Lithuania and berated members of Einsatzkommando 9 because they had been slovenly in liquidating 'only 96 Jews'. On 9 July when the two SS chiefs returned, they were mollified to discover that the shootings had increased 'considerably'.[85]

Until the present, historians have not been able to complete the trail of blood left by Einsatzkommandos in the eastern Baltic region, White Russia, Moldavia, the Ukraine and Russia itself. No more than three thousand men, supported by Waffen-SS, regular police units and Wehrmacht troops killed more than half a million men, and from October 1941, also women and children. The worst massacres find their place today on the monuments to genocide in Europe, the United States and Israel: Kamenez-Podolsk 23,600 dead; Babi Yar 33,700; Vitebsk 17,000; Dniepropetrovsk 10,000; Odessa 27,000; Dalnik 20,000; Rovno 21,000; Minsk 19,000; Riga, 38,000; Vilna 33,500 . . .

The cold-blooded and fastidious manner in which such mass executions were planned is depicted in a so-called infantry report: 'The performance of such *Aktionen* is primarily a question of organisation.

The decision to make each particular area Jew-free systematically demands a thorough preparation of each individual *Aktion* and intelligence of the prevailing situation in the area concerned.'

If the 'intelligence' was satisfactory, the Jews would be assembled at one place, or at several different places. Bearing in mind the numbers, the location for the burial trench had to be found and excavated. The distance from the assembly point to the trench would be four to five kilometres on average. The Jews were transported to the place of execution in batches of five hundred, each batch at least two kilometres apart.[86] What happened next was established by the Kiel *Landesgericht* in 1964 during the investigation into Einsatzkommando 8:

> In the opening shooting *Aktionen* (Bialystok and Baranowice) execution squads would be formed from members of the Einsatzkommando and attached police. They would be equal in number to the group of people being taken to the shooting trench, or in some cases up to twice as strong so that sometimes a victim might be shot by one or two squad members. These Kommandos were issued with carbines and consisted mostly of police officers and members of the SS squads led by an SS-Führer appointed by the commander of Einsatzkommando 8.
>
> At these executions undertaken by shooting squads it would occasionally be arranged for the victims to line up along the trench edge so that they could be 'pushed in' easily afterwards. For the later *Aktionen*, at the latest from the time of Baranowice, the victims had to lie face down inside the trench and were then shot in the back of the head. During the shootings at Bialystok, Novgorod and Baranowice, the corpses were well covered over, more or less, with sand or chalk before the next batch was brought up. In the later shooting *Aktionen*, this was done only rarely so that the next batch of victims, if they were to be shot in the trench, always had to lie down on the corpses of those who had just been killed before. But even in those cases where the corpses had been covered with sand or

chalk, the next victims often saw them, because body parts would frequently be jutting out of the thin layer of sand or earth.[87]

In this manner on 29 and 30 September 1941, 33,771 people died in the gorge at Babi Yar near Kiev. A survivor recalled:

> In the cemetery the Germans took away from us and the other citizens all our bags and valuable articles before leading us in groups of forty to fifty people through a so-called 'corridor' about three metres wide lined by Germans armed with sticks, rubber truncheons and dogs. Everybody who went down the corridor was cruelly beaten by the Germans. They thronged into a place at the end of the corridor where the police took them and forced them to strip to their underwear while being beaten. Many people were killed just going through the corridor. Then those who had been beaten and stripped were taken in groups to the Babi Yar gorge, to the place of the shootings. I saw myself how the Germans took children from their mothers and threw them into the gulley. I saw women, old and sick, who had been beaten, and beaten to death. Young people went grey before my eyes.

One of the riflemen present that day confirmed the scale of the horror:

> The Jews had to undress in a sandpit. There were children, men and women. From this sandpit they had to descend the steep sides into the gulley. There were bodies there already, how many layers I do not know. I also had to climb over these bodies, as did my comrades. The Jews had to lie down on the corpses, then they were shot dead.

Three days later, according to another witness, the mountain of bodies was still 'shrugging'. Those who had survived being shot would certainly suffocate or die of thirst under the weight of the dead above them.[88]

The murderers had compassion, but only for their own. 'Our men were more nervy than those who had to be shot,'[89] stated Paul Blobel, who ordered the massacre of Kiev's Jews at Babi Yar. 'The death we handed out was a short, fine death.'[90] Viennese Secretary of Police Walter Mattner wrote home describing an *Aktion* at Mogiliov in White Russia: 'Suckling children were thrown up in the air and as they came down we shot them before they landed in the trench or the water. Let's be rid of this brood! By the devil, I have never seen so much Soviet blood, filth, flesh and bone! Now at last I can understand the meaning of the word "bloodlust".'[91]

True to Heydrich's requirement for 'outstanding appearance on and off duty', his mass-murderers turned their faces away from 'inappropriate and sadistic executions'.[92] To the indignation of a German Sonderkommando, their Rumanian ally celebrated its arrival at Kishinyov by shooting down at random people visiting the Jewish cemetery or walking in the street. The bodies were left where they fell. German commander Paul Zapp demanded from the Rumanian district commander a public admission that his troops had been responsible for the undisciplined shootings, so that 'the blame for this atrocity' should not be attributed to his Sonderkommando.[93]

SS execution troops did not operate in a vacuum, for wherever they did their work there would always be Wehrmacht soldiers close by. Fifty years after the war's end, the myth persisted that German infantrymen had played no part in the killing orgies arranged by Heydrich. This was changed finally by the exhibition *Vernichtungskrieg – Verbrechen der Wehrmacht 1941–1944* (War of Extermination – Wehrmacht Crimes 1941–1944) at the Hamburg Institute for Social Research in 1995. There was a widespread public outcry and protest against the exhibition.

In the spring of 1941, therefore before the Russian campaign, the SS and Wehrmacht High Commands had agreed their respective spheres of operations. 'The Einsatzgruppen and their Kommandos are justified, in the framework of the duties for which they are responsible, to carry out execution measures against the civilian population.'[94] This secret order of the day by Oberkommando des Heeres C-in-C Walther von Brauchitsch, issued on 28 April 1941, proves that the Wehrmacht heads knew of the

SS murder plans from the outset. The generals approved these plans in principle, which even wrested from Hitler and Himmler the right to supply the Einsatzkommandos with binding instructions, but only expressly if the military situation made it necessary.[95] The authority to order a halt to mass executions was practically never used. All the generals asked for was that 'if at all possible, the executions will be undertaken away from the troops'.[96]

From 11 June 1941, Generaloberst Franz Halder set out the respective roles of SS-Einsatzgruppen and Wehrmacht: 'For carrying out their special assignments, the instruction of troops, showing identity documents, provision of auxiliary personnel, sharing of vehicles and other help, insofar as the fighting situation permits, is to be provided in every way to lighten the burden of the Kommando.'[97]

In the operational area of Einsatzgruppe C, many infantrymen interpreted the phrase 'other help' for Heydrich's Kommandos so enthusiastically that the C-in-C 6th Army felt compelled to intervene. Generalfeldmarschall Walter von Reichenau in August 1941:

> In various localities of the Army area, organs of the SD, RF-SS and heads of the German police are carrying out necessary executions of criminal, Bolshevik, mostly Jewish elements. It has come to notice that off-duty soldiers are volunteering to assist the SD in this work, or are attending these measures as spectators and taking photographs. The C-in-C 6.Army has issued the following instruction: 'All participation by Army personnel as spectators or helpers at executions not ordered by a military superior is forbidden . . . Should the SD make a request to the district commander for men to cordon off against spectators an area to be used for an SD execution, this request is to be complied with.'[98]

The 'necessary' destruction of 'criminal, Bolshevik, mostly Jewish' lives did not concern the field marshal, but since the Einsatzgruppen operated autonomously, he recalled the division of labour laid down by those above him: executions on the one hand, giving help on the other.

Heydrich, in Berlin or Prague, was able to keep abreast of the situation through the 'Event Reports USSR' provided him by 'Gestapo' Müller and could rest content that the Wehrmacht, apart from a few cases, was going along with the 'cleansing *Aktionen*' without protest. An example here was at the Babi Yar massacre near Kiev in September 1941. Units of 6th Army sealed off the Ukrainian capital and, under threat of death, ordered the city's Jews to assemble at a certain place on the outskirts and watched as a German police regiment and Ukraine police auxiliaries escorted them to the executions areas. Similarly at Lubny, the Wehrmacht assembled almost two thousand persons for execution by a Sonderkommando.

At Minsk in July 1942, thirty thousand Jews were killed to 'cleanse' the ghetto. 'The butchery was carried out by an SS-Sonderkommando but soldiers of the German Wehrmacht stood guard around the ghetto to ensure that nobody ran off and so escaped death.'[99]

According to information from the Ludwigsburg Central Office for the Investigation of National Socialist Crimes, Wehrmacht units were directly involved in mass shootings. Acting under the orders of Sipo and SD, No. 7 Company, 727 Inf. Rgt murdered over eight thousand Jews in October and November 1941 in White Russia.

Otto Ohlendorf's Einsatzgruppe D killed several thousand persons at Simferopol in the Crimea at the end of 1941. On 15 December they were able to notify Heydrich that the city was 'Jew-free'. Two Wehrmacht units, Feldgendarmerieabteilung 683 and Geheime Feldpolizei 647 helped in the shootings. A few months later, the Simferopol district commander enquired on behalf of the C-in-C 11th Army, General Erich von Manstein, if the Army could retain watches 'from the Jewish *Aktion* for service purposes'. Heydrich's departmental aide replied by sending 120 watches of victims murdered earlier and suggested that in the case of need additional supplies could be delivered. Valuable chronometers of gold and silver were absent, however, since Einsatzgruppe D had 'forwarded these to the *Staatskasse* Berlin as ordered'.[100]

Heydrich had never watched a massacre on location. Once in Berlin he had been shown a film of a mass shooting and, springing to his feet in excitement, had demanded that another method be found. Since

Himmler had also come to the same conclusion, Heydrich's henchmen, led by Arthur Nebe, set out to find the most effective way of killing people in bulk and, as mentioned earlier, experimented with dynamite and stable gas chambers.

The problem was that the death squads needed mobile execution locations to enable them to start work immediately after German troops had captured a particular district, and while Nebe had to persevere for the time being with shootings, his criminal-police technicians at RSHA in Berlin were assembling a prototype DIY gassing lorry. A hose was led directly from the vehicle exhaust into the sealed box structure behind the driving cab. SS-Sturmbannführer Friedrich Pradel explained that members of shooting squads in the East frequently suffered nervous breakdowns or were permanently on the verge of one, and therefore it was necessary 'to use a more humane method of killing'.[101] Execution expert Dr Albert Widmann experimented with vehicle ignition systems to find ways of enriching the carbon monoxide content of exhaust gases. Various measurements of the atmosphere in the interior of the lorry during these tests, carried out by assistants of the KTI wearing gas masks, were found to be 'satisfactory'. However, the RSHA did not want to send its 'new humane development' to Russia before testing it 'under clinical conditions' and in November 1941 at Sachsenhausen concentration camp thirty inmates were selected for the final trial. The prisoners had to undress and board the lorry 'as if they were getting on a bus'. Then the engine was started up. One of the chemists involved, Dr Theodor Leidig, made this statement in 1959:

> I was told that the people who would be getting into the lorry were Russians who would have been shot anyway. The higher-ups wanted to find out if there was a better way of killing them. Then we went to another spot where we found the lorry ... I still remember that you could look inside through a peephole or window. The interior was lit. Then they opened the lorry. Some of the bodies fell out, others were unloaded by prisoners. As we technicians confirmed, the bodies had that

pinkish-red hue which is typical of persons who have died of carbon monoxide poisoning.[102]

The designers and those who had placed the order were satisfied. Himmler ruled that the mobile gas chambers were to be kept clean and in good running order. According to his romantic notions, death by carbon monoxide poisoning would not be painful suffocation but a simple 'falling asleep', a gentle twilight. From Hitler's Chancellery came a telephone call with more practical suggestions: the police technical unit would fit the interiors with grilled floors to facilitate cleaning urine and excrement.[103] From December 1941 these gassing lorries were tried out by Einsatzkommandos in the East.

Concurrent with the introduction of these mobile units, fixed gas chambers were set up in the concentration camps. On 3 September 1941 at Auschwitz, vastly expanded on Himmler's orders given in March (Heydrich knew in January about Auschwitz II), the SS tested out the installation on Russian prisoners of war. Commandant Rudolf Hoess employed the Zyklon B insecticide which used hydrocyanic acid crystals. The majority of the 1.1 million victims at Auschwitz were disposed of by this method. In October, Himmler told Einsatzkommandos at Mogiliov, 'Soon, Jews will be killed by gassing only'.[104]

The first mass extermination centre from 7 December was Chelmno near Lodz. This camp, unlike Auschwitz or Treblinka, was run by the SD. In fifteen months 150,000 persons died there. At least initially there were three mobile gassing units disguised as furniture removal lorries.

Upon the outbreak of war, Heydrich had sought experience 'of a sporting nature' at the fighting front in accordance with his unceasing urge to achieve. Serving with the Kriegsmarine, which had thrown him out in 1932, was out of the question. He rejected brusquely conciliatory gestures from former colleagues of 'Crew 22', and attempted to discredit the Navy commander-in-chief with Hitler, but Admiral Raeder 'constantly refuted the false accusations'[105] and Heydrich found that he had reached his limits: Hitler stood by his naval chief.

In 1939, therefore, Heydrich went into the Luftwaffe. Although already thirty-five years old, he was trained on the Messerschmitt Bf 109D fighter aircraft at Werneuchen aerodrome near Berlin. During the Polish campaign he flew his first enemy missions as an air-gunner. In 1940 Heydrich operated solo over Norway and Holland with Jagdgeschwader 77 and in 1941 flew coastal patrols over the Frisian island of Wangerooge in an Me 109E-7 with 'SS' markings.

He was no stranger to accidents due to his own negligence. On 13 May 1940 at Stavanger he overshot the runway because of excess gas. The aircraft was a write-off and Heydrich had to be cut free. He sustained injuries to his left arm. In June 1941 at Wangerooge he damaged his machine while manoeuvring in a hangar. Official propaganda saw these errors in a different light. 'In an accident with an aircraft – and even the best fighter pilots had the occasional bad luck – Heydrich received a far from minor lesion to his hand. His hand freshly operated on and bandaged with emergency dressings, he then took off on a new mission.'[106]

There was, all the same, something heroic about the manner in which he discharged his duty to his country.

> When, as night fell, the German aircraft landed on the grass airstrip, and the pilots threw themselves into an exhausted sleep, the Home Front awaited Major Heydrich. There were despatches to read, telephone calls to be made, appointments to arrange and courier mail to send. The chief of Sipo and SD was no less on duty at the front than the Luftwaffe major. His comrades would often ask themselves, however, when Major Heydrich found the time to sleep.[107]

Although Himmler stopped him from flying on a number of occasions, at the beginning of Operation *Barbarossa* he was at the front secretly, flying his private Me 109 with JG 77 at Balti in Moldavia. To astonished pilots of the squadron he described how he had been given the machine by Luftwaffe General Ernst Udet in exchange for a police badge which Udet could use for permission to drive about at night and during enemy bombing raids.[108] During an attack on a bridge over the Dniester near Yampol on 22 July 1941, Heydrich's machine was hit by Soviet anti-aircraft fire and he was forced to make an emergency landing between the lines.

Anton Mader, his squadron chief, was beside himself with anxiety. If the RSHA head fell into Stalin's hands, there would be hell to pay from Hitler. At last there came a telephone call from a front unit: 'One of your pilots has come down near here. He must have had a bang on the head, he keeps insisting he's Reinhard Heydrich!'[109]

The German Press, quickly notified, gave this disaster a halo: 'In action on the Eastern Front, his Me 109 was forced to land after a stubborn fight. Using all his skill, his determination resulted in his landing the aircraft close to the German lines. As he came down, he watched the Soviets fleeing.'[110]

The Germans who spirited the unharmed Heydrich to safety were his own subordinates: a troop of Sonderkommando 10a, Einsatzgruppe D under SS-Hauptsturmführer Otto-Ernst Prast brought him to Kommando leader Heinz Seetzen. Heydrich knew Seetzen, who had been Gestapo chief at Hamburg. After 'fighting partisans' that day, Sonderkommando 10a had just finished off forty-five Jews and thirty hostages.

After this crash, Himmler banned Heydrich from any more flying. 'As an aviator he had no great experience and claimed no victories,' pilot Georg Schirmböck related. 'He got the Iron Cross I and II and the Front clasp in silver, and that was it.'[111] In the evening double-header, Heydrich would often hold forth to his fellow Luftwaffe pilots with his vision of a Greater German 'Paradise' in a Russia made fruitful, something of which the Russian masses and in particular their Communist leaders were incapable. The hell to be gone through on the way was discreetly glossed over.

Back from the front, Heydrich now began to assume an ever more central decision-making position regarding the Holocaust. Historian Eberhard Jäckel wrote: 'The chief architect of the genocide was not Himmler but Heydrich. He even motivated Hitler.'[112] After obtaining Hitler's agreement, on 26 March 1941 Heydrich presented to deputy leader Goering a draft plan for 'The Solution of the Jewish Question' and received in reply on 31 July a written instruction requiring him 'to submit in the near future a full plan concerning the organisational, objective and material preconditions for the carrying out of the projected Final Solution to the Jewish Question',[113] the *carte blanche* for genocide.

Those in the know at the time knew that the mass-murders in Russia were the prelude to the general genocide. In a letter dated 6 August 1941, the head of Einsatzgruppe A, Heydrich's confidant Walther Stahlecker, referred to 'fundamental orders in writing which are not to be discussed' from the Sipo leadership alluding to 'the total cleansing of Europe of all Jews' which would soon 'mature'.[114] Others, such as the SD chief of Posen, Rolf-Heinz Höppner, was puzzled as to whether the Jews were to be allowed 'a certain life' or would be 'totally wiped out'.[115]

In summer 1941 Heydrich summoned his RSHA departmental head for Jewish Affairs, Adolf Eichmann, to inform him: 'The Führer has ordered the physical destruction of the Jews.' Then the fast-talker made a long and unusual pause 'as if he wanted to examine the effect of his words',[116] as Eichmann stated later at the Israeli police hearing. 'C' ordered him to speak to SS- and Polizeiführer Odilo Globocnik at Lublin: 'The Reichsführer-SS has already given the corresponding orders. Find out how far he has got with his intentions.'[117] In fact, Himmler had entrusted Globocnik with the expansion of a conglomerate embracing within a year the death camps at Belzec, Sobibor, Treblinka and Maidanek which would be responsible for terminating two million Jews.

On 15 October 1941, as Heydrich informed Himmler four days later, the long-planned mass deportations from German-controlled territory 'had begun daily runs in transports of 1,000 persons each.'[118] By the time winter arrived, more than fifty thousand German Jews had been transported to Lodz, Riga, Kaunas and Minsk, where most were crammed into ghettoes. On 30 November, however, SS-Führer Ostland, Fritz Jeckeln, took 1,035 Berlin Jews straight from the train at Riga into the nearby Rumbuli woods. He had them shot there, contrary to Heydrich's order, and was threatened by Himmler with a criminal trial. Already too many subordinate officers were making decisions to execute people on their own initiative, a sign that contempt for humanity at the higher levels stirred up the lust to kill among the lower ranks. This did not concern

Hitler unduly, however: 'It may be a good thing if the terror precedes us, that we are destroying Jewry' he told Himmler and Heydrich during the table talk of 25 October at Führer-HQ.[119]

For Hitler, 'World War II' began after the attack on Pearl Harbor, when he declared war on the United States as a sign of his loyalty to his Japanese ally. On 12 December 1941 in the privacy of the Reich Chancellery he reminded the Gauleiter of his 1939 'prophecy', while Goebbels wrote afterwards in his diary: 'We have the World War and the destruction of Jewry must be the necessary consequence.'[120] Another participant at the meeting, Poland-Gouverneur Hans Frank, told his staff at Cracow on 16 December 1941 that the plans for the deportation of the Jews to 'Ostland' had been shelved following the Red Army counter-offensive before Moscow, which had dealt the prospects of victory on the Eastern Front a severe blow. At a loss as to how to proceed, in Berlin he was told, 'Liquidate them yourself!' Frank's interpretation of this was: 'We must exterminate the Jews wherever we find them.'[121]

On 18 December 1941, Hitler discussed the fate of the Jews with Himmler at Führer-HQ Wolfsschanze in East Prussia, after which Himmler made a cryptic note in his service calendar: 'Jewish Question/to be destroyed as partisans.'[122]

What that meant in finer detail was to be made clear at a conference of the State Secretaries which they were accordingly invited by the RSHA to attend at the SS guest house Am Grossen Wannsee 56–58 in Berlin on 20 January 1942. Here it was Heydrich's purpose to leave nobody in any doubt as to how the Jewish Question was to be solved.

Chapter Four

The Military Governor
1941–1942

The crown jewels of the kingdom of Bohemia are put on display in the Prague Cathedral of St Vitus only on the most special occasions. 19 November 1941 was one such occasion: the symbolic subjugation of the Czech nation to German military supremacy. In the Wenceslaus Chapel, close to the golden gates of the cathedral, Czech State President Emil Hacha handed to the acting Reichs-Protektor, SS-Obergruppenführer and General der Polizei Reinhard Heydrich, the seven keys to the Coronation Chamber. Hachs retained three keys 'in loyal hands', as Heydrich emphasised, 'as symbols of the loyalty of Bohemia and Moravia to the Reich'.[1] Then the men stood before the crown of Wenceslaus, the holiest relic of the Czechs.

The crown has a bejewelled cross, set upon a thorn, said to be from Christ's crown of thorns. The crown is endowed with a curse that 'whoever should wear it without authority will die violently within a year, followed in death by his eldest son'.

121

Heydrich, Lord of Life and Death, was surely above such superstitions, his officers thought. The 38-year-old raised the relic and crowned himself, to the utter horror of the Czechs. Nobody was allowed to film or photograph this act of 'coronation'.

On this day Heydrich felt well-established. He had demonstrated almost childish pleasure when on 24 September he had been summoned to the FHQ Wolfsschanze in East Prussia to receive notification from Hitler that he had been appointed successor to Statthalter Konstantin von Neurath, who had been sent on permanent sick leave, having not been found sufficiently strict with the Czechs. 'I have become It,' he joked in Berlin as his friend Schellenberg cracked open a bottle of champagne.[2] In order to maintain diplomatic protocol, he was officially to be known as the 'acting Reichs-Protektor' since von Neurath had not been discharged from his position, but effectively Heydrich was now the absolute ruler of Bohemia and Moravia. The new position finally gave him that direct access to the Führer for which he yearned. All power in the Third Reich flowed out from that source, for as Armaments Minister Speer explained after the war, 'In Hitler's Germany, no measure of any significance was thinkable without Hitler knowing about it, if he had not actually ordered it himself.'[3] Previously, Heydrich had had to channel his ideas to Hitler through Himmler or Goering, and received the latter's wishes relayed down in the same way. He had risen from a minor NS-report collator in 1931 to head the RSHA, the terror-administration centre of the Nazi State, but always he stood in Himmler's shadow. Now he had the opportunity to draw level. Those members of the German public who dared to make their opinions known believed it probable that the idolator of the *Germanen* would soon be manipulated by the smart, Machiavellian Heydrich: this was expressed by the acronym 'HHHH' – *Himmlers Hirn heisst Heydrich* – (Himmler's brain is called Heydrich): Heydrich called himself 'Himmler's mainspring'.[4] Although outwardly loyal, Heydrich was easily the match of SS-1 intellectually. 'I have had enough of your cold, rational criticism,' Himmler would growl, and then out of spite postpone all decisions he had just made with Heydrich as soon as the latter left the office. At the same time, Himmler admired his colleague as a successful fencer, horseman and swimmer who had won the Reich Sport Badge at age thirty-six. For his part, Heydrich found it 'very advantageous', being a person eternally 'struggling for position below the Führer-level' in the Third Reich, 'to have someone in front of him to ward off the blows'.

As Reichs-Protektor of Bohemia and Moravia in Prague, but also RSHA head in Berlin, Heydrich had more occasion than anybody else to wire directly to the Reich leaders: he reported frequently to Hitler's representative Martin Bormann, who controlled access to the Führer and had recommended Heydrich for the Prague post, and he had also impressed Goebbels: 'He has absolutely what I did not suspect, a clever political head.'[5]

This was exactly the recognition he was aiming for: to discard his evil reputation as 'the rubbish dump of the Third Reich' and 'bloodhound' and so rise from being a State criminal to statesman. Prague seemed ideal for his 'carrot-and-stick' methods. While the war raged elsewhere, Czechoslovakia existed almost as it had done in peacetime: the men, released from military duty, ate at home with their families, the cities were spared the attentions of Allied aircraft and the Resistance was lame. Nevertheless, Heydrich could not afford to have anybody think the Reich 'was soft': scarcely had he taken over his new seat of power at the Hradshin Palace than he had Czech Prime Minister Alois Elias arrested, tried and sentenced to death for treason, all within a week. In the era of Reichs-Protektor Neurath, Elias had had contact with the Czech Government-in-Exile in London, and this was known to the Nazis. Neurath had not considered it politically useful to make the arrest, whereas the new man at the Hradshin thought otherwise. For him, the condemned Elias was a man in pledge whom he could operate.

Heydrich ensured that the lightning prosecution of the Prime Minister was not a 'show trial' but was 'especially solemn, correct and so generously conducted' that Elias, after his conviction, was full of praise for his treatment 'at the hands of Gestapo and court'.[6] The candidate for death read out in court a personal statement admitting his guilt and distancing himself from the idea of an independent Czech State outside the German Reich. 'Whenever we have set ourselves against Germany in the past, our political and economic situation became unsure and weak,' he said: he, Elias would happily die for his people 'if it served as a last appeal to reason and helped us find the way to an honourable and honest co-operation with the German people.' After the war it was revealed that Elias had made this statement under the threat that twenty thousand Czechs would be executed if he did not sign it.[7]

Heydrich requested Hitler not to exercise his right of reprieve but to postpone execution so that Elias might be further interrogated since he was intending to make further major disclosures about his Government colleagues and the State President. Politically it was valuable 'to get these incriminating things . . . on record'. Heydrich believed that this would provide him with something in reserve for when he needed a hold over State President Hacha. The removal of Hacha did not seem opportune for the time being. Heydrich was much more in favour of 'postulating Hacha as the wise and clever President of the Czech Protectorate', using 'his certain prestige among the Czech people' to create the illusion that he 'is visibly going along with us'.[8] Behind the facade of the puppet government under Hacha, Heydrich believed he could gouge out any remaining autonomy it might have without it coming much to notice, while at the same time keeping the population docile.

The Reichs-Protektor even found words of praise for the unfortunate Hacha. He was going to speak out against the Czech Government-in-Exile abroad and recognise Hitler as his Führer, according to Heydrich. He had received some coaching on correct procedure in the Nazi manner.

> I had Hacha informed that I considered the raising of the right arm with a *Sieg Heil!* for the Führer as proper form. After all, the Protectorate belonged to the German Reich and the Führer was accordingly also Führer of the Protectorate. Confidential enquiries later revealed that the presiding official of the Czech Government, and his cabinet . . . had been practising the Hitler salute.[9]

The stubborn Czechs had no real yearning to fall in with Heydrich, and when they continued to agitate against the occupation and commit acts of sabotage, Heydrich declared a state of emergency under which, up to 29 November 1941, 404 Czechs were executed. More than four thousand persons disappeared into Gestapo cellars below the Pecek Palace while deportations of the Prague Jews began, first into the 'assembly camp' at Theresienstadt, later to the East for extermination. At the same time, Heydrich increased the food ration for propaganda purposes, set up soup kitchens and hunted down black-market profiteers. By giving workers 'their daily bread', he was hoping to keep the important armaments industry of Bohemia running.

Since the central figure of Czech history had been King Wenceslaus (also a German king), and he had never courted the East,[10] Heydrich made no secret of the fact that 'when all is said and done in this area, the Czechs have lost nothing'. This was the long-term objective. For 'important war and tactical reasons', as Heydrich explained to senior Protectorate officials on 2 October 1941 in chambers before his appointment, 'in certain things one should make efforts not to get the Czechs all stirred up and force them – because they can see nothing else for it – to make the great bid to oust us.'[11] For that reason, Heydrich said later, it always had to be perfectly clear who was in charge.

> The Reich will not allow itself to be made a fool of, and is master in the house, which means that a German will overlook no wrong committed by a Czech in the same way as with Jews in the Reich we will never allow a German to say, 'this one is decent, in his case we will make an exception' . . . if we do not stick together inwardly and outwardly, and build a front against the Czechs, they will always find back doors through which they can get up to tricks.

Convinced of the towering cultural superiority of the Germans over the Slavs, Heydrich then warned his senior administrators, in an unintentionally comical passage of his speech indulging his Nordic cultural beliefs:

> The German must not get pissed in a bar. We are not saying he must not get pissed, and if he does, nobody will have any

objections provided it is within his own four walls or in the mess. The Czechs must get the impression that whether on duty or in private, the German remains a gentleman from top to toe.[12]

Every German in the Protectorate had to be aware, Heydrich explained later, that the Czech is a slave and interprets any kindness as weakness. The idea of germanising this riff-raff *en bloc* was false: and to his colleagues he set out the following ludicrous explanation why the germanisation of the people of the Protectorate would not succeed in the long term:

We have the following types of people. First, those of good race and good intentions. That is simple, these people can be germanised. Then we have the rest, starting with those of bad race and bad intentions. I have to move these people out. There is plentry of room in the East. Next we have a middle layer which has to be investigated thoroughly. This layer has well-intentioned people of bad race (a), and mal-intentioned people of good race (b). Group (a) will probably have to go somewhere in the Reich where we can make sure they cannot procreate. As for (b) they are the most dangerous, being the upper layer of good race. Since they have evil intentions, there is only one thing left, which is to resettle them in the Reich in a pure German environment, hoping to germanise and edu-cate them to think correctly, and if that doesn't work, put them against the wall. I wouldn't be able to resettle them else-where, you see, because if they went to the East they would develop into a layer of leaders to oppose us.[13]

The 'non-germanisable' element, which he estimated to be half the population of Czechoslovakia, 'could live out its existence in the Arctic once we take over the Russian gulags.'[14]

The contents of this secret ground-laying speech, only for service use, leaked out. Next morning a senior Czech police officer called on the

German chief of the Prague civilian police and enquired, with horror in his voice, 'If I may be permitted to ask, Herr General, do my family and I belong to the "Czechs of good race and good intentions" whom it is proposed to germanise, or to the intelligentsia of good race but evil intentions who are to be liquidated?'[15] Heydrich's cynical guidelines to resolve the Czech problem were quickly broadcast far and wide and stiffened the resistance to the Nazi occupation.

In the winter of 1941, Heydrich saw no further advantage in continuing to spare the condemned Elias. Konrad Henlein, Gauleiter of the Sudetenland, the northern region of Czech territory reannexed by Hitler in 1938, had pushed strongly for the execution of Elias at the end of November. The risk of making a martyr of Elias was probably not a valid argument, he said, because the outstanding number of condemned Czechs renders the death of Elias insignificant. 'On the other hand, the carrying out of the sentence would be seen by the Czechs as a sign of our strength and determination to take ruthless measures against all internal enemies of the Reich.'[16]

Heydrich pursued this line of argument in letters to Hitler and Bormann on 30 December 1941 in which he pleaded 'most respectfully' that the Führer release Elias to him 'for the execution of the sentence of the People's Court'. Heydrich promised himself 'that by the execution of the sentence and the short, laconic announcement of its performance, the Czech people will be clear that the Reich will be just and help the small man by providing him with his life necessities provided he is loyal and basically speaks out expressly and frankly against the opponents of the Reich.'[17] A week later he repeated his plea to Hitler, adding the argument 'that because of the war situation in the East, in the Mediterranean and in Africa, the attitude of the Czech people has stiffened considerably.'[18]

Until the assassination of his man in Prague, however, Hitler restrained himself from granting Heydrich's wish, the reason being that the leadership in Berlin was convinced Heydrich had the Protectorate firmly in his grasp. In February 1942 Goebbels noted in his diary: 'As it happens, the danger of the Czechs threatening German security in the Protectorate has been completely overcome. Heydrich has been successful. He is playing cat-and-mouse with the Czechs and they swallow everything he tells them.'[19]

To his Protectorate officials at the end of November 1941, the highly praised Heydrich showed himself to be a fanatic so convinced of victory that he had already cut the map of Europe into neat slices. Scandinavians, Flemings and Dutch belonged among the *Germanen*: the Near East and Africa was Italian, the Russians were to be 'forced back behind the Urals, their lands taken over by German *Wehrbauer*. 'The Urals will become our eastern border. Our recruits will soon be spending their first year there training in anti-partisan warfare as border guards.' Whoever did not want to be part of this struggle could go, Hitler's Statthalter promised, 'I will do nothing to him.'[20] Nobody took him up on his offer.

Heydrich handled his twin positions in Prague and Berlin with proven élan. Three times weekly he made the round trip by Ju 52 aircraft with his staff. He used all modern aids, as would a business manager of the time: radio, Dictaphone, couriers, Lufthansa express post, diplomatic mail. He was so conscious of the need to protect the secrets which made him so powerful that he would write messages in 'secret ink', on microdot or in cypher. He used a team of secretaries, for he liked going into exhaustive detail: arrest warrants, responses to applications for mercy and exemptions, salary and pay lists, procurements.

Together with Himmler, Heydrich concerned himself with peripheral matters such as the protection of German youth against external malevolent influences. In a police raid in Hamburg in 1941, the police arrested nearly five hundred young people dancing to 'swing music' at a party. This resulted in a letter from Himmler in 1942:

> I am against us taking only half measures here. All ringleaders are to go to a concentration camp. There the youths will have to have beatings. The stay in the camps must be long ones, two to three years. It must be made clear that they will not be allowed to resume their studies. Only by taking brutal measures can we avoid a dangerous growth in these anglophile tendencies.[21]

In June 1942, about the time of Heydrich's assassination, forty to seventy young Hamburg 'swing fans' were transported to youth concentration camps at Moringen and Uckermark, where they remained until the war's end.

Now as before, Heydrich sniffed enemies everywhere. A typical order: 'I request information on what kind of guy the so-called historian Panitzer von Patzan is. He seems a pretty oblique sort of bird who is additionally very pro-Czech.'[22]

He collated information endlessly. Not only were conversations in his office in the Prinz-Albrecht-Strasse eavesdropped secretly, he even ordered SD-Führer Schellenberg to set up a high-class brothel at Giesebrechtstrasse 11 in Berlin, equipped with the most modern eaves-dropping equipment.

> One day he remarked to me it was time to trawl for better information all round, including among 'prominent people' and foreign guests. He was thinking of setting up a well-appointed, cosy restaurant with attractive women in attendance in a prestigious district of Berlin . . . so I rented a place through an intermediary. The best architects were appointed for the conversion work and the fittings. Double walls, modern listening equipment and automatic transmission devices ensured that every word spoken in this 'saloon' was recorded and relayed to a monitoring centre.[23]

Since Schellenberg considered that the recruitment of the ladies was beyond his jurisdiction, Heydrich got Kripo chief Arthur Nebe to do it. Nebe scoured Europe for prostitutes of the right calibre and also interviewed amateur courtesans from German high society who were prepared to 'do a turn' for Greater Germany. Heydrich gave the establishment the cover name 'Salon Kitty' after the lady in charge, a Berlin hairdresser in her thirties, although officially it was known as 'Pension Schroeder'. Sixteen girls were employed who, among their other talents, had above-average command of foreign languages. The password for guests was 'Rothenburg'. Heydrich was very proud of this Gestapo love-nest and told Felix Kersten, Himmler's masseur, not long after the grand opening that the concern was a sideline which he hoped would soon pay for itself.

> When I laughed aloud, he smirked and told me that since the opening of the brothel, Ciano (the Italian Foreign Minister) was much keener on coming to Berlin, and it also had a definite attraction for Germans in high places. Heydrich reckoned it was justified 'because otherwise foreigners in Berlin would fall into the clutches of the most evil whores'.[24]

Heydrich then asked Kersten what would be his opinion of a similar institution for homosexuals. According to his memoirs, Kersten would not let himself be drawn and with a sarcastic smile Heydrich told him, 'Herr Kersten, if you would like to look over the Giesebrechtstrasse place, naturally from purely medical interest, it is always at your disposal.'[25]

In 'Salon Kitty' the SD kept watch for several years on the bedroom whisperings of Nazi big-wigs and diplomats without ever managing to pull off a great coup. Once, Heydrich, known to his staff as 'the Don Juan of Sex and Licentiousness'[26] was eavesdropped in his own brothel after his instructions to shut down the system were ignored accidentally. Schellenberg was extremely upset about this for some reason.

It speaks volumes for Heydrich's energy that he was able to find the time and enthusiasm for sport in his sixteen-hour working day. He wanted to be an example: he recommended wrestling to the SS as giving 'a permanent claim to body and character development'.[27] His photo as victor of the Reich Full-Pack March was hung in more SS barracks than portraits of Himmler, while his success in fencing made banner head-lines. 'Suddenly he would interrupt his work schedule on an impulse to go swimming, or horse riding or to fly an aircraft,' Ernst Hoffmann, an acquaintance, stated. 'The appropriate clothing always had to be ready. Afterwards he would still be fit to put in more office work.'[28]

Without doubt, Heydrich was a talented and thoroughly ambitious sportsman. In 1925 as a 21-year-old midshipman he won first prize for the 100-metre breaststroke at the SV *Flensburg* swimming tournament, but his favourite sport later was fencing, especially with the sabre. At Kiel in 1927 'Lt Heidrich [*sic*] had entered the city championships', but what place he achieved in the competition is not known.

His rapid political rise in the National Socialist State went hand in hand with a meteoric fencing career. In the journal *Leibesübungen und Körperliche Erziehung* ('Aerobics and Corporal training'), Herbert E. Daniels enthused about Germany's greatest fencer:

> Bad Kreuznach in August 1941: for the second time the German Wartime Fencing Championships have come to a successful conclusion. The Reich Special Class, the twelve best, has been declared, and they will receive the gold and silver pin of the NSRL (Nationalsozialistischer Reichsbund für Leibesübungen). In fifth place came an SS-Obergruppenführer and Chief of Police. He is Reinhard Heydrich, Chief of Security Police and SD. With great joy he received the congratulations due him yet his whole attitude manifests the modesty of the victor. Those who know him also know that he will not be resting on his laurels. 'Neither rest nor relax, always keep working on yourself and strive to advance,' that is his basic creed whether in sport or duty.[29]

Heydrich's rise into the fencing Special Class was due in part to his talent, but the fact that the 37-year-old sportsman was Hitler's most feared thug must certainly have contributed to his 'unstoppable advance' as a veteran. In the age before electronically signalled hits, fencing was a discipline in which the event umpires were required to decide whether a competitor had obtained a hit or not, and 'in the major competitions it was extremely difficult to find somebody to referee a bout in which Heydrich was a participant.' The determination not to force Heydrich into a corner resulted in his achieving remarkable success. In December

1941, the German sabre-fencing team met for an international against Hungary. The *Völkischer Beobachter* had assessed the meeting with the Hungarian 'brothers-in-arms' as 'difficult' and 'lacking all prospects for victory'. The German team had been weakened: the 1940 champion, Georg Frass from Friedenfeldt, had fallen on the Eastern Front and the No. 2, Josef Losert, could not be released from the Russian campaign. 'Under these circumstances, it is especially appreciated that the acting Reichs-Protektor, SS-Obergruppenführer and General der Polizei Reinhard Heydrich, has stepped into the breach and will accompany his three fencing comrades in their difficult task.'[30]

As expected the competition was lost 11:5, but one German shone. 'In the individual ratings, Germany had the best man, and this was the Reich Sports Office leader, SS-Obergruppenführer and General der Polizei Heydrich who won all his bouts. He beat Rajczy 5:2, Rajcsan 5:4 and Berczelly 5:1,' according to the *Völkischer Beobachter* on 16 December 1941. The Hungarian brothers-in-arms knew the score.

A sporting partner in occupied Belgium apparently did not. In 1940, Heydrich had been desirous of expanding his administrative activities in the international sphere and become president of the international fencing organisation in addition to his many positions in the sporting circles of the Nazi State, such as president of the national fencing body in the NSRL as well as being Himmler's Inspector for Body exercises. Belgian Paul Anspach was President of the International Fencing Association. After the military defeat of Belgium in June 1940, Anspach, who had acted as Military Judge Advocate, was arrested by the Wehrmacht for alleged war crimes and incarcerated. Heydrich had the stockholding and funds of the Association sequestered and transferred from Brussels to Berlin. After a few months, when it was clear that Anspach was innocent, he was released, but then recalled to Berlin, where Heydrich gave him an ultimatum to surrender the fencing presidency to Heydrich. After thinking it over for twenty-four hours, Anspach declined, but Heydrich, though infuriated, allowed him to return home. In June 1941, Heydrich had the satisfaction of informing Anspach that he had been deprived of the presidency after consultations with the fascist

Italian President of Fencing, Giulio Basletta, but with the outbreak of war against the Soviets, Heydrich had more important things on his hands than running the honorary office of an international sporting administrator.[31]

Within the sport Heydrich conducted himself on the whole with sporting fairness even if somebody dared withhold his customary bonus: when he called for a meeting to discuss an umpire's decision, the team leader overruled him in public: 'In the sport of fencing, the only rules which apply are sporting rules and nothing else.' Heydrich commented admiringly to a friend on this courageous attitude: 'I never thought such a thing was possible!'[32]

Within the fencing fraternity, Heydrich also showed mercy to Jews. He facilitated the departure to the United States of the former German champion Paul Sommer, a Jew, apparently at the request of SS team members, and once war broke out, on his express instruction none of the 1936 Polish Olympic fencers was harmed.[33]

Sporting camaraderie towards a Jew was one side of the coin but the 'Jewish Question', central to RSHA affairs, had moved increasingly to the forefront of his considerations and appeared to require more ruthless measures for a solution, this being, according to French historian Edouard Husson, 'the constant driving force of Heydrich's most radical objectives',[34] and he attempted to expand his jurisdiction at the expense of Eastern colonisers Alfred Rosenberg, Poland-Gouvernor Hans Frank, and Oswald Pohl, Inspector of Concentration Camps.

Although Heydrich maintained close relations with Abwehr chief Admiral Wilhelm Canaris, his former naval superior, Berlin neighbour and horse-riding companion, he relieved him of his SD responsibilities in military espionage because Canaris had spoken out on behalf of the Wehrmacht against massacres in the East and Jewish deportations. When in October 1941 the military complained at bomb attacks against seven Paris synagogues by RSHA agents, Heydrich replied that he did not expect understanding for 'such measures in the conflict with political enemies' and he knew what he was doing: it had been his mission 'for years' to bring about 'the Final Solution to the Jewish Question in Europe'.[35]

For this specific mission, Heydrich was insisting on a 'parallelisation of the lines of leadership'. On the snowy early afternoon of 20 January 1942 in a villa at Berlin's Wannsee, fourteen Secretaries of State, departmental leaders and police chiefs of the competent districts for 'Jewish affairs' – but no military men – convened to discuss 'the Jewish Question'. Heydrich did most of the talking while Amt IV B4 head SS-Obersturmbannführer Adolf Eichmann had prepared the agenda and, on Heydrich's instructions, would be responsible for producing the conference protocol, limited to thirty copies.

The Wannsee Conference was not the beginning of the genocide; Heydrich had initiated that with the Einsatzgruppen in Poland in 1939 and in the Soviet Union in 1941. The death camps at Auschwitz, Belzec, Maidanek and Maly Trostinez had been in existence for some time. After several inspection trips by Eichmann to the camps concerned, it was confirmed that gas chambers and crematoria was the most effective method of mass-murder: Zyklon B had been tested successfully at Auschwitz in September 1941.

For his part, however, Hitler did not take the decision to adopt a comprehensive extermination policy until the autumn of 1941, and only then after much vacillation and hesitation, as the American Holocaust historian Christopher Browning has convincingly argued. Hitler's underlying intention to eliminate the Jews does not appear ever to have been in doubt, and in July 1941, after the beginning of the Russian campaign, he was once again expressly in favour, but his assent to mass deportations and death camps seems to have hinged on the military situation in the East, and he would not give the green light until he was sure. As 'victor' he would take decisive steps towards the Final Solution, but while uncertain of military victory he held back, even with regard to the Jews.

On 6 October 1941, Hitler still had his doubts about beginning the deportations to the East. They were 'not to be carried through for the moment on account of the great need (of the Wehrmacht) for the means of transportation.'[36] Yet next day, when the German panzer armies succeeded in encircling Wiasma and Biansk, and almost 700,000 Red Army soldiers surrendered, Hitler appeared 'very confident of victory' and forgot his doubts about the transport situation.

The first deportation trains left from Vienna for Lodz, and shortly afterwards three more 'Jew transports' left Prague, Luxemburg and Berlin. The extermination programme had finally come to life. Browning: 'One can draw a noticeable parallel between military successes of the German armies in the East and Hitler's key decisions.'[37]

In November 1941 Hitler's luck changed. Catastrophic weather, blocked highways, shortages in supplies, exhausted German troops and the fierce resistance of the Red Army brought the Wehrmacht advance to a standstill. A quick, triumphant conclusion was beyond reach. Might Hitler now – in a state of dejection – have brought the deportations to a stop too? 'Just as Hitler later was never prepared to consider a strategic withdrawal from a piece of conquered territory, neither could there be any going back in the "Jewish Question" once the decision had been made. The death camps were being built and expanded, and the trains kept rolling,' Browning commented.[38]

The conference of fourteen distinguished departmental heads at Wannsee on 20 January 1942 did not open the doors to the Holocaust, they were already wide open, but the conference was an important stage on the slippery road to murdering six million Jews – and there was no way back. What had gone on before had been, according to Heydrich, only 'practical trials' for the Final Solution. Now it was set down in writing.

The atmosphere at the conference was tense but almost friendly. 'It went off very quietly, very friendly, very polite, very formal and nice, and not a great deal was said: it did not last long either, a tray of cognacs was handed round and then it was over,' Eichmann, drafter of the protocol, told the court in Jerusalem.[39]

It was in this cordial environment that the death sentences for millions of people were set down in respectable, bureaucratic phraseology and euphemism. 'Instead of (enforced) emigration, there is another possible solution in which, having previously obtained the approval of the Führer, the Jews will be evacuated to the East,' the protocol states. 'In large work columns, separated into the sexes, Jews fit for labour will be put to work on highway building projects in these regions, whereby undoubtedly a major proportion will be lost to natural wastage.' The remaining survivors, undoubtedly the most resistant group, would 'have to be dealt with correspondingly' since they represented 'a natural selection', a possible 'nucleus' of a Jewish renaissance.[40]

For the purposes of the Final Solution, 'all Europe would be combed from west to east' for the up-to-eleven-million Jews – including those who, in January 1942, were not yet living in territories under Nazi control or influence. When Eichmann was asked by his Israeli captors in 1960 what the term 'have to be dealt with correspondingly' meant, he replied, 'Killed, killed, definitely'.[41]

Behind the niceties of protocol language, it would appear that the Wannsee Conference participants talked turkey in murderous terms throughout. Eichmann to the Jerusalem tribunal:

> The particulars of the thing are no longer clear to me today, Mr Chairman, but I do know that the gentlemen sat down together and talked in very forthright words – not in the words I set down in the protocol, but in very forthright words, putting the thing bluntly, without dressing it up. Certainly I cannot recall any more, except that I said at the time, 'Watch, watch Stuckart', who was always thought of as a very precise and very awkward lawyer, yet he set the tone and put the formulations in a very unlawyer-like way.[42]

Wilhelm Stuckart, State Secretary at the Interior Ministry, was a 39-year-old career lawyer and surprised all those present by suggesting more extreme methods than Heydrich in the detailed discussion on the question of how to handle German-Jewish persons of mixed blood. After the war he defended his intervention by explaining that he had gone radically beyond the position of Heydrich and the SS participants in order to gain time for those concerned. In his opinion, the forcible sterilisation of persons of mixed blood was a technical impossibility, and that was why he had suggested it. In all probability it was Stuckart's intention, however, to bolster up the steadily diminishing influence of his Ministry on the question of Jewish policy *vis-à-vis* Heydrich and the RSHA.

Anxieties about loss of prestige and jurisdiction may have been a contributory factor in the decision of many ministerial officials at the conference table not to oppose Heydrich's proposals. Quite naturally after the war all denied that there had ever been any talk at Wannsee of 'killing' Jews, and most certainly none of them had ever spoken out on any such subject himself. It is true of course that the protocol does speak only of Jews 'having to be dealt with correspondingly' or becoming 'natural wastage' through forced labour, yet what else than 'murder' can these expressions be interpreted to mean?

The conference concluded to Heydrich's satisfaction: except for the secondary matter of persons of mixed race, nobody had challenged his competence to set the parameters. Furthermore all the 'experts' on Jewry from the various Party and State offices had now been drawn into the genocide plot as accomplices. In good humour after the meeting, Heydrich, Eichmann and Gestapo chief Müller sat before the fireplace in the RSHA guesthouse. Eichmann:

> It was then that I saw Heydrich smoking, a cigarette or cigar, for the first time, and I thought, 'today Heydrich is smoking, something I never saw before, and he is drinking cognac. It is years since I ever saw him touch alcohol' . . . After this Wannsee Conference we just sat together quietly, not to talk shop, but simply to relax after the long and strenuous hours.[43]

The Wannsee agreement was not a blank cheque for the extermination of the Jews. In the future, Hitler and Himmler would mix in orders to fit each particular wave of killings. Browning: 'During all 1942 the awkward balance between the requirements of the work force and the genocide project was being constantly juggled.' Thus there were no decisions about whether the murders were to go ahead or not, but only when and in what order they should take place. The protocol was to some extent a notice that the genocide had become official policy.

On his visit to Paris on 7 May 1942 Heydrich came right out with it when at the Hotel Majestic he told high-ranking SS officers of the occupation army that the gas-lorries in the East had proven 'inadequate technically' for the liquidation of Jews and 'larger, more perfect, countless more fruitful solutions' were coming: 'The death sentence has been passed on the totality of European Jewry.'[44]

The large-scale extermination programme got under way at Auschwitz-Birkenau at the end of January 1942, and at Belzec in mid-March. By June another fifty-five thousand Jews had been deported from the Reich to Eastern Poland prompting Goebbels to comment that a 'fairly barbaric' process would be being applied 'and of the Jews themselves there will be very few left'.[45]

If Heydrich had had his way there would be none of them left. At the beginning of 1942, however, the German advance into the Soviet Union had been stemmed and the possibility had now to be considered that 'racially cleansed' areas of the East might eventually have to be abandoned. The organisers now feared that the discovery of mass graves by Germany's enemies would cause an outcry of world opinion and so, shortly before his death, Heydrich had begun an exhaustive programme to clear away the traces. All photographs of the executions and graves were to be destroyed. SS-Oberführer Paul Blobel was given a special unit to command and told to use it to clear away the existing mass graves. The Düsseldorf architect was a good man for the job, having proved himself very competent in extermination questions, being a designer of the gas chambers.

Blobel's first attempts to blow up the burial sites with explosives proved inadequate, and he experimented next with mass-produced bone-grinders, but the best solution proved to be cremating the remains with wood or oil and carefully scattering the ashes. Blobel's unit was known as Sonderkommando 1005, so named for the number of inmates under his control. One thousand were ordinary camp prisoners, mostly Jews, the other five being 'experts', inmates who had taken part in extermination 'actions' as assistants. As the Russian offensive approached the work area of Kommando 1005, the thousand auxiliaries had to be put to death with a shot to the back of the head, but Blobel permitted the five 'experts' to survive, since their experience was indispensable to the SS project leader.[46]

During his sojourn in France in May 1942, Heydrich was preparing his next operation, in which he would introduce his Prague methods into France. He considered his work in the Protectorate completed. 'If he had done so, the story of the French Resistance would have had a quite different outcome,' says the American Heydrich-biographer Charles Sydnor, 'and Heydrich would have built himself a springboard to the highest positions.'[47]

Heydrich had probably admitted to himself privately that it was his ambition to become 'The First Man of the German Reich'. The Führer would then adopt a ceremonial position. Two sporting colleagues are even said to have told Heydrich during the 1941 fencing championships at Bad Kreuznach that first of all he would have to make Hitler harmless in case 'the Old Man stirred up the shit'.

Whilst her husband made his murderous plans, Lina Heydrich was enjoying 'the most wonderful time of our marriage'. As wife of the Reichs-Protektor, the teacher's daughter from the lower nobility lived in style in the Prague fortress, and later in *Schloss* Jungfern-Breschan (Panenske Brezany) twenty kilometres north of the capital. 'I am a princess and live in a fairytale land,'[48] she enthused. For the first time, Reinhard cared for his children like a father should, 'idolised' his little daughter Silke and dined at home almost every evening. Frustrations at the constant absence of the 'workaholic' who 'had dined at the office for seven of his ten years of marriage'[49] were now a thing of the past, as were the anxieties about his extramarital escapades, which had provoked her flirting with Schellenberg, aimed at arousing Heydrich's jealousy. In public in Prague she was usually at his side, as on 26 May 1942 in the Waldstein Palace when the music-loving Reichs-Protektor threw a concert in memory of his father, the composer Bruno Heydrich, deceased in 1938, and for which he had engaged old music teachers from the Halle Conservatory.

Heydrich felt good: master of the situation in the Protectorate of

Bohemia and Moravia, even if he felt that there was more bubbling below the apparently calm surface than he cared to admit. A few hours before the concert he had said to journalists:

> I have to mention that discourtesy, tactlessness even, if not to say impertinence, towards Germans is on the rise again . . . small sabotage acts, which do less harm than the spirit of opposition, have increased . . . You should be aware, gentlemen, that I would not hesitate to respond with unheard-of violence if I should gain the feeling and impression that the Reich is considered weak, and the loyal conciliation on my part is interpreted as weakness.[50]

It says much for Heydrich's state of mind that, despite the thousands of Czechs whom he should have had on his conscience, he believed himself to be, if not actually loved, then at least respected, by the majority of the Protectorate population. In his opinion he had done much to improve the work and living conditions of the labour force, and he saw them as being out of the argument. Therefore he felt he could move about Prague without concerns. At factory meetings he mixed among the workers without protection. When Armaments Minister Albert Speer visited Prague in the spring of 1942, he was horrified to learn that Heydrich was driven through the streets in an open car without bodyguards. To his concerned enquiry, Heydrich countered, 'Why should my Czechs shoot me?' He actually said 'my'. Besides, he said, it was unsporting to be protected by armed bodyguards. This was *petit bourgeois*, something for 'the Party big-wigs'. On 27 May 1942, the heroic pose would come to an end.

Chapter Five

The Assassination
1942

Jozef Gabcik glanced at his watch nervously. Quarter past ten! He had been waiting at the Klein-Holeschowitz Street tram stop in the Prague suburb of Lieben since nine o'clock, and there was still no signal from Josef Valcik. The latter was waiting further up, in Kirchmeyer Street, keeping watch for the 'target'. According to his information, the Reichs-Protector was due to pass by there at any moment. A Czech watchmaker who had been called to Heydrich's office to repair an antique grandfather clock had discovered on Heydrich's desk a screwed-up slip of paper with his itinerary for 27 May 1942, and passed it to a charlady, who let the Resistance have it.[1]

Gabcik, a partisan trained in England, had to keep wiping the sweat from his forehead, his body overheating from excitement and standing in the May sun. Despite the warm weather, he carried a raincoat over his arm. Its purpose was to conceal a Mk II FF 209 sten gun. On the opposite side of the street, his friend Jan Kubis, leaning against a lamp standard, two highly sensitive bombs in his briefcase, gave him an enquiring glance. With a gesture of irritation, Gabcik signalled him to be patient.

Suddenly everything happened at once – swiftly and not as planned. Just as the No. 3 tram came rattling up to the stop, from Kirchmeyer Street Valcik's shaving mirror flashed in the sun – the signal! 10.29 a.m. Gabcik ran to join Kubis on the inner pavement of the hairpin bend, where the road bends sharply towards the banks of the Moldau.

A dark-green Mercedes 320 with the registration plate 'SS-3' was approaching, an open convertible with two occupants, the driver and, seated behind him, the tall figure of Reinhard Heydrich. The chauffeur, SS-Oberscharführer Johannes Klein, decelerated for the bend as the tram came to a stop opposite, allowing passengers to board and alight. The Mercedes was now three metres from Gabcik. Dropping his raincoat he aimed the machine-pistol at Heydrich and squeezed the trigger. The mechanism was clogged with greens and the gun jammed – Gabcik had kept it dismantled in his inner coat pocket where he also put vegetable matter for his rabbits.

'Stop!' Heydrich shouted, and stood upright in the convertible. Drawing his pistol, he aimed at Gabcik and pulled the trigger. Nothing happened – the weapon was not loaded. Chauffeur Klein, instead of stepping on the accelerator to get his chief to safety, braked. While the dejected Gabcik fumbled to clear his sten gun, Kubis, unnoticed by either Heydrich or the driver, stepped forward and tossed a bomb towards the car. It fell short and exploded near the rear right wheel, metal splinters entering Heydrich's back together with fragments of horsehair from the upholstery.

A skirmish now ensued. While the wounded Heydrich brandished his empty pistol at Kubis, the bomber, Gabcik threw away his useless sten gun and ran for it, pursued by Klein, who cornered him in the Brauner butchery. Gabcik drew his pistol and, after shooting the SS driver in the leg, escaped. Kubis, his face cut and bleeding from bomb splinters, fled down the hill on his bicycle. The third man, Valcik, who had signalled Heydrich's arrival with his shaving mirror, also vanished. These were the dramatic moments which heralded the demise of Reinhard Heydrich.

It remains a mystery why two such mediocre soldiers as Kubis and Gabcik should have been selected by the Czech Government-in-Exile in England for the assassination attempt, which was codenamed 'Anthropoid'. In the British training reports, chimney-builder Kubis had rated a 'five out of ten', and the locksmith Gabcik 'six out of ten'. On explosives-handling, Gabcik had earned the observation 'slow in practice and reaction'. The two partisans had been dropped by parachute by RAF aircraft, over the wrong spot near Prague, on 29 December 1941. The Prague Resistance provided them with false papers.

Meanwhile, Heydrich had collapsed near the tram stop, bleeding from a small hole in his back. A woman passer-by, recognising him, cried: 'Heydrich! Jesus Maria!' It was almost half an hour before Heydrich was brought to the Bulovka hospital, barely a kilometre from the hairpin bend. No ambulance came. Passers-by stopped cars. The first, a baker, refused to transport the injured man when he saw the SS uniform. He didn't have time and had to work, he said. The next vehicle, a delivery van, was stopped by a Czech policeman. The officer helped Heydrich into the narrow cabin beside the driver, a very painful procedure for the wounded man.

With the bleeding Reichs-Protektor at his side, the driver took the wrong road and had to make a three-point turn and return to the tram-stop. Here Heydrich said he would prefer to lie in the back of the van. In the rear were cartons of floor wax. The driver got out and redistributed them before helping Heydrich to lie in the rear. Because of the injury to his back, he lay face down. The driver set off and arrived at the hospital at around eleven o'clock.[2] Later a passer-by brought Heydrich's attaché-case containing secret documents for a conference with Hitler.

Heydrich should have survived this injury, but in the next two hours his fate was decided on the operating table. Czech surgeon Alois Vincenc Honek recalled what happened.[3] He was halfway through a stomach surgery when an orderly rushed in: 'There's been an assassination attempt on Heydrich. He's lying half-dead in the ambulance.' Shortly afterwards leading surgeon Walter Dick appeared and asked Honek to vacate the operating table. He stopped the stomach operation and then waited in his private room while SS and Gestapo occupied the building. A half hour later Honek was requested, the only Czech doctor present, to assist in the surgery 'because only I was properly acquainted with the British anaesthesia equipment'.

He continued: 'When I entered the operation theatre, Heydrich had already been undressed. He was wearing a bullet-proof vest but only to the front. He had not said whether he was in pain. I asked him, "Do you have all your own teeth?" but he made no reply, and so I opened his mouth and checked everything.' Metal splinters and horsehair from the car upholstery had entered his back on the left side above the diaphragm, destroying his spleen. Prague's leading internist, Professor Walter Hollbaum from the German Clinic on the Karlsplatz, was to lead the surgical team.

Hollbaum began with a large longitudinal incision above the navel. Honek:

> At once he saw that it was not correct. He had sweat on his forehead. Professor Dick reacted quickly: 'You are not looking well. If you will permit me, I will carry on.' Hollbaum stepped back, and Dick made a diagonal incision to the side, extracting the spleen, stitched the diaphragm and closed the wound. After this, Heydrich's collapsed lung was pumped out again. The consequences developed because the first access incision was too large [Honek recalled]. We had not expected any great problems because the original wound was so small.

There was now an infection in the stomach cavity, a perisplenitis, which gained hold rapidly. Himmler's surgeon, Karl Gebhart from Berlin, ordered it fought with sulphonamides (penicillin was not available in Britain, its country of origin, until late 1943). Seven days after the attempt, at nine o'clock on the morning of 4 June 1942, Heydrich died in the Bulovka hospital. The reason for his death was given as 'bullet wound/murder attempt/wound infection' in the hospital report.

Seeing Heydrich facing death, the Man Without A Heart became maudlin. Himmler, who visited him in hospital, recited some lines from an opera by his father:

Yes, the world is just a barrel-organ
which our Lord God himself turns over
everyone must dance to the tune
that happens to be on the cylinder.[4]

Accounts of the assassination have made much of an alleged death wish lurking behind Heydrich's banal fatalism. Hellmut G. Haasis, in his study of the man, perceived the 'necrophilia' of the 'young, evil god of death' as the psychological key to Heydrich's whole existence. According to Haasis, the Reichs-Protektor was not merely light-headed and reckless to drive around Prague without bodyguards: he was inviting a duel probably knowing that in the end he would draw the short straw. Haasis: 'He enjoyed an almost erotic lust for extreme danger.' This flirting with death could be offset against his murderous activities. 'Perhaps he was sublimating the idea of a death which might strike him at any moment into an unsuppressable consciousness of guilt about the murder of the Jews, nothing of which could be allowed to leak out.'

Did the Lord over Life and Death experience any premonition that his drive that day led nowhere, and encompassed his own death?[5] On sending his subordinates to active mass-murder operations in Russia, he asked of them that they 'not only give death' but 'receive it' too. Most of all he would have liked to have sent all his RSHA departmental heads to the front to lose their lives in order to proudly inform the Führer: 'All Sipo office heads have fallen on the field of honour', Karl Brandt, Himmler's personal aide, confided to Felix Kersten. Heydrich was actively seeking the ultimate duel. 'Day by day he sat at his desk while others were at the front fighting. He was making decisions of life and death, and therefore had to stare death in the face himself and so prove his courage.'[6]

Thirty years later, Lina Heydrich supported this theory.

I tend to believe today that he wanted this end. It seemed to me he had long embraced the idea of dying soon. Apparently he knew that he, who had to decide whether other people lived or died, would soon have his own 'death-warrant' handed to him. I know it sounds trite, but I believe he wanted to sacrifice himself.[7]

Sacrifice himself for what? In his study of Heydrich, Haasis cites Erich Fromm, who wrote about Mussolini and Hitler: 'They had no creative ideas, and never introduced major changes which might have been of use to humanity. What they lacked was the true criterion of the revolutionary spirit: the love of life, the desire to serve its development and growth.'[8] These sentences also apply to Heydrich.

Nowhere does one find within Heydrich a positive vision. The state of the nation was, as Günther Deschner wrote, understood by him to be one of permanent crisis. In times of crisis nothing is built. Huge sums of money have to be set aside, all spending ruthlessly cut back. In future, preventive measures were to be taken against 'parasites' to render them harmless.[9] Even the parting letter which Heydrich sent his wife at the outbreak of war as a contingency is, in its content, bleak and negative.[10] Apart from showing 'generosity towards the people of one's own race', he emphasised the three 'harsh rules' in the rearing of his children: harshness in imposing the basic SS regulations, harshness with themselves, harshness against all enemies at home and abroad. Impacability as a principle in handling people.[11] Contempt for humankind on the path to the goal, a racially pure, engineered European State: 'Of what concern is it if this or that Fräulein Meier is happy at this or that time? It is not our personal happiness which matters, but only whether we achieve our goal or not.'[12]

Heydrich's thinking was destructive and devoid of a future. If by some mischance he thought in a creative way, his fantasy would nevertheless be an inhuman one: 'For the superfluous Czechs who could not be "germanised", he had conceived a nice job for them as pioneers or supervisors in the Arctic, the "future ideal homeland for Europe's 11 million Jews".'[13] The extermination of the Jews and the course of the war dictated that this creative plan would be eventually laid aside.

Even close colleagues of Heydrich never gained the impression that hate lay behind his frequently mentioned 'unheard-of harshness'. Even in the Final Solution of the Jewish Question, the technocrat of might was not, according to Werner Best, motivated by personal aversion to the arch-enemy of National Socialism:[14] he simply believed that genocide was a necessary duty to be carried out in the service of the – nebulous – National Socialist Germanic Greater Reich.

The absolute racist egotism expressed by Himmler with graceless brutality in 1943 had justified every excess for Heydrich beforehand.

> The SS man must abide absolutely by the basic principles to be true, honest, decent, loyal and comradely to members of our own blood, but to nobody else. What happens to Russians or Czechs is utterly irrelevant to me . . . whether other peoples live in comfort or die of hunger interests me only to the extent that we need these people as slaves for our culture, otherwise I do not care.[15]

This way of looking at things reduced people to objects, mass-murder victims waiting for death.

According to his wife, Lina, it was by this way of thinking, so Heydrich asserted frequently, that he was enabled to feel 'free of all guilt'.[16] Yet this self-justification by the Lord of Life and Death left him damaged spiritually. Himmler at the State funeral in Berlin: 'From numerous conversations with Heydrich, I know what this man, outwardly so hard seeming, has achieved, and what it often cost him. Nevertheless under the SS laws we are duty-bound "to spare neither our own nor foreign blood if the life of the nation demands it": to decide is to act.'[17]

Many Czechs believe that Heydrich fell victim to the curse associated with the crown of King Wenceslaus. In the year after his own violent end, on 24 October 1943 Heydrich's eldest son, Klaus, also died. At an unguarded moment, the ten-year-old cycled past the SS guard at the gates to *Schloss* Jungfern-Breschan into the main road, straight into the path of a lorry carrying local children home from a Sunday football match. In an obituary in the SS journal *Das Schwarze Korps*, Lina Heydrich lamented the loss of her 'blossoming child'. The Gestapo let lorry-driver Karel Kaspar go almost immediately, for he was obviously free of any blame for the accident. When Lina Heydrich was preparing to flee from the Red Army in April 1945, she hired Kaspar for the transport of her effects. He never returned.[18]

The death of Heydrich, according to Himmler, 'hit Hitler harder than a lost battle'.[19] For his paladin he staged the most magnificent State funeral that the Berlin Nazis had ever seen. The pompous ritual in National Socialist style began in Prague. A death mask was made on the day of Heydrich's decease and an SS guard stationed in his hospital room. During the night of the following day an SS detachment, accompanied by torchbearers, bore the coffin on a gun carriage to the Hradshin Palace, where the body was laid out. Next day, 6 June 1942, the Catholic Vicar-General asked if four Church dignitaries of high rank could participate in the mourning ceremony. Heydrich had been baptised into the Catholic faith. They also wanted to toll the bells of St Vitus's Cathedral. The SS declined.

In his regular table talks at Führer HQ Hitler mocked the servility of the Czech clergy. The Episcopate of Bohemia and Moravia had asked permission to ring the bells for Heydrich and read a requiem. Hitler had pointed out to the gentlemen, however, that it would have been better if they had occasionally said a prayer for the survival of the representative Reichs-Protektor.[20]

Heydrich's coffin was put on display at the Ehrenhof courtyard of the Hradshin Palace, behind it a giant Iron Cross, flaming torches set in wall sconces and the black-and-white SS flag at half-mast. Among those personalities who formed the guard of honour was the later-Resistance-conspirator, Arthur Nebe. Thousands paid their respects by filing past the sarcophagus, among them numerous Czechs. The funeral service in Czechoslovakia was accompanied by much Beethoven, the *SS-Treuelied*, the German national anthem and the *Horst Wessel*, and the usual bombast. Here we had a deceased who had been 'a thinker', whose name was worthy to be 'engraved in stone in the proud *SS-Ehrenhalle*' and, high point of the verbiage, he was a man 'who had won the love of simple people in this land of Bohemia and Moravia'.[21]

The coffin was then borne to the main Prague railway station and put aboard a special train for Berlin, where the ritual of honour guards, flaming torches in wall sconces and soft drum beats was continued. The main funeral ceremony was held in the Mosaic Room at the New Reich Chancellery. This splendid hall, built for Hitler by Albert Speer, was half the size of a football pitch, and throughout its existence it saw nine ceremonies of this kind.

For the prelude, the State Orchestra played the Funeral March from Wagner's *Götterdämmerung*: leading the eulogies, Himmler praised Heydrich's 'character of rare purity'. From the depths of his heart and blood, he had understood, fulfilled and made reality the world vision of Adolf Hitler.[22] According to Himmler's masseur, Dr Felix Kersten, however, 'Reichs-Heini' looked back on his closest helper with a far more jaundiced eye than he cared to admit at his funeral. No matter what the specialists and technical people might say, the Reichsführer-SS himself was convinced that Heydrich 'had a trace of Jewish blood'.

> Heydrich suffered endlessly from the stigma that he was not of pure blood. Through great achievements in sport, in which Jews as a rule do not excel, it was his purpose to furnish the proof that the Germanic proportion in his blood must be overwhelming. He displayed childish pleasure at winning the Equestrian Badge, and the Sport Badge in Silver, also when he was awarded the Iron Cross, First Class. But it was all to prove a point, the thing itself gave him no real pleasure . . . I have been able to observe him for years in my closest circle and know this for a fact. I often conversed with him and tried to help him, against my personal convictions, speaking of the practical possibility of overcoming the Jewish biogenetic element by means of mixing it with a superior Germanic blood, and I cited his own case as evidence for that fact. He was very thankful for such help, and appeared relieved, but in the long run did not use it.[23]

Following Himmler's eulogy, Hitler also paid homage to Heydrich with a wreath and a solemn declaration:

> I have only a few words to dedicate to the deceased, [he began, turning to face the mourners.] He was one of the best National Socialists, one of the strongest defenders of the concept of the German Reich, one of the greatest opponents of all enemies of the Reich. As Führer of the Party and the

> German Reich, I decorate thee, my dear comrade Heydrich, the second German to receive it following Todt, with the highest award in my gift, the highest stage of the German Order.[24]

The orchestra emphasised the solemnity of the bald few words by breaking into The Dead Soldier's Song – *Ich Hatt' Einen Kameraden* – before the coffin was borne from the Mosaik Room to the strains of Beethoven's *Eroika*. Among those in the cortège were Himmler and Generaloberst Kurt Daluege, chief of police and Heydrich's rival, and a Czech deputation from the Protectorate Government. These gentlemen had already condemned the assassination in the strongest terms in Prague when Heydrich was still hovering between life and death, and called for pro-German demonstrations.[25]

Heydrich's body was interred at the Invaliden Cemetery in a simple grave. In 1943 at the hairpin bend in Prague where the assassination attempt was made, the Nazis erected an impressive memorial adorned with a bust of Heydrich, and this had an ever-present SS guard until the Germans abandoned the city in 1945.

To his intimate circle, Hitler raged against Heydrich's categorical refusal to use bodyguards and protected vehicles.

> Heroic gestures such as driving around in open, unprotected cars or walking through the streets of Prague without an escort is a stupidity of no use to the nation. Men of the political stature of Heydrich must be made aware that people lie in wait for them as if in pursuit of game, that countless people spend their time thinking of nothing else but how they can kill them.[26]

Two hours after the attempt, Hitler had called Karl Hermann Frank, Heydrich's deputy, with the immediate enquiry as to whether Heydrich had had an escort vehicle. Frank: 'I said no. The Führer condemned that very forcibly.'[27] Hitler ordered Frank never to drive around 'without a security escort' and promised to put an armoured car at his disposal. He also ordered reprisals. That same day Hitler suggested that Himmler should send SS-General Erich von dem Bach-Zelewski to Prague 'because he knew for certain that the General was harder and more brutal than Heydrich and would wade happily through a sea of blood without the least scruple. The Czechs had to learn that if they shot down one man, he would be replaced at once by somebody even worse.'[28] As a direct measure, Hitler was in favour of shooting ten thousand 'suspected' Czechs 'or similar, who have political irons in the fire'. Himmler suggested it was better to shoot just a hundred at once and ordered Frank by telex to arrest ten thousand hostages 'starting with all the Czech intelligentsia who oppose us. Of those, the top 100 opponents are to be shot dead tonight.'[29]

One of the first to be executed was the Czech Prime Minister Alois Elias, whose death sentence was carried out almost immediately Heydrich died, but Frank convinced Hitler against the major reprisals on 28 May, at a meeting at Führer-HQ. They would be contrary to Hitler's policies, cause more unrest than ever and give the enemy ammunition for his allegations that mass executions were the only way left to counter the broad resistance of the Czech population.

In his written interpretation of the situation, Frank stated that so far the search for the assassins had been limited to rabble-rousers and saboteurs in the Protectorate. By mid-June 1942, the police had arrested a thousand Czechs, but none of these was suspected to be one of the assassins.

At Heydrich's funeral, Hitler demanded of Emil Hacha, President of the Protectorate, greater declarations of loyalty to the Reich. These were delivered. 'Hitler informed Hacha that it would not please us to see any more grave injuries to Reich interests in the Protectorate, and if necessary he would consider resettling the population, something which would be no problem for us, since we had already resettled several million Germans. At this offensive, Hacha gave in.'[30]

Prague Sipo chief Horst Böhme was in favour of making an example, however: according to a Gestapo report from Kladno, the mining settlement of Lidice north-west of Prague was suspecting of harbouring Czech partisans parachuted from British aircraft. This allegation was false: two young Czech army officers who came from the village had left for Britain in 1939, but neither had any connection with the assassination, nor were they hiding in Lidice. Nevertheless their families, a total of fifteen persons, were liquidated.

On 9 June 1942 Hitler accepted Böhme's suggestion and ordered the eradication of Lidice. The SS executed all 184 men of the village, deported the 198 women to Ravensbrück (of these, 143 eventually returned) and sent the 105 children to Lodz (of these only 17 survived). Lidice was razed to the ground. An official Nazi Press report from Prague on 10 June 1942 justified the reprisal in the following terms:

> During the search for the murderers of SS-Obergruppen-führer Heydrich, irrefutable evidence was discovered that the population of the village of Lidice had provided support and help to the circle of individuals under suspicion. Other evidence came to light without the assistance of the local population, although they were interrogated. Their favourable attitude to the assassination was confirmed by the intention to commit further hostile acts against the Reich, as evidenced for example by the discovery of anti-German pamphlets, of weapons and ammunitions dumps, illegal transmitters, while residents of the village are active overseas against the German Protectorate.[31]

The 'weapons and ammunitions dumps' contained two hunting rifles, a revolver and a shotgun loaded with bird pellets.[32] On 24 June 1942 the revenge of the Germans fell upon the village of Lezaky, where the Gestapo did at least discover the Resistance transmitter 'Libuse'. This time the women were also shot: the toll of victims was thirty-three persons.

None of the assassins survived June 1942. Their military comrade Karel Curda, part of the partisan team dropped by parachute but not directly involved in the assassination, although he cashed five million kronen for the operation, went to ground at his mother's house after the event. Fearing for her life should he be found there, Curda decided to betray his accomplices. (He worked subsequently as a Nazi informer within the Resistance and was executed in 1947.)

Kubis, Gabcik and Valcik had sought sanctuary together with four other parachuted partisans in the orthodox church of St Cyril and Methodus. Vladimir Petrek, the parish priest, hid them in the crypt, the entrance to which was hidden below a flagstone in the nave. Over the next few days Petrek supplied the seven with newspapers and food. Bishop Gorazd, head of the Prague orthodox community, was also in the picture.[33] Once it became obvious that the Gestapo was suspicious of the church, the Resistance made desperate plans to smuggle Kubis and Gabcik out of the city, favouring empty wine barrels or coffins for the purpose, but the police controls throughout Prague were by now too tight. Instead the two assassins decided to go out in a blaze of glory. They had heard about the massacre at Lidice and felt responsible for the death of so many innocent people. They considered sitting on a park bench with a placard reading 'We are the assassins!' hung around their necks and committing suicide, or requesting an audience with Emanuel Moravec, Propaganda Minister for the Protectorate Government, shooting him dead and then taking a suicide pill. Both ideas were rejected, for they would do nothing to mitigate the scale of the German revenge.

At two o'clock on the morning of 18 June 1942, eight hundred Gestapo and SS men surrounded the church and stormed it at 4.15 a.m. Their orders were to take the partisans alive. The seven Czechs fought a valiant but hopeless battle. Adolf Opalka, Jaroslav Svarc and Kubis had the night watch in the nave as the Germans burst into the church on two sides. From the choirstalls the partisans opened fire; the SS responded energetically and forced the Czechs into cover. Their accurate fire kept the SS troops at bay for three hours, and only when the SS began to lob hand grenades did they gain the upper hand. By 7 a.m. the first Czech was dead; the other two, including Kubis, seriously wounded, shot themselves in the head. They were carried out alive and brought to the SS military hospital but died there without regaining consciousness.

Initially the Germans were not aware of the other four partisans in the crypt, but on searching the choirstall they found a suit which had not belonged to any of the three dead. The Gestapo made a closer search of the building and found the trapdoor. The priest Petrek was brought in handcuffs to persuade the men in the crypt to surrender. Petrek, his face showing signs of a beating, shouted through the hatch: 'These people say you should give yourselves up, nothing will happen to you, and you will be treated as prisoners of war.' This was received with mocking laughter from below and the retort: 'We are Czechs. We will never surrender.' Later the traitor Curda attempted to convince his colleagues to lay down their weapons, but in vain.

Two SS volunteers were now lowered by rope through the entrance and into the crypt. The partisans opened fire, hitting the Germans in the legs, and they were hauled back up hastily. Next tear gas was used against the Czechs, but they managed to return the grenades. Outside, the local Czech fire brigade was ordered to pump water into the cellar in an attempt to drown the incumbents, but the latter ejected the hose using a wooden ladder. On the second attempt the hose was cut through to the accompaniment of loud laughter. Water and tear gas prevented the SS from entering the crypt for some time, but eventually they succeeded after enlarging the access by use of hammer and chisel, and finally a dynamite charge.

The SS commander reported:

> A broad stone stairway led from the altar side of the church into the catacomb. Shortly before the flagstone was broken away there was a brisk exchange of fire and some hand grenades were thrown. Four criminals were found dead in the cellar. Besides serious wounds, some had been shot in the head so that apparently they committed suicide when the cellar locks were broken down.[34]

Autopsies revealed that all four had self-inflicted head wounds while two of them had additionally taken poison. The Gestapo arranged for the identification of the seven dead by their families in a particularly gruesome manner, the corpses being decapitated and the heads impaled on a stake, the relatives and friends then being invited to file past the display.

During the fighting in the church, the Gestapo had arrested the priest Petrek, several congregational workers and their families: next day Bishop Goradz, still at liberty, wrote to the Protectorate Government: 'I place my person at the disposal of the relevant authorities and will accept any punishment, including the death penalty.'[35]

On 1 September the accomplices and those accused of having knowledge of the activities of the dead partisans were tried. Gorazd, Petrek and two members of the clergy were sentenced to death and shot. Over the next few weeks, 236 other supporters of the partisan group were taken to Mauthausen concentration camp and killed there on 24 October 1942.

Thousands of Czechs lost their lives in the reprisals that summer, and the word *Heydrichiade* was coined to describe the wave of terror which followed the assassination. Mere approval of the assassination was punishable by death. Hana Vorel, née Kopecka was nine years old when two courteous gentlemen asked for her father, 42-year-old senior forester Cyril Kopecky. Here, representative of hundreds of similar accounts, is Hana Vorel's memory of that day, written down in 2004.[36]

That lovely summer morning, 27 June 1942, my mother listened with tears in her eyes to the radio broadcast announcing the names of the men and women, whole families, who had been executed the previous day. In that terrible time of the *Heydrichiade*, the victims were numbered in hundreds, maybe thousands. Suddenly she noticed a car drawing up outside our house in the quiet little town of Protivin in southern Bohemia. She thought it strange because all private cars had been confiscated after the German occupation. Two men, whose names we discovered after the war to be Bacher and Ehrensberger, got out and entered my father's study in the basement. He was Dipl. Forestry Eng. Cyril Kopecky, head of the forestry office. Shortly afterwards my father appeared in the front doorway, led by the two men, and my mother realized that something terrible was going to happen. It was in the time of martial law after the assassination when over 3,000 people were arrested and more than 1,300 executed, 477 of them for 'Approving of the Assassination'. The previous evening, Thomas Mann at the BBC London had said of the situation: 'Since Heydrich's violent death, the most natural

155

death that a bloodhound such as he can die, the terror rages everywhere more wildly, more unrestrained, than ever before.'

The two Gestapo men allowed my father a brief leave-taking of my mother. She told him in Czech: 'Be strong.' Then he embraced my seven-year-old brother and myself in a last cuddle before they led him to the waiting car and drove off. They also took some of my father's hunting weapons and his dog. The whole thing went ahead completely calmly: Nobody shouted, nobody made a scene, the Gestapo didn't hit anybody, nobody fired shots into the air. There must be order, for the Germans had a civilized rule in our country, you see.

Even today I can picture the scene in my mind's eye: we children, terribly shocked, and my crying, trembling mother holding us out of the window so that we could see our father for the last time. In that moment of despair, my mother remembered my father saying recently that in an emergency she was to ask for help from his German supervisor called Sladek at the Forestry Directorate in Trebon, about 60 kilometres away – all the senior officials in the Protectorate had to be German. 'Ask for help from him, he is a decent man,' he had said. But it was Saturday: Herr Sladek was not in his office and could not be found.

They shot my father next day, 28 June 1942 at Tabor. My mother read it in the newspaper. In the column listing the executions, all carefully categorized into type and extent of anti-State activity, the name of engineer Cyril Kopecky appeared with nine others under 'Approved the Assassination of SS-Obergruppenführer Heydrich and provided encouragement and support to the assassins.' That terrible moment, my mother recalled how, a few days before, in the presence of the whole family, my father had spoken out against the assassination. Such attempts were pointless in the Nazi world, one tyrant would simply be replaced by another. Probably he had come to attention because he was chairman of the Czech association Sokol, which the Nazis had banned for anti-German activities.

A few days later three Gestapo came in a lorry and took away all my father's personal belongings down to the last toothbrush, even though they must have known he had been executed. But there must be order. They drafted a long list of the carpeting, paintings and other valuables they were confiscating. They even took my father's wedding ring, but correctly not my mother's, for they could only impound the property of a traitor, not that of his wife. Two of the Gestapo were caught after the war. When they were tried it came out that the valuables of executed people were put in a warehouse where Gestapo people could buy them cheaply and send them home.

Three Gestapo – once again they were courteous and correct – brought my mother the official death certificate, issued on 18 June 1942, bearing an entry in box 22b 'Nature and Method of Death if Violent': 'Death by Shooting (Execution). Date of Death 28 June 1942, 1900 hours.'

Twenty-nine Gestapo personnel, uniformed and in civilian dress, two of them female, were employed at Tabor. In a single month, from 3 June to 3 July 1942, they succeeded in arresting 156 persons, shooting them, confiscating their property and taking it to store, burning their corpses and casting the ashes to the winds, so that today they have no known grave.

My mother was obliged to evacuate the six-roomed tied cottage within seven days, could not find work and received no widow's pension. It was the second time that the Nazis had forced us out of our home, the first time in 1938 a few days after Munich we were driven out of Zakupy. After my father's death we lived fror three years with my mother's parents on their small pension and with the support of relatives and friends.

In the summer of 1945 after the end of the Third Reich, we moved into an empty flat in Prague once the German occupants had fled. Every week a German girl, who had remained behind in Prague, came to teach German to my brother and me. Our neighbours and relatives protested to my mother: 'How can you let your children be taught German when they killed your husband?' But my mother said German was the language of a great culture and had nothing to do with Nazi atrocities.

Despite the reign of terror which succeeded the assassination in the Protectorate of Bohemia and Moravia, the Czech Government-in-Exile in London since 1939 considered Operation *Anthropoid* a political success. The local partisan fighter Ladislav Vanek, whose Sokol group had sheltered Kubis and Gabcik, attempted by radio shortly before the attempt to persuade the Czech leader in exile, Eduard Benes, against it. The Nazi reprisals would cost 'thousands of lives' he warned. Benes remained firm, for the murder of Heydrich would bring worldwide recognition of his exiled regime as the Government of a fighting nation prepared to take action in peaceful Bohemia, where the Allies, particularly the Soviets, were loath to become involved: the likely death toll was taken into account. His calculations were correct. The massacres at Babi Yar or Riga were far greater, but Lidice became the rallying cry of the Resistance mainly because the Nazis spoke out about this reprisal whilst not mentioning the excesses of which they were the perpetrators in the Soviet Union. 'Lidice will live!'[37] became the international cry against the Hitler regime. Scarcely had the SS wiped the village off the map when there came into being in the United States, Mexico, Peru and Brazil new Lidices. In California, exile Heinrich Mann wrote his novel *Der Protektor*, director Douglas Detlef Sierk the film *Hitler's Madman* and Berthold Brecht his play *The Song of Lidice*.

In the East, the waves of exterminations for which Heydrich had planned so meticulously began in earnest after his demise. Holocaust researcher Dieter Pohl mentions the period between July and October 1942 as 'the bloodiest weeks of the 20th century': in the death camps in Poland more than 1.5 million Jews were killed off. In honour of the murdered Reichs-Protektor, the extermination programme under Himmler's executioner Odilo Globocnik at Belzec, Sobibor, Treblinka and Maidanek was given the operational name *Aktion Reinhard*. When it tailed off in October 1943, two million people had been eliminated.

How the Nazis envisioned the future is recalled in a conversation at Auschwitz in 1944, shortly before the withdrawal, when an inmate asked camp doctor Mengele, 'When is all this killing going to stop?' Mengele told him, 'It will just keep on, just keep on.' [38]

Chapter Six

The Man with the Iron Heart and the Unregenerates 1942 to the Present

'Go back to Fehmarn!' was apparently Reinhard Heydrich's last piece of advice to his wife, Lina, before he sank into a coma on 4 June 1942 at Prague's Bulovka Hospital and died.[1] The widow did not show any particular keenness to follow this instruction and decided to become the Lady of *Schloss* Jungfern-Breschan.

'On 7 December 1942 we moved back into Breschan *Schloss* permanently, or so I hoped,' she wrote in her memoirs.[2] Meanwhile a central heating system had been installed in the Talschloss in the valley, until then fitted out only as a summer residence, while Heydrich's successor Karl Hermann Frank occupied the Bergschloss higher up. Further improvements, such as the new swimming pool in the extensive parkland behind the main building, indicated that Lina Heydrich was not contemplating abandoning her privileged life in still-peaceful Bohemia for her home island of Fehmarn. Even the death of her ten-year-old son Klaus in a road traffic accident on 24 October 1943 did not shake her in this resolve. She had the dead boy laid to rest with a torchlight procession of the local Hitler Youth organisation. Heinrich Himmler, self-appointed tutor to the Heydrich children, escorted the coffin to the grave, the grieving mother in mourning on his arm. From Adolf Hitler there arrived only the barest essential, as she complained: 'Herr Hitler had a typed condolence sent.'[3]

Hitler had already proved his generosity, however, when on 20 April 1943 he announced from Führer-HQ:

> SS-Obergruppenführer and General of Police Reinhard Heydrich, chief of Sipo and SD, Reich Protector in Bohemia and Moravia, fallen in loyal and fearless fulfilment of his duty in the struggle against the enemies of the State, has rendered unsurpassable service to the Greater German Reich. In order to express visibly the gratitude of the nation for the outstanding achievements of the deceased, I have decided that the *Schloss* property of Jungfern-Breschan at Prague, of which he had become so fond, with all its terrains and installations pertaining thereto, shall be transferred into the possession of his widow Lina Heydrich and his children as a gift. It is my wish that the ancestral line of Reinhard Heydrich will be linked for ever through this property with his life and death.[4]

Lina Heydrich declined the gift, explaining to Himmler that 'the estate was too big having regard to her expected widow's pension and the future income of the family,' as Hans Lammers, Secretary of State at the Reich Chancellery, reported after the war. Moreover, according to Himmler, she had 'turned down the offer because of the condition imposed (by Hitler) that she should not remarry'.[5] Accordingly, the estate remained the property of the Third Reich, while Lina Heydrich stayed on as administrator with all rights.

Former employees of 'the Lady' recalled Lina's conduct fifty years after the event. Helena Vovsova lives today in the village of Panenske Brezany twenty-five kilometres north of Prague. From her garden she can see the Talschloss, which 'became her life's work'. She was employed there from 1941 to 1985, first for the Nazis, then for the Red Army, which set up in the grounds, and after that for three decades in the Metals Experimental Institute of the Czech armed forces. Helena was just sixteen when taken on as a house-and-garden help in March 1941 in the service of the 'landlord', Reichs-Protektor Konstantin Freiherr von Neurath. She hardly knew Heydrich: 'He was rarely there, and then always on horseback.' Of Lina Heydrich she knew more: 'In the presence of visitors one day, Lina sat on a chair in front of the *Schloss* and made a sweeping gesture with her arm. "All that is mine," she said.'[6]

The German mistress, always referred to by the castle staff among themselves as 'Our Old Lady', was never brutal. 'She had a loud voice,' Helena remembered, 'and she liked ordering people around. Lina had her moods. If she hadn't slept well, she would go about shouting at everybody, telling them they were all lazy and so on, even the SS guards. When she was in a good mood, she ignored us all.'[7]

Once when Helena Vovsova had an eruption on her arm she went to the office to request permission to go to the surgery. 'What's wrong, Helena? You don't need a doctor, come with me!' Lina cried. Because Helena was 'frightened of being left alone with Lina', she asked the maid, Marie, to accompany her. Marie was sent to fetch some sugar, and Lina made a sugar poultice, which she renewed regularly. The eruption showed no signs of improvement, and when by the fifth day it was visibly worse, Helena was at last given leave to consult a doctor. He prescribed her an ointment which soon cleared up the condition. 'Nevertheless,' Helena said, 'Lina always used to say afterwards, whenever she saw me, "That is the girl whose arm I cured".'[8]

In October 1942 at Lina's request, around 120 inmates from the concentration camp at Theresienstadt arrived at Jungfern-Breschan. 'We weren't allowed to speak to them,' Helena said, 'but we did so secretly. I helped them, mostly with gifts of food.'[9] The prisoners had to help landscape the parkland. It was a well-laid-out English-type park, but the estate manager wanted a meandering stream through it, and a few orchards, vegetable and flower gardens. The prisoners – there were Jews among them – were 'housed in inhuman conditions' in the stables near the *Schloss*, 'all crammed together in the smallest possible space', as one of them, Walter Grunwald, reported. 'The bugs ensured that we got no rest after each day's 14 to 18 hours' toil. The food was deficient in all respects. We got what was laid down officially in the Long-Day Supplementary Menu, so what we got was the supplement only.'[10] The food parcels sent by friends, from which the SS guards had first choice of the contents, ensured that the prisoners did not starve to death. 'All these regulations, from the long hours of labour to the setting of completion dates, the inhuman treatment and the constant threat of deportation to Auschwitz if the job was not carried out satisfactorily and so on,' said Grunwald, 'all this was the exclusive handiwork of Lina Heydrich. The camp inmates were supposed to look lively whenever they were in her presence.' Grunwald continued: 'It often happened that we would be insulted in the most vulgar manner, such as "Jewish pig, get out of my way", or by some comment about our children.'[11]

The prisoners were guarded by a dozen SS men. According to Helena Vovsova, nobody was killed there, although the prisoners reduced in numbers with the passage of time, and it was known in one case that a Czech worker at Breschan had been sent to Auschwitz on Lina's orders.[12]

After the war, Lina disputed such accusations vehemently. She emphasised to the contrary that she had negotiated with Himmler the release of a group of Jehovah's Witnesses.[13] As for what went on at Theresienstadt, she only happened to learn from an SS officer: 'It made me gasp.'[14] Another Jewish prisoner, Milan Platovsky Stein, who by his own admission owed his survival to the kindness and contraband food smuggled to him by Helena Vovsova, described Lina Heydrich thus:

> The attitude of Heydrich's widow towards me was relatively good. She strode about like an Amazon, whip in hand. She loved the crack of it against her riding boots. My impression of her was that she was cruel and arrogant. She never actually hit anybody, but liked people to fear her. Later, when the situation normalized, she left the whip indoors. She gave us our orders directly, not through the SS.[15]

Lina Heydrich was close to the officer in charge of the SS detachment, Obersturmbannführer Fritz Brandstädtler, whom the former inmates accused of brutality. He was almost a substitute father to her children. An official report about him states: 'To the sons of the Obergruppenführer he gave successful instruction in horse-riding and swimming and combined this into their upbringing. His whole approach was such that he would be invited to dine regularly with the family.'[16]

While Lina Heydrich played out her role, visiting former colleagues of her husband like Werner Best, Reich Plenipotentiary in Denmark, or receiving home visits at Jungfern-Breschan, such as that of Reich Minister Albert Speer, the portents of the approaching collapse could no longer be ignored, not even in the apparently peaceful world of Bohemia. Ever more refugees from the East, and the ruined cities of the Reich, sought and found sanctuary on the estate. A 'bombed-out' family from Duisburg, for example, stayed there from 1942 until the end of the war. At this time Himmler wanted no politicising widow and Lina was warned to be restrained in her public utterances.[17]

Between June 1942 and October 1943, Lina Heydrich lost her husband and eldest son, but in her own sorrow she showed little sympathy for the cruel blows of fate which struck other members of her family. On the night of 19 November 1944, her brother-in-law, Heinz Siegfried Heydrich, committed suicide. A journalist and publisher of the soldiers' newspaper *Die Panzerfaust*, he shot himself in a special train fitted out with its own print-shop near the front in East Prussia. Lina Heydrich commented: 'He did not have the necessary armour to survive it without psychic damage.'[18]

Heinz Heydrich's son Peter Thomas interpreted the suicide in retrospect rather differently. Since the death of his brother (Reinhard Heydrich), his father had become 'another person, always depressed, melancholy, of grave demeanour, whereas before he had been light-hearted, full of humour and temperamental, a man who clearly loved life.'[19]

Peter Thomas Heydrich attributed the sudden change to an event of which his mother, Gertude, had described to him. Before the State funeral in Berlin in June 1942, Heinz Heydrich had been given a large packet containing his brother Reinhard's files, released from his strong-box at Gestapo headquarters, 8, Prinz-Albrecht-Strasse. He had shut himself away in his room with the papers. Next morning his wife noticed that her husband had sat up all night burning the documentation from the mysterious package. 'I remember only that my father, who was on leave from the front, could not be engaged in conversation,' Peter Thomas said, 'he seemed to be elsewhere mentally, and like stone.'[20] His mother would never speak of the documents in the packet. ' "I can't say anything about it until the war is over," she always used to say, but when the time came, even then she refused to talk.' Peter Thomas Heydrich presumed 'they might have been my uncle's personal files, from which my father understood for the first time in all its enormity the systematic extermination of the Jews, the so-called Final Solution.'[21]

After that, Heinz Heydrich helped many Jews escape by forging identity documents at the print works. Many escaped to Sweden through Denmark, among them the Jewish wife of the actor Karl John. When in November 1944 an economic commission headed by a State Attorney investigated the editorial staff of *Panzerfaust*, Heinz Heydrich thought the game was up and shot himself in order to protect his family from the Gestapo. The attorney knew nothing about the forgeries, however, and was only trying to find out the reason for shortages in paper supplies.

In January 1945, Peter Thomas Heydrich, then fourteen years old, visited his aunt at Breschan for the last time. He felt like 'a Crown Prince'. An SS officer showed him around Prague, taking him to his uncle's former offices at the Hradshin, whilst a whole cinema was made available to show him a documentary film about Reinhard Heydrich. In his memoirs he commented: 'I often think back with horror on what would have been made of me if the Third Reich had not ended.'[22] After a short while he returned to his family, evacuated to Wreschen in the Warthegau. Gertrude Heydrich declined to seek refuge with her sister-in-law Lina, and at the beginning of January 1945 reached Berlin in a cattle-truck.

Lina was not to be lured away from her estate. She raised rabbits, chickens and poultry, lopped park trees for firewood and hunted hare and pheasant. In January 1945 she still had plans to take her children for a short skiing holiday to 'Frankstadt in the Beskiden'. Previously she had sown leek and celery.

> At the moment I wouldn't know where we could be safer than right here, [she wrote to her parents on Fehmarn on 6 February 1945:] to flee, as other women do, is out of the question for me. By my decision to remain here after Reinhard died, I made a political commitment. I am here what I always was, perhaps the only woman in public life who has not disappeared into anonymity through the death of her husband. It is therefore pointless to do what the others do. If we lose the war, the Russians will know where to find us to liquidate us. There will be no pardon for anybody who was active nationally or bandied himself about. Either that or the British and Americans will come. And with them the Jews. With our Jewish laws we burned our bridges. The Jews will also be able to get at us. There is no point in deluding ourselves. All this we know.[23]

Despite the veiled references to the maltreatment of the Jews and the expected revenge-seeking of the victors, she added:

> I have things to take care of and my work, and that is the important thing. Above all I have a clear conscience. My people depend on me, even today they work reliably and willingly. I have made a success of the concern. Work was all my life together with great belief in our quality, our purity. If Fate does not recognize the German people, then there is no justice, and life on this Earth has no pleasure.[24]

'Go back to Fehmarn!' Heydrich had advised her, but not until March 1945, when Germany's enemies were converging on the Reich from west, east and south, did Lina Heydrich consider making a move – to the west, to Bavaria. According to her memoirs, a farewell visit by the Reichsführer-SS made up her mind for her. Himmler came to Breschan and agreed her plans. During the conversation, Heider Heydrich, his godson, came into the room and sat with 'Uncle'. 'I will never forget that moment,' Lina recalled, 'Himmler looked at Heider, slowly raised his right arm, stroked Heider's hair and said only, "*Ach ja*, Heider!" For me, that was the hour of total capitulation. I needed to know nothing else. It was enough. I knew then that we were quite alone, and had to finish everything.'[25]

Shortly afterwards, Lina Heydrich bought a *Maringorka*, a circus caravan, and had all her animals slaughtered and the meat preserved. Her staff realised that her departure was imminent. Helena Vovsova asked little Silke, 'Where are you headed for?' The five-year-old replied, 'We're taking a trip.' A few days lated the child added, 'We are scared of the Russians because they eat little children.'[26]

In mid-April 1945 after the refugees camping at Breschan had withdrawn, Lina Heydrich assembled the *Schloss* staff and thanked them for their work, shaking the hand of each individually and promising them a small gratuity after the war. Together with her chauffeur, Hauptscharführer Herbert Wagnitz, and tutoress Gertrude Schillung, Lina, Heider, Silke and Marte Heydrich left the Bohemian estate in two cars. The caravan was hauled by a tractor-driven vehicle which Karel Kaspar drove. He never returned. Beforehand, according to Helena Vovsova, Lina had had the tin coffin containing the remains of her son Klaus disinterred from the park grounds and loaded aboard: 'I didn't see him being brought up, but I saw the empty, open grave.'[27] Other Czech witnesses reported that the empty coffin was found abandoned by the roadside. It is possible that the corpse of Klaus Heydrich was reburied at some unknown place in the woods in order that the body should not be desecrated after the family had left. The caravan was destroyed during a low-level attack by Allied aircraft at Pilsen.

A few days after setting out, Lina and her entourage arrived at Rottach-Egern on Tegernsee. She was given shelter in the house of Frieda Wolff, the estranged wife of Himmler's adjutant Karl Wolff. At the beginning of May the US Army arrived, requisitioning the house. Frieda Wolff moved into the poultry house; her guests lived in their vehicles until finding more suitable accommodation in a hospital.

Lina expected to be arrested at any moment. 'The word "war crimi-nal" pursues me wherever I surface,' she wrote, 'ever since I have had to live as the wife of a war criminal . . . we carry the mark of Cain on our foreheads.'[28] For this reason she channelled her children to her parents in north Germany. A couple of acquaintances, two soldiers and a Hitler Youth boy returning north offered to take the older children, Heider and Silke, to Lübeck. Descher, the Hitler Youth, eventually took them the whole way to Fehmarn, delivering them into the custody of grandparents Jürgen and Mathilde von Osten, who since the mid-1930s had lived in retirement at Burg on Fehmarn Island.

Lina's homeward journey was rather complicated, according to her own account. She forged her identity documents with the help of an unsuspecting friend by the name of Lisa Hunger, whose initials coincided with her own, and arranged for Lisa Hunger to take little Marte to Esslingen. Lina followed, first by train from Tegernsee to Munich, from there by bicycle, past numerous US Army checkpoints, to Augsburg, from where she hitch-hiked, and got a lift on a lorry to Stuttgart and Esslingen. The final stretch, reunited with Marte, she made by train in time-consuming stages via Hanover and Lübeck. On 7 September 1945 she knocked on the front door of her parents' house, Staakensweg 30 at Burg, and to her relief found that Heider and Silke had arrived safely long before.

The British military authorities on Fehmarn, who requisitioned the family's holiday home at Burgtiefe, left her in peace. In 1946 she went through the first denazification procedure of the British military author-ity in Germany.[29] Besides her personal details, education and overseas visits (here she mentioned a Mediterranean cruise between 1 and 19 May 1937, and her visit to Werner Best in Denmark in the summer of 1943), she admitted to drawing a widow's pension between 1942 and 1945 of 52,798.35 Reichsmarks and had inherited 'house and land Sahrendorf/Summer house 1942 from my husband'. As proof she fur-nished an extract from the journal of the Burg *Amtsgericht*, Vol. 1, folio 53, proving that SS-Obergruppenführer and Minister of State Reinhard Heydrich had procured a parcel of land at Burgtiefe, fourteen hectares in size plus six hectares for a house, paid for with fifteen thousand gold marks and another twenty thousand gold marks mortgaged to Consul Willy Sachs at Schweinfurt. Besides this, she stated that in 1935 'secretly and without her husband's knowledge' she had left the Evangelical Church, although her son Heider had been baptised in it before she did so. This had been a 'purely personal decision'. Reinhard Heydrich did not leave the Catholic Church until 18 October 1936.

At this time Lina Heydrich had unfounded fears that the British would deport her to Czechoslovakia to stand trial on indictments outstanding there, and at the beginning of April 1946 she decided to flee. With the help of former SS men at Hamburg she got to Munich, where a helpful friend from the time of her husband's death in Bohemia, the Austrian Leopold von Zenetti, got her work as a milkmaid on a farm at Wels in Lower Austria. For some time she considered marrying Zenetti but decided against it once she realised he was a heavy drinker. The work of a milkmaid, the foreign surroundings and the unaccustomed diet she found not to her liking, and then intolerable, and eventually she returned to Fehmarn to face the music. There was none to be faced, however, for the British had their hands full with the maritime black market and con-traband operations along the coast. Even when, on 19 October 1947, the People's Special Court, Department XIII, at Prague found her guilty, in the name of Marketa Heydrich, of 'Supporting the Nazi Movement' and 'Mistreatment of Jews' during her occupation of *Schloss* Panenske Brezany and sentenced her to life imprisonment, twenty years of which was to be spent at forced labour, the British took no interest.[30] All her Czech properties were held forfeit to the Czech Soviet State. The sentence recognised the absence of the accused, whose whereabouts were 'unknown'. The specification tabulated various offences: starving prisoners, allowing their guards to beat them with rifle butts and whips: refusing medical help to a prisoner who fell from a tree, as a result of which he died of his injuries: conspiracy with her husband's successor, Reichs-Protektor Karl Daluege, and his representative Karl Hermann Frank, to execute under martial law in force at the time all persons sus-pected of complicity in the assassination of her husband.

That this sentence was never mentioned in any subsequent legal proceedings against Lina Heydrich speaks volumes for the new climate of confrontation which had developed between East and West. 'So I became one of the few Nazi women who never got locked up,' Lina Heydrich commented, 'and I was a bit sorry not to have had to do some time, for I certainly wasn't spared anything else.'[31]

On 29 June 1949 Lina Heydrich appeared before the Main Denazification Commission for the district of Oldeburg/Holstein. She entered a plea of 'ignorant of any guilt'. She had been 'a member of the NSDAP from 1933 to 1945 and of the Deutsche Jägerschaft – the hunting organisation – from 1943 to 1945'. She had entered the Party 'at my husband's wish'. The Commission was not impressed by her protestations of innocence and in file H15159/48 awarded her a place on the list for decisions in Group IV 'Collaborators'. This meant automatically that 'the valuable benefits which accrued to you as a participant in National Socialism are forfeit.'[32] Lina lodged an appeal against the ruling, which was heard by the Schleswig-Holstein Denazification Appeals Commission at Kiel and ended with the public prosecutor backing down. Lina's attorney, Wilhelm Massmann, produced a string of rebuttal witnesses to whom the Commission gave more credence than the statements of former prisoners, such as Rita Griebel, a friend of Lina from Grossenbrode: 'I never saw Jews being struck or mistreated, although I was always out in the open with the children . . . they [the prisoners] were all healthy and well fed.'[33]

The decision of 12 January 1951 transferred Lina to Group V, 'Discharged', and so she was no longer 'Brown'. The Commission found that 'she was no longer a participant in National Socialism', which she had been since 1949 because she had not owned the property at Jungfern-Breschan and was only 'the administrator of the Government estate', although she had invested money in it. Moreover, the Appeals Commission was not convinced that having Czechs or concentration-camp inmates working on the estate amounted to 'exploitation', and after seeing photographs of the stables in which they were accommodated considered that they appeared almost like 'a gentleman's lodge' and in any case were 'suitable for housing a large number of people and animals'.[34]

It was argued to be 'characteristic' of her treatment of prisoners that Lina Heydrich had intervened personally for the liberation of fifteen 'bible bangers' who had even brought their families to Jungfern-Breschan. Finally, the Fehmarn summer house was not in her possession 'improperly' since all debts had been discounted with Consul Sachs, and the remaining debt of five thousand gold marks in April 1945, immediately before the capitulation. Consequence: 'The embargo on benefits and the fiduciary agency fall away.'[35] The sequestration of the Fehmarn property was thereby lifted.

Lina Heydrich was not finished yet. For several years she had been filing suit against the new Federal Republic of Germany for a widow's and orphans' pension for herself and her children. Her initial application of September 1950 had been thrown out by the Schleswig-Holstein authorities two years later on the grounds that, contrary to the widow's claim, Heydrich had not 'fallen victim to an immediate effect of warfare' and had in fact not been a soldier at all but a *Reichsbeamter* – Reich official – which was not covered by the regulations.[36] The Lübeck office and the Schleswig Appeals Commission also came to the same conclusion.

On 9 February 1952, No. 8 Judicial Chamber of the Schleswig Obersicherungsamt – Higher Social Security Claims Office – ruled that the Prague assassination had been 'a military action' within the meaning of the legislation, and awarded Lina Heydrich a pension backdated to 1950. The provincial and federal authorities appealed, but after long drawn-out proceedings in three senates the Schleswig *Landessozialgericht* found in favour of the claimant on 20 June 1958.

In this process, all expert evidence damaging to Lina's case was discarded, including the opinion of the Kiel historian Michael Freund, which had been requested by the court, and of which extracts appear in the Introduction. Freund thought that the assassination was 'a completely isolated occurrence' and the court should not take into account 'war events'. The court had to ask itself 'if the criminal doings of Heydrich should be placed squarely alongside the wartime sacrifice of honest German soldiers'.[37] The Federal Labour Ministry argued the same:

> It was much more a political assassination which Heydrich brought upon himself by virtue of his brutal political handling of affairs . . . it is the sense and purpose of the Federal Social

Security Law, officially designated as 'Law for the Social Security of War Victims' . . . and it would be false and contrary to equate the assassination of the tyrant Heydrich with the sacrificial deaths of millions of respectable German soldiers.[38]

The *Landessozialgericht*, influenced by its official adviser Waldemar Meinicke-Pusch, a former Nazi lawyer and later deputy to the Kiel provincial parliament, brushed all these pleadings aside. 'The decision in favour of the claimant,' the final ruling decreed, 'would only be justified if the death of Heydrich occurred as the result of an immediate act of warfare, and was a military act in connection with the Second World War.'[39] This was obviously what the assassination at Prague had been. It had not been a tactic of the Czech resistance movement internally, which would have made it the mere 'murder of a tyrant' and of 'internal Czech origin'.

What is decisive is if those persons who killed Heydrich were members of the enemy forces, were deployed from an enemy centre, were therefore following orders, and their act had as its objective the weakening of the German war potential. It is clear from the evidence that such was the case.[40] It was carried out by Czech soldiers trained in England and who participated on the Allied side in the war against the Third Reich.[41]

The ruling enabled Lina Heydrich a relatively carefree, if modest, existence on Fehmarn on a State pension, which she continued to draw until her death in 1985. She did not enjoy her house on the much-frequented southern side of the Burgtiefe peninsula for long. She was having the thatched building, since 1954 a guesthouse, converted into a modern hotel to which she gave the name 'Kleine Kimbern', praised by the local Press as 'a touristic jewel of our Baltic coast'. On 18 February 1969 the structure was gutted by fire after the thatch caught fire from a welder's spark in the new north-west wing. Neighbours helped save furniture, wickerwork beach chairs, paintings and documents but the building, valued at 750,000 Deutsche Marks, was lost, and apparently not fully covered by insurance. The payout was only sufficient for a very modest guesthouse at Todendorf, 'Das Gehege', well off the beaten summer tourist track on Fehmarn.

By the time the Federal Republic 'came to terms with' its past, Lina had become a quite normal citizen: she was 'denazified', her husband a man who had 'fallen in the war', and after her marriage to Finnish theatrical director and painter Mauno Manninen between 1965 and 1969 was no longer 'Frau Heydrich', although she never really ceased to be 'Brown'. In the private quarters at the Burgtiefe guesthouse, and later at Todendorf, numerous nostalgic reunions were held over the years. 'When these old scar-faces ranted over their exploits,' local historian Karl-Wilhelm Klahn reported, 'we young men listened with such intensity that our ears burned.'[42] Even foreign sympathisers were received at Fehmarn in her parlour, directly beneath Reinhard Heydrich's bronze death mask, as in 1973 the Italian neo-fascist Michele Sakkara. He wrote later a fictionalised diary of Heydrich under the title *L'uomo dal cuore di ferro* (The Man with the Iron Heart).

Lina Heydrich would allow nothing to be said against her husband. In 1962 she wrote to a Dutch historian on her old typewriter, equipped with a special 'runic SS' key, on the subject of Heydrich's guilt:

> Why is he so important today! Why so discussed? Is it so unusual that my husband is absolute, that he utterly is. I ask you, is a warlord brutal because many people die under his command? Why is sadism, brutality, perversion, read into those decisions which my husband dictated in the course of his duties and which perhaps in his eyes were an unavoidable political necessity of State? We have all become accustomed to judge the decisions of those times from today's warm bed.

She also went into the question of whether her husband had ever had contact with the German resistance movement against Hitler and answered: 'Never. He knew the names of all those of 20 July and had condemned them already as unreliable soldiers.'[43]

In 1965 she told a reporter of the Dutch newspaper *De Nieuwe Dag* that her husband had 'not been anti-Jewish': 'Reinhard had nothing against the Jews and he had nothing to do with the campaign of extermination.'

She was still enthusiastic about the Third Reich ('National Socialism meant the solution to almost all our problems') and the Führer ('Hitler was a fantastic man . . . he was charming, courteous and very intelligent.')[44]

In 1969 after her remarriage, she told the German woman's magazine *Jasmin* 'with tears in her eyes' about Heydrich: 'Even today I still dream about my husband nearly every night. He wants to separate himself from me. He wants to leave me. I reproach him that he has deserted me. Almost every night it is the same.'[45] And in 1979, when the US television documentary drama *Holocaust* created a furore in West Germany, she told the *New York Times*: 'I do not associate the character called Heydrich in that play with my husband.'

She knew nothing about the murder of the Jews, the Final Solution: 'My husband had nothing to do with it, he was falsely accused of that. The European Jews were all taken to the Urals.'[46]

She sent a copy of her book *Leben mit einem Kriegsverbrecher*, from which a number of extracts are quoted in this book, to the American reporter. It was published in 1976 at Pfaffenhofen by Wilhelm Ludwig with a commentary by the Hitler-biographer Werner Maser. The historian found a hefty 'discrepancy between poetic licence and truth': 'Quite clearly, Lina Heydrich has embellished many of her husband's doings with rich fantasy, rigorously distorted, knowingly glossed over or simply attributed his misdeeds to other leading figures of the Hitler regime.'[47]

Whenever Lina Manninen-Heydrich sent out a complimentary copy of her book, the forty pages of Maser's observations would have been excised meticulously beforehand. Even her son Heider voiced the opinion later that the memoir contained 'fairly enormous distortions of history, and she even bent things about herself'.[48]

At the end of her life did Lina Manninen have anything approaching insight? The Hamburg mathematics professor Arno Ausborn, who got to know her during his holiday visits to Fehmarn, and had rendered help when the owner was attempting to evict her from the rooms she had at Todendorf, found that he could rarely bring the 'always distrustful' old lady to talk about the past, and when he succeeded, it was always more of the same: the murder of the Jews had only been 'partisan actions', the type of thing that happened in war. In a telephone conversation two weeks before her death, however, when according to Ausborn she was in 'a pretty poor state', she reportedly said: 'The thing about the persecution of the Jews and the mass-murders, that must probably have been true. But all National Socialist leaders put the blame on Heydrich because he was dead.'[49]

She died in her seventy-fourth year on 14 August 1985 on her home island. The *Fehmarnisches Tageblatt* honoured her with the headline 'A Life Heavy with Destiny', describing her as an avid amateur archaeologist of the coastal mudbanks and as an 'outstanding storyteller'. Above the obituary notice her family had inserted: 'May Heaven give her Peace.'[50] On the morning of 17 August she was buried in the St Georg Rural District new cemetery at Burg in the family vault below a stone bearing the coat of arms and the inscription 'Family Grave v. Osten'. On her memorial plate is engraved 'Lina Manninen, widow of Heydrich, née von Osten, 1911–1985'.

On the island it is rumoured that the vault contains not only the remains of her parents and five-year-old brother Klaus von Osten (who died in 1919), but also her second brother Hans and his wife – and Reinhard Heydrich. In the confusion of the immediate postwar period, the widow allegedly had the corpse of her husband disinterred by former SS men and brought to Fehmarn, but there is no proof of this. The rumour results from the fact that Heydrich's grave at Berlin's Invaliden Cemetery no longer exists. The Berlin historian Laurenz Demps, author of a book on the Heldenfriedhof – 'heroes' cemetery' – emphasises that Heydrich's grave is still registered as being in Sector A, unmarked because the simple wooden cross erected in 1942 disappeared at the war's end. In the epoch of the DDR, within whose territory the Invaliden Cemetery lay, close to the demarcation line between West and East Germany in 1949, 'nothing had been removed.' And before? 'Anything is possible,' Demps declared, 'but somebody would have noticed.'[51]

The competent Gardens and Cemeteries Office of the Berlin-Mitte district replied to my enquiry: 'The bones are present. No exchange of remains is known of. That is pure speculation.' All the same, no check has been made of the contents of the Heydrich grave so that 'some uncertainty remains as to whether, in the confusion of the immediate postwar period, somebody interfered with the bodies.'[52] In 2001, the descendants of Heydrich renounced 'for ever' all interests in connection with the Berlin grave.

The authorities want no sensationalism about Heydrich's last resting place. The last thing anybody needs in Germany is a new pilgrimage site for new and old Nazis at the Invaliden Cemetery similar to that of the NSDAP martyr Horst Wessel in Berlin, or of Admiral Dönitz at Aumühle, Hamburg.

For many unregenerates, Heydrich, the never-convicted mass-murderer, remains the Greatest. More so than Rudolf Hess he is to neo-Nazis 'the ideal National Socialist' or, as the US racist Rob Fenelon put it, 'the Naziest Nazi of them all'. On an American Internet website, H. H. Norden published in several languages an article eulogising Heydrich's 'exemplary life':

How can we National Socialists of the 21st century follow the example provided by Reinhard Heydrich in his lifetime? First of all we must assent uncompromisingly to the National Socialist doctrine, and be ready to do whatever is necessary for the victory of the Aryan race. It is our holy duty to engage our enemies ruthlessly. If necessary, we will avail ourselves of conspiratorial methods, while in other cases we shall take up arms. We do not recognise the legitimacy of democractic systems which came to power in Europe after 1945, and our objective is accordingly the utter annihilation of the democracies and the removal of the leading political voices of this ghastly age.

The article is peppered with tirades against the Jews as 'the worst enemy of the Aryan people', against democratic politicians and publishers, with denials of the Holocaust, with respect to which the Wannsee

Conference had only worked towards 'the evacuation of the Jews from Europe', and the role of the SS. Norden's conclusion is that: 'The life of SS-Obergruppenführer Reinhard Heydrich shows us the path to follow. We will never leave this path. Only then will victory be ours.'[53]

Through the medium of the Internet similar texts and books are offered in numbers, among them a biography of Heydrich, a pictorial volume about the assassination and even a computer game of the *Sim City* genre called *The Sims,* which features a family, consisting of 'Reinhard Heydrich' and 'Lina von Osten', together with their children, whose house can be built. Among the 'heroes' on the website of American neo-Nazi Gerhard Lauck, Heydrich ran Hitler a close second in 2002. In a modern racist twist 'the Jew' is replaced by 'the Turk': 'Sleep, Turk, sleep, sleep well. Soon an SA man will arrive and stuff you in the oven. Reinhard Heydrich gives us his blessing to simply, simply, kill you.'[54]

The Berlin neo-Nazi Arnulf Priem, sentenced to three years six months in prison in 1995 for raising an armed troop, was described as 'an enthusiastic arsonist' in the indictment. He named Heydrich as his great role model. His intended insurrection and bomb-making were described by the State Attorney as 'unsurpassed in their damnability'. To the victims of the Third Reich and their descendants, such activities sixty years after its twilight and destruction are incomprehensible. The lack of insight and ignorance of the heirs to the Nazi Reich reduced the Jewish author and Nobel Peace Prize winner Elie Wiesel, a survivor of Auschwitz, to despair. 'One and a half million Jewish children were murdered. How could the murderers murder them? How could the world let it happen? I can't understand . . . If Auschwitz and Buchenwald have really not changed people, whatever can?'[55]

The fact that the crimes of the SS-Obergruppenführer murdered in 1942 were never fully investigated by the justice system has contributed to the uncritical veneration Heydrich's memory receives. Many files related specifically to Heydrich's work were never looked at after the war and disappeared within the mass of archive material sent off to Washington, London and Moscow, where they remain today under lock and key. The War Crimes trials of the victorious Powers at Nuremberg between 1945 and 1949 delivered no posthumous condemnation of Heydrich nor against those others principally responsible who escaped justice through suicide: Hitler and Goebbels in the Reich Chancellery, Himmler in British custody at Lüneburg. In the first hearings before the International Military Tribunal (IMT) the twenty most important men of the Third Reich sat in the dock for months while the repugnant crimes of National Socialism were revealed to the world public. None showed remorse with the possible exception of the recently pious former Governor-General of Poland, Hans Frank: 'A thousand years will pass and Germany's guilt will still not have been extinguished.'[56] There was instead, as in the next twelve cases against various organisations, that secret understanding which even Lina Heydrich proclaimed: 'Blame everything on the dead! Blame everything on Heydrich!'[57] This went so far that Ernst Kaltenbrunner, from January 1943 chief of the RSHA, in dismissing a comparison of his work with that of his predecessor as 'completely unfair', complained: 'I object in the strongest terms to being described as Heydrich's successor.' He had had to get by on the salary of a police general of about 1,320 Reichsmarks per month while Heydrich drew 30,000 Reichsmarks monthly 'and not as remuneration for his high service rank, but in recognition of the quite different employment he had.'[58] The tribunal would not wear it, however, and Kaltenbrunner numbered among the ten principal defendants sentenced to death (nine were hanged; Goering took a suicide pill to avoid execution).

Although the IMT declared as 'illegal organisations' parts of the Nazi State apparatus including the SS, Gestapo and SD groups controlled by Heydrich, the RSHA was not mentioned even though its role, for instance as the controlling body of the Einsatzgruppen in the East, was obvious in the first trial.

One of the most shocking cross-examination revelations at Nuremberg was brought out by US prosecuting attorney Colonel John Harlan Amen on 3 January 1946 while questioning the former leader of Einsatzgruppe D, Otto Ohlendorf. Even this former SS-General pointed to Heydrich as the source of the order for the mass-murders.

> **Amen:** What were your instructions with regard to the Jews and Communist functionaries?

Ohlendorf: The instruction stated that in the Russian territories where the Einsatzgruppen operated, the Jews and Soviet political commissars were to be liquidated.

Amen: When you use the word 'liquidate', do you mean 'kill'?

Ohlendorf: By that I mean 'kill'.

Amen: Do you know how many people were liquidated by Einsatzgruppe D, and particularly under your authority?

Ohlendorf: In the year bewteen June 1941 and June 1942, about ninety thousand were reported liquidated by the Einsatzgruppen.

Amen: Does that number include men, women and children?

Ohlendorf: *Jawohl* . . . some Einsatzgruppe leaders rejected the military method of liquidation and carried out the killings with a bullet to the back of the head.

Amen: And you were opposed to that procedure?

Ohlendorf: I was against that procedure, certainly.

Amen: For what reason?

Ohlendorf: Because it caused enduring psychic harm to both the victims and those who were ordered to do the killings.[59]

Ohlendorf was the only Einsatzgruppe leader to be brought before the Nuremberg tribunals: Otto Rasch (Einsatzgruppe C) fell ill during the preliminary hearings and was declared unfit to stand trial: he died of Parkinson's Disease in custody in 1948. Walther Stahlecker (Einsatzgruppe A) died in March 1942 while being borne away from the

Eastern Front with serious wounds. Reichskriminaldirektor Arthur Nebe (Einsatzgruppe B) joined the German Resistance in 1944 and paid for it with his life on 3 March 1945. Consequently Ohlendorf, the shining intellectual without a scruple, the principal accused in the so-called Einsatzgruppe prosecutions, was sentenced to death by the US Military Tribunal on 10 April 1948 together with thirteen others of the twenty-two accused. Yet even these trials had a 'cold amnesty' in due course: only four of those sentenced to hang as leaders of Hitler's murder-commandos in the East, Ohlendorf, Erich Naumann (Einsatzgruppe B), Paul Blobel (Sonderkommando 1005) and Werner Braune (Sonderkommando 11b) were executed, at Landsberg prison on 8 June 1951. The leader of Einsatzkommando 2, Eduard Strauch, was extradited to Belgium and died in prison there in 1955. All the remaining candidates for death had their sentences commuted by US High Commissioner John McCloy to life imprisonment or other specific prison terms. This was at the urging of the German Federal Government which had abolished the death penalty under the 1949 Constitution. Six of the convicted were released in 1951 but two, Ernst Biberstein (Einsatzkommando 6) and Adolf Ott (Sonderkommando 7b) completed thirteen years each. Heydrich's sociology professor, Franz Alfred Six, leader of Einsatzkommando 7c, was sentenced to twenty years' imprisonment but walked free in 1952.

Smaller fry had to hang: the concentration-camp guards, the torturers, those in charge at the lower levels. Between 1945 and 1948, the US military authorities instituted 489 trials against 1,672 accused. Of these, 256 were acquitted and 426 condemned to death, of whom 152 were -execu-ted. Of the twenty-six commandants of the largest death camps, ten were executed by the Americans, one before the war's end by the SS: four fell at the front and four committed suicide: eight died of natural causes, two received life sentences. The great majority of prosecutions were initiated before responsibility for justice passed to the two new German States.

The Federal Republic, bent on achieving an economic miracle and reintegrating into the West, wanted the Nazis as far out of sight and mind as possible: the DDR used trials and investigations to demonstrate how old Nazis were back in the ranks of power in Konrad Adenauer's CDU

Government. A number of Heydrich's grim reapers got away very lightly for this reason. One of these was Bruno Streckenbach, former head of Hamburg Gestapo, responsible for massacres in Poland and Russia, Amtschef I at RSHA and executive head of the office in the half-year after Heydrich's death. In 1945 as commander of 8 SS-Kavallerie Division Florian Geyer he was captured by the Russians, a fact which proved very useful in the Einsatzgruppen trials at Nuremberg, since the accused could heap the blame on Streckenbach as being the prime source of the orders before the Russian campaign in 1941 to murder Jews there. On 9 October 1955 he appeared in Hamburg suddenly a free man (his file at the Russian Federation Special Archive bears the endorsement 'material unsuitable for release to the public').[60] Streckenbach enquired at once of the State's Attorney if there were any claims outstanding against him, but apart from a complaint of grievous bodily harm from his Gestapo days his record was clean. One year later a process contemplated against him was abandoned by the justice authorities: despite all the allegations made at the Einsatzgruppen trials, whatever had gone on in the East they were no longer interested. Not until two more years had passed, on 30 June 1973, was Streckenbach charged in Hamburg with having 'caused the deaths of at least one million persons'. Since he had now developed a serious heart condition, on 20 September 1974 the *Oberlandesgericht* declined to proceed with the specification, and from then until his death on 28 October 1977 he never came before a court, and so nobody could pin on him the label 'convicted murderer'.

Heydrich's deputy at RSHA Sipo, Werner Best, also slipped through the net. Extradited to Denmark in 1948 and condemned to death there, he was reprieved and returned to the Federal Republic in 1951. Condemned as a 'Principal in Guilt' at Berlin in 1958, but not proved a murderer, he was ordered to make a payment in expiation of 70,000 Deutsche Marks, and only 100.40 Deutsche Marks remained outstanding by the time his appeal was heard in 1962. Rearrested in March 1969 on a charge of having passed down orders for the murder of 8,700 Poles in 1939, Best was found unfit to stand trial in 1972 and released: he lived quietly for another seventeen years.

Not a single head of the RSHA Polish Division IVD2 ever came before a court. In 1968 in Berlin while the criminal proceedings against the three consecutive divisional chiefs Joachim Deumling, Berhard Baatz and Harro Thomsen were pending, West German law was changed requiring the prosecution to prove 'base motivation' in cases involving murder. This made a conviction for murder unlikely, and since everything else was out of time under the Statute of Limitations, the trial was never convened, and neither were eighteen other prosecutions against about three hundred RSHA accused which the Berlin State Attorney General had had in preparation since 1963. Deumling later became a judge in the labour courts system, Baatz a businessman and Thomsen a notary public. A subsequent allegation against Deumling alleging complicity in the murder of 3,823 persons also came to nothing.

Other RSHA desk-bound officials made careers within State organisations. Walter Zirpins, criminal police (Kripo) chief at Lodz, headed the Kripo at Hanover after the war. Karl Schulz, adjutant to Einsatzgruppe leader Nebe, had risen by the end of the 1950s to head the Landeskriminalamt at Bremen. Heinrich Malz, an SD man from 1935 and by 1944 adjutant to Kaltenbrunner, became head of affairs at the German Federation of State Officials. In the Bonn republic, 'coming to terms with the past' meant only too frequently repressing, colouring or forgiving it. Historian Jörge Friedrich told the author in an interview: 'The Final Solution ended with the disappearance of the executioners.'[61] His colleague Michael Wildt of the Hamburg Institute for Social Research, investigating RSHA career-men, concluded that the old Nazis, even if their rise was 'a scandal', were 'unable to do any more damage' once employed in State offices.

> Men like Karl Schulz have not turned into democrats, [Wildt stated in an interview] but it proves the strength of democratic institutions since 1945 that men like him can take State jobs without the Federal Republic becoming 'Brown'. So long as we ensure that our democracy has State offices where all are treated the same under the law, even in the practice of taxation

and gifts, then we are protected against extremists in those offices from doing harm. They remain paper tigers. If this layer of society were to become an institution, radicalized in the manner of the RSHA, however, then that would be enormously dangerous – political plutonium.[62]

The best example here is Adolf Eichmann, a mass-murderer wearing the disguise of a respectable gentleman, who in his manner exemplified 'the banality of evil', as Hannah Arendt expressed it in her book. No war crimes trial had electrified world opinion since Nuremberg as did the Israeli prosecution of the former 'Jewish Office IV B4' head in Heydrich's RSHA. Abducted in the Argentine capital, Buenos Aires, by Mossad agents in May 1960, Eichmann was given a show-trial in the Jerusalem House of Justice, Beth Hamishpath.

All Nazis acted only under orders. None ever admitted to blood on his own hands. Here was a chance to set the record straight, for now there stood, in an Israeli courtroom, in a cage of bullet-proof glass, a wishy-washy man in spectacles who could have put his hands up to something, anything, before the hangman took him. But he never did. He had no personal regrets for anything.

'I was never anti-Jewish,' Eichmann told the court, 'I was a nationalist.' Almost without emotion, as if it had nothing to do with him personally, he added: 'I regret it and do condemn those of the German leaders of that time who *ordered* extermination activity against the Jews. For myself I would not wish to overstate my own situation. I was no more than a tool in the hand of more powerful forces and more powerful powers and of implacable destiny.' When asked if he felt any guilt he replied, 'Guilt as a human being, yes . . . ' Did he regret anything? 'There is no point in regret, regret is for tiny children.'

In a psychological test he compared himself to Pontius Pilate, whom he acquitted of any guilt in the death of Jesus Christ. 'Pilate acted from political duty, and in washing his hands he demonstrated that he was not involved personally in the act. If I am permitted to compare myself to an historical figure, I was also, in the final analysis, in his situation.'[63]

Even Eichmann's finger always pointed to Himmler, Heydrich and 'Gestapo' Müller as the source of his orders. Contemporary documents and more recent research prove, in the opinion of Viennese Eichmann-expert Hans Safrian, 'that he was an over-zealous Jew-hunter who often exceeded his authority in order to make the methods of persecution and deportation more efficient.' Would he have been a good bureaucrat if not in Hitler's service? 'The mechanism for assembling the victims and for mass-murder required not solid civil servants but administrators at key points who acted as path-finders. Eichmann was one of the latter.'[64]

On 15 December 1961 Eichmann was sentenced to death and hanged on the night of 1 June 1962. The Eichmann trial gave an injection of adrenalin to West German justice still hamstrung by attempts to lift the statute of limitations for murder. The trials of the accused who had served at the extermination camps of Auschwitz and Treblinka attracted great attention and helped weaken the persistent taboo of 'coming to terms with the past' by not mentioning it.

National Socialism and the Holocaust remain to this day 'irons in the fire' of public debate in Germany, always controversial, as the disputes related to 'the Historical Argument', 'the Auschwitz Lie', about Daniel Goldhagen's *Willige Vollstrecker* – Willing Executioners – the question of Wehrmacht involvement and the Berlin Holocaust memorial prove. Even if many of today's Germans, old and young, lack insight and continue to follow Hitler's ideology, and in the year 2000 committed fourteen thousand 'extremist' offences, the judgment of the majority of Germans on the darkest epoch of their history is unequivocal. Bundespräsident Johannes Rau summed it up in a memorial speech to the Bundestag on 26 January 2001 thus:

> One need never have heard anything about the Third Reich and its henchmen to know that persecution, mistreatment and mass-murder are wrong. We must ensure that Right-extremist force and anti-human thinking do not deter us from enquiring into National Socialism. There are Right-extemists who know more than many other people about the Third Reich, but

neither personal morals nor ethical convictions can arise out of knowledge alone. Remembrance can help us understand. It can show us what happens when the value of people is debased, when the destruction of the worth of people is the goal and content of the politics. When the National Socialists declared certain people or groups unworthy to live, they turned on humanity itself.

For that reason, the parental figures of our Constitution inserted the inviolability of the value of every individual person at the very beginning of the legislation. That was the consequence inferred essential from National Socialist rule. That is the basic consensus of politics in our Republic.

For a long period of time, the Third Reich seemed to us to be a retrogressive epoch. In the foreground of our mental image of National Socialism were the phrases of Blood-and-Soil propaganda, or the *Germanen*-cult. That was a mistake, for National Socialism consisted not only of insane ideas: on many points it stood squarely on what seemed to be scientific possibility at that time – in medicine, in history, in law and many other disciplines. Science and ideology were linked into the belief that one should do anything that was possible, provided it was useful to one's own group, one's own folk, one's own race. The end justified the means. The memory of it stands as an enduring appeal to all those born afterwards that the freedom and worth of individual people is inviolable.[65]

The sorrow and the shame remain with some, however, and not only those who took part in it. It is the heaviest burden of that evil past, and psychologically affects the descendants of the main participants. Reinhard Heydrich's nephew is considered by many historians to be a case in point. In 1950, when Peter Thomas Heydrich was sent to Switzerland for treatment for suspected tuberculosis, he received from his doctor for the first time comprehensive literature about the Third Reich. He came to realise his uncle's role and also that 'the name of Heydrich would always be associated with these terrible things.' The horror worked itself into his psychological make-up: 'Suddenly, I felt guilt.' For years the fact tortured him that nobody, beginning with his mother, would talk to him about it: 'I was confined in an inner prison.'[66] His first contact with philosophers and writers such as Gottfried Benn, Helmut Gollwitzer and Karl Barth broke the spell. In his career as actor, cabaret artist and singer, he made the centrepoint recitals from the 'burnt literature' – the books which the Nazis had banned and burned. For peace of mind he took his mother's maiden name and became Thomas Werther, but could not escape the curse of the name: Radio Bremen had to let him go because 'such a small station could not afford to employ somebody from that family',[67] listeners would have complained at having to hear a Heydrich at the microphone. Even though he was able to write a family history decades later, his friend the Düsseldorf pastor Hans-Georg Wiedemann did not believe 'that he ever managed to defeat the legacy'.[68]

'Somebody had to assume guilt for the evil my uncle did,' Peter Thomas Heydrich told the journalist and Speer-biographer Gitta Sereny a few years earlier. 'I felt myself to be the representative of all the others: of my aunt Lina Heydrich, who was so proud of her husband: of his three children (Heider, Silke and Marte) who, and this I cannot understand, felt and feel nothing.'[69]

Thomas Werther died in Düsseldorf on 22 November 2000.

The trail to Heydrich's children led back to Fehmarn. His youngest daughter, Silke, settled there, married a local farmer from Johannisberg and bore five children. She named her eldest son Reinhard. The lady at the Burg Heimatmuseum was happy to provide information. Frau Marte Beyer kept a fashion shop just around the corner, where she could be found most days: 'You will recognise her at once.' In front of the building with its white-painted walls and small display windows stood a board announcing 'Exclusive Fashions "at Marte" since 1970'. Inside, a woman in her mid-fifties, dressed in a colourful blouse and bright beige jacket, was arranging clothes on a rack. She had short, shining, blonde, permed hair, and on her slender body sat the head of the Reich Protector: long nose, angled features, grey-blue eyes. At first evasive, eventually she agreed to answer a few questions.

'I still suffer from it today,' she said. 'I had to have treatment for a long time. I had trouble sleeping. He was there in my dreams. You have no idea what it means to have such a father.'[70] Actually she never knew him, for Marte was born on 23 July 1942, nearly two months after his death. As a schoolgirl on Fehmarn, as she once told a reporter, 'the other children would spit at us'.[71]

'My own children have all gone through the hoop at school,' she continued, 'and then come the journalists, who are always surfacing, with their investigative eye. Many come pretending they want to buy a frock, just to talk to me. Others overwhelm you. 'Oh, how much you resemble your father,' they say. How should one react to that? Once she went to the Czech Republic, after the Wall came down, to see if she could find the grave of her brother Klaus. She scrambled over the walls surrounding the *Schloss* at Panenske Brezany but saw nothing: 'Apparently they had some kind of secret armaments project there. Everything was sealed off.'[72] If I wanted to know more about the family I should contact her brother Heider, who lived in Munich, she told me. He was an expert on the documents and would certainly be willing to supply further information.

I did not find that to be the case. On the contrary, he wanted to have nothing to do with journalists researching his family history. In a fax produced by his computer, with computerised signature, the now-retired former director of the Dornier aircraft company, Dipl.-Ing. Heider Heydrich, wrote to me from his Bavarian home at Wörthsee:

> As is known, I was born in 1934 and cannot speak from my own experience about those times. I have respect and esteem for historians and their conclusions about the period of the Third Reich and who maintain a professional position one way or the other. Personally I have pursued other professional goals in my life and considered that I am not sufficiently competent to explain historical events and processes.[73]

And the next generation? Reinhard (Beyer) Heydrich, who takes the surname of his grandfather, also lives on Fehmarn, where he sells wind turbines. He slithered like an eel through all questions requiring his assessment of Nazi war crimes. Despite sixty years of research into the Gestapo, Sipo, RSHA and Einsatzgruppen he prefers to reserve his opinion. 'Nobody really knows for sure what Grandpa did.'[74]

Silke Heyrich's son Ingo Wischnewski, who lives in Hamburg, threatened to set the police on anybody who telephoned and mentioned the name 'Heydrich'. 'It gets him into a state,' his wife apologised.[75]

It is clear that of all the direct Heydrich descendants, not one has ever uttered publicly a word of regret about the crimes committed by their ancestor. Never have they furnished a gesture towards the Jews, Poles or the survivors of Lidice. They have simply withdrawn behind a veil of silence or, if not, then like Lina Manninen-Heydrich-von Osten, attempted to cast a net of distortions and lies over the truth about Reinhard Heydrich. Peter Thomas Heydrich despaired of them and many years before his death broke off all contact with Lina, her children and grandchildren. Her lack of sympathy and interest was incomprehensible to him.

Were they frightened they might come in for rough justice if they exposed themselves too much? Did they fear the wrath of the victims of the Reich Protector? They had no cause to think so for, as the Israeli historian Tuviah Friedmann emphasises, 'The Jews have taken no revenge on Heydrich's children or his wife, who brought her fourth child into the world at a time when every day Jewish children and their mothers were being shepherded into the gas chambers.'[76]

Notes

Introduction

1. The scene from a German wartime newsreel is reproduced in the Heydrich documentary film *Opus pro smrtihlava* (Opus for the Death's Head) by Karel Marsalek, Czechoslovakia, 1985.
2. Bundesarchiv Berlin-Lichterfelde, Abt III (Drittes Reich), *SS Akte Heydrich* under PA No. H222A.
3. Shlomo Aronson, *Reinhard Heydrich und die Frühgeschichte von Gestapo und SD*, Stuttgart, 1971, DVA.
4. Interview with Eberhard Jäckel, 8 April 2002.
5. Alan Burgess, *Sieben Männer im Morgengrauen*, Gütersloh, 1961: Bertelsmann, p. 77f.
6. Written opinions of Prof. Dr Michael Freund (Christian Albrechts-Universität, Kiel) dated 5 May 1956 and 23 November 1956: Landesarchiv Schleswig-Holstein, Sig. LAS Abt. 794 Schleswig 2.
7. Charles W. Sydnor, 'Executive Instinct, Reinhard Heydrich and the Planning for the Final Solution' in Michael Berenbaum and Abraham Peck, *The Holocaust and History, The Known, The Unknown, The Disputed and the Re-examined*, Bloominton, 1998: Indiana University Press, p. 159f.
8. Interview, 6 April 2002.
9. Hans-Georg Wiedemann: 'Peter Thomas Heydrich's Recollections of his Uncle Reinhard Heydrich', Unpublished Manuscript, 2002, p. 5f.

Chapter One

1. *Hallescher Central-Anzeiger*, 10 March 1904, Stadtarchiv Halle a. d. Saale, portfolio 5502.

NOTES

2. StAr Halle, portfolio 5502.

3. Baptismal register 1904, Propstei Church Office, St Franziskus und Elisabeth, Halle (p. 356, entry No. 154).

4. Anon.: anonymous undated letter to the publisher W. Ludwig, Pfaffenhofen as a reaction to the publication of the memoirs of Lina Heydrich, IfZ Munich, Sig. ED 450.

5. StAr Halle, portfolio 2571 FA.

6. *Saale-Zeitung*, Easter 1904, StAr Halle, portfolio 2571 FA.

7. '*I.Bericht des Bruno Heydrich'schen Konservatoriums für Musik und Theater, speciell Hochschule für Gesang zu Halle a. d. Saale*' (1903), StAr, portfolio 2571FA.

8. Anon., as (4) above.

9. Aronson, p. 27. The description of Heydrich's childhood and youth follow eyewitness accounts quoted in Aronson, Deschner and Calic, see Bibliography.

10. StAr Halle, portfolio 2571 FA.

11. Advertisements from *Hallesche Nachrichten*, 3 and 7 May 1919.

12. NARA Washington, Sig. T-175, film 257, document 19b ('Personal files of Frau Lina Heydrich').

13. Description per details in *Hallesche Nachrichten*, March 1919, and in Georg Soldan: *Zeitgeschichte in Wort und Bild*, Berlin, 1931, National-Archiv, p. 256ff.

14. *Hallesche Nachrichten*, 5 March 1919.

15. As (12), NARA, document 12.

16. As (12), document 19.

17. Anon., as (4).

18. Description of the unrest including the quote per *Hallesche Nachrichten*, March 1920, particularly *Die Schreckenstage in Halle vom 13 bis 23 März 1920*, in H.N., 30 March 1920 (1.Supplement) and in Soldan.

19. Photocopy in: Max Williams and Ulric, *Reinhard Heydrich, The Biography*, Vol. 1 *Road to War*, Church Stretton, 2001, Ulric Publishing, p. 12.

20. Aronson, p. 23.

21. Felix von Luckner: *Seeteufel, Abenteuer aus meinem Leben*, Leipzig, 1921, Koehler, p. 307.

22. Aronson, p. 27.

23. Heinz Höhne: *Canaris, Patriot im Zwielicht*, Munich, 1976, Bertelsmann, p. 91.

24. Edouard Calic: *Reinhard Heydrich, Schlüsselfigur des Dritten Reiches*, Düsseldorf, 1982, Droste, p. 38f.

25. Günther Deschner, *Reinhard Heydrich, Statthalter der totalen Macht*: Esslingen, 1977: Bechtle p. 32 and Aronson, p. 30f.

26. Photocopy of Naval Service Record, 30 April 1931 in: Lina Heydrich: *Leben mit einem Kriegsverbrecher*, Pfaffenhofen, 1976: W. Ludwig, opp. p. 31 (plate section).

27. Reader's letter, *Der Spiegel*, 2 March 1950.

28. Lina Heydrich, *Jasmin* interview, April 1969, p. 70f.

29. Hugo Riemann: *Musik-Lexikon*, Berlin/Leipzig, 1916, Max Hesse, p. 467.

30. StAr Halle, portfolio 2571 FA, letter dated 6 July 1922.

31. Aronson, p. 258, footnote 29.

32. Interview with Harry Lichtenstein, Paris, 26 April 2003.

33. Adolf Hitler, *Mein Kampf,* Munich, 1940, Franz Eher Nachf., p. 69f.

34. See Lawrence Stokes, *Kleinstadt und Nationalsozialismus, Ausgewählte Dokumente zur Geschichte von Eutin,* Neumünster, 1984: Wachholtz, and Lina Heydrich, p. 26.

35. Quoted in *Mitteilungen* of the *Hochseesportverband Hansa,* Neustadt/Holstein, No. 1, p. 3.

36. Jörg Hillmann and Reinhard Schreiblich (photos): *Das rote Schloss am Meer: Die Marineschule Murwik seit ihrer Gründung,* Hamburg, 2002: Convent.

37. Article *Friedrich-Carl Freiherr von Eberstein, Führer des neuen SS-Oberabschnitts "Mitte" zu Dresden,* in: *Saale-Zeitung,* 27 March 1934.

38. The description of the first meetings follows the memoir of Lina Heydrich. Some details have been corrected as a result of the author's research in Kiel and Fehmarn, as for example 'Wicht's Weinkeller' and not 'Wick's Weinkeller'.

39. Files respecting the former Kolonialen Frauenschule Rendsburg, which existed from 1927 to 1944, can be found in Stadtarchiv Rendsburg. Only the 1930/1931 course is absent from newspaper accounts of the time which parodied the school and its pupils. One of the girls who passed through its portals was Hannah Reitsch. The school buildings, used from 1946 as a *Heimvolkshochschule,* were torn down in 1977. As regards the Heydrich girlfriend, see Aronson, p. 34f: Deschner, p. 38 and Jochen von Lang, *Die Gestapo, Instrument des Terrors,* Munich, 1993: Heyne, p. 12.

40. Reader's letter, *Der Spiegel,* 2 March 1950.

41. *Marineverordnungsblatt,* Vol. 12 (Year 62), 1 May 1931, p. 75.

42. *MOV-Nachrichten,* No. 10 (13th Year) 15 May 1931.

43. *Dienstleistungszeichnis,* as (26) above.

44. See Deschner, p. 40f., Lina Heydrich, p. 26f.

45. Bundesarchiv Berlin-Lichtefelde, SS personal file Heydrich, Sig. PA No. H222A.

46. Lina Heydrich, p. 26.

47. From Himmler's speech, 30 January 1943 at RSHA, quoted in VfZ (Year 38), No. 2 p. 343.

48. Heinrich Fraenkel and Roger Manvell: *Himmler, Kleinbürger und Massenmörder,* Herrsching, 1981, Pawlak, p. 14.

49. Guido Knopp, *Hitlers Helfer,* Vol. 1, Munich, 1996: C. Bertelsmann, p. 149.

50. Fraenkel and Manvell: *Himmler,* p. 81.

51. Calic, p. 59.

52. Lina Heydrich, p. 29.

53. Quoted in: Arthur Böckenhauer, *10 Jahre SA Hamburg in Bildern mit verbindendem Text,* Leipzig, 1932, J. J.Weber, p. 1.

54. *Hamburger Tageblatt,* 3 September 1931.

55. *Hamburger Echo,* 3 June 1931.

56. Charles Sydnor: 'Reinhard Heydrich, Der ideale Nationalsozialist' in Ronald Smelser and Enrico Syring: *Die SS: Elite unter dem Totenkopf,* Paderborn, 2000, Schöningh, p. 211.
57. Photocopy of a letter in: Lina Heydrich, plate section opp. p. 33.
58. Deschner, p. 46.
59. Felix Kersten: *Totenkopf und Treue: Heinrich Himmler ohne Uniform,* Hamburg, 1951: Robert Mölich, p. 130.
60. Aronson, p. 317f.
61. Aronson, p. 318.
62. Lina Heydrich, p. 28ff.
63. Lina Heydrich, p. 34f.
64. Deschner, p. 58ff.
65. Bundesarchiv, Berlin-Lichterfelde, SS personal file Heydrich, Sig. PA No. H222A.
66. As above, opinion, on 22 June 1932.
67. Kersten, p. 128.
68. Letter from Heinrich Hoffmann dated 9 March 1871 to IfZ Munich regarding the search for Heydrich's Jewish ancestry, IfZ Sig. ED 450.
69. For genealogy see family tree in Aronson, p. 310 (also at IfZ under Sig. ZS/A 34) and Williams/Ulric, p. 41, also Karin Flachowsky, *Neue Quellen zur Abstammung Reinhard Heydrichs* in: VfZ, Vol. 48 (April 2000), p. 318ff.
70. NARA, Sig. T-175, film 257.
71. Heinz Höhne, *Die Machtergreifung: Deutschlands Weg in die Hitler-Diktatur,* Reinbek, 1983: Rowohlt p. 260.
72. Manfred Oversch and Friedrich Wilhelm Saal: *Das III Reich 1933–1939, Eine Tageschronik der Politik, Wirtschaft und Kultur,* Augsburg 1991, Weltbild, p. 9f.
73. Höhne, p. 265.

Chapter Two

1. Lina Heydrich, p. 38.
2. Reinhard Heydrich, handwritten letter to Kurt Daluege from the Berlin Savoy Hotel, 5 March 1933.
3. Lina Heydrich, pp 39.
4. Guido Knopp, *Hitler – Eine Bilanz,* Munich, 1997, Goldmann p. 187.
5. Heydrich's explanation to General von Epp, Governor of Bavaria, 12 July 1933.
6. Rudolf Diels, *Lucifer ante portas – es spricht der erste Chef der Gestapo,* Stuttgart, 1950, Deutsche Verlagsanstalt, p. 328.
7. Heinrich Fraenkel and Roger Manvell: *Göring,* Herrsching, Pawlak, p. 95.
8. Diels, p. 408.
9. Political decision of Heinrich Müller of 28 December 1936, issued by *Amt fur Beamte der NSDAP Gau München-Oberbayern:* Bundesarchiv Berlin, personal file, Müller.
10. Walter Schellenberg: *Memoiren,* Cologne, 1956, Verlag für Politik und Wirtschaft, p. 288.

11. Opinion of Munich Kriminaldirector G, February 1945, ZStL, 415 AR 422/60.
12. Statement by Horst Kopkow, 9 May 1961: ZStL, AZ 415 AR 422/60.
13. Lina Heydrich, p. 182f.
14. See Schellenberg, *Memoiren*, pp. 163–168 and Igor Lukes; *Stalin, Benesch und der Fall Tuchatschewski* in *VfZ* pp. 527–547.
15. Speech by Heinrich Himmler, Gruppenführer meeting, Posen, 4 October 1943.
16. Notes by Rudolf Hoess about Heinrich Müller, IfZ Munich, F13/Vol. 6, sheet 340.
17. List of recommendations for award of Knights Cross of the War Service Cross with Swords (originating office, RFSS, Reichsminister for the Interior) 7 October 1944: SS personal file, Müller.
18. Lang, *Die Gestapo*, p. 54.
19. Kersten, p. 130.
20. Lina Heydrich, p. 69.
21. Hans-Bernd Gisevius, *Adolf Hitler, Versuch einer Deutung*, Gütersloh, Bertelsmann, p. 263.
22. Gisevius, p. 264.
23. Kersten, p. 118f.
24. Miroslav Kárný with Jaroslava Milotová and Margita Kárná: *Deutsche Politik im Protektorat Böhmen und Mähren unter Reinhard Heydrich, 1941–1942*: Berlin, 1997, Metropol p. 109.
25. Fraenkel and Manvell: *Himmler*, p. 48.
26. Otto Gritschneder: *Der Führer hat Sie zum Tode verurteilt, Hitlers 'Röhm-Putsch'-Morde vor Gericht*, Munich, 1993, Beck, p. 18.
27. IMT Nuremberg: *Der Nürnberger Prozess gegen die Hauptkriegsverbrecher vom 14. November 1945 – 1 October 1946*. Nuremberg, 1947, IMT (31 volumes). These reports were signed by Heydrich.
28. Hans-Bernd Gisevius: *Bus zum bitteren Ende, Vom Reichstagbrand bis zum 20 Juli 1944*, Gütersloh, 1961, Bertelsmann Lesering (special edition) p. 168.
29. Gildisch prosecution case file, from Robert M. W. Kempner, *SS im Kreuzverhör*, Munich, 1964, Rütten + Loening, p. 257.
30. Friedrich Zipfel: *Kirchenkampf in Deutschland 1933–1945*, Berlin, 1965: Walter de Gruyter, p. 64.
31. Kempner, p. 255ff.
32. Kempner, p. 255ff.
33. Gritschneder, p. 29.
34. RGBI.I, 1934, p. 529, quoted in Norbert Frei, *Der Führerstaat – Nationalsozialistische Herrschaft 1933 bis 1945*. Munich, 1987m dtv, p. 33.
35. Gritschneder, p. 51.
36. Carl Jacob Burckhardt: *Meine Danziger Mission*, Munich, 1960, dtv, p. 57.
37. Ulrich von Hassell: *Vom anderen Deutschland. Aus den nachgelassenen Tagebuchern, 1938–1944*. Zurich/Freiburg, 1946, Atlantis p. 94.

38. Bella Fromm: *Als Hitler mir die Hand küsste*, Reinbek, 1994, Rowohlt, p. 213.

39. Burckhardt, p. 57.

40. Reinhard Heydrich, *Wandlungen unseres Kampfes*, Munich/Berlin, 1935, Franz Eher Nachf. (photocopy), p. 18ff.

41. Reinhard Heydrich, *Wandlungen unseres Kampfes*, p. 18ff.

42. Friedrich Wilhelm: *Die Polizei im NS-Staat, die Geschichte ihrer Organisation im überblick*, Paderborn, 1997, Schoningh, p. 74ff.

43. Michael Wildt: *Die Judenpolitik des SD 1935–1938*, Munich, 1995: Notes from the IfZ Quarterly Journal (Vol. 71) p. 118ff.

44. Reinhard Heydrich, p. 7.

45. Reinhard Heydrich, p. 7.

46. Interview by Günther Deschner with Lina Heydrich, 20–22 March 1973.

47. Burckhardt, p. 53ff.

48. Burckhardt, p. 53ff.

49. Burckhardt, p. 53ff.

50. Quoted in Burckhardt, p. 55.

51. Jochen von Lang, *Der Adjutant Karl Wolff: Der Mann zwischen Hitler und Himmler*, Munich, 1985, Herbig, p. 65ff.

52. Interview with Lina Heydrich, *Jasmin*, 4/1969, p. 70ff.

53. Kersten, p. 120.

54. Aronson, p. 254.

55. Kersten, p. 120.

56. Ulrich Popplow: *Reinhard Heydrich oder die Aufordnung durch den Sport*, in: *Olympisches Feuer, Zeitschrift der Deutschen Olympischen Gesellschaft*, Vol. 8/1963, p. 15.

57. Horst Naude: *Erlebnisse und Erkenntnisse als politischer Beamter im Protektorat Böhren und Mähren, 1939–1945*, Munich, 1975, Fides, p. 120.

58. Quoted from Hellmut G. Haasis, *Tod in Prag – Das Attentat auf Reinhard Heydrich*, Reinbek, 2002, Rowohlt, p. 119.

59. Lina Heydrich, p. 59.

60. Schellenberg, p. 36.

61. Fraenkel and Manvell: *Himmler*, p. 167.

62. Johannes Tuchel and Reinhard Schattenfroh: *Zentrale des Terrors – Prinz-Albrecht-Strasse 8: Hauptquartier der Gestapo*, Berlin 1987, Siedler, p. 214.

63. See H. S. Hegner: *Die Reichskanzlei von 1933–1945 – Anfang und Ende des Dritten Reiches*, Frankfurt/Main, 1959, Verlag Frankfurter Bücher, p. 214ff.

64. Schellenberg, p. 41.

65. Edouard Calic, *Reinhard Heydrich, Schlüsselfigur des Dritten Reichs*, Düsseldorf 1982, Droste, p. 268.

66. Reinhard Heydrich, 'Kripo und Gestapo' in: *Düsseldorfer Nachrichten*, 29 January 1939.

67. Gestapo file, Alfred Oppenheim.

68. Author's research.
69. Joachim C. Fest, *Gesicht des Dritten Reiches – Profile einer totalitären Herrschaft*, Munich, 1993, Piper, p. 139.
70. Speech by Reinhard Heydrich on German Police Day, 1941, quoted in Günther Deschner, p. 135.

Chapter Three
1. Lina Heydrich, p. 51.
2. Hans-Jürgen Döscher, *Reichskristallnacht, – Die Novemberpogrome*, Munich, 2000, Propylaen, p. 65.
3. Interview with Eberhard Jäckel, 8 April 2002.
4. Lina Heydrich, p. 49.
5. Hermann Graml: *Reichskristallnacht: Antisemitismus und Judenverfolgung im Dritten Reich,* Munich, 1998, dtv, p. 17ff.
6. Döscher, p. 98.
7. Copy of signal, Döscher, p. 95–97.
8. Reinhard Heydrich: Erlebnisse und Erkenntnisse als politischer Beamter im Protektorat Böhren und Mähren telegram with orders for all Stapo centres: *Massnahmen gegen Juden in der heutigen Nacht*, 9 November 1938 (IMT document 3051 PS).
9. Stenographic copy of a part of the discussion regarding the Jewish question chaired by Feldmarschall Goering at the Reich Air Ministry, 12 November 1938 (IMT document 1816-PS), quoted in Deschner, p. 170.
10. Quoted in Deschner, p. 142.
11. As above, p. 143.
12. Lina Heydrich, commentary of Wilhelm Ludwig, p. 143.
13. Ian Kershaw: *Hitler 1936–1945*, Stuttgart, 2000, Deutsche Verlagsanstalt, p. 183.
14. Alfred Spiess and Heiner Lichtenstein, *Das Unternehmen Tannenberg*, Wiesbaden, 1979, Limes, p. 26f.
15. Spiess and Lichtenstein, p. 129.
16. NS newspaper report on the Gleiwitz raid.
17. Ulrich Herbert, *Best: Biographische Studien über Radikalismus, Weltanschauung und Vernunft, 1903–1989*, Bonn, 1996, Dietz p. 241.
18. Hans-Bernd Gisevius, *Wo ist Nebe? Erinnerungen an Hitlers Reichskriminaldirektor*, Zurich, 1996, Droemersche Verlagsanstalt, p. 184.
19. Michael Wildt, *Generation des Unbedingten: Das Führungskorps des Reichssicherheitshauptamtes*, Hamburg, 2002, Hamburger Edition, p. 283ff.
20. See Hans Mommsen, *Auschwitz, 17 July 1942*, Munich, 2002, p. 97.
21. Interview with Michael Wildt.
22. See Christopher R. Browning, *Der Weg zur Endlösung: Entscheidungen und Täter*, Hamburg, 2002, rororo, p. 115.

23. Hans Jansen, *Der Madagaskar-Plan, Die beabsichtigte Deportation der europischen Juden nach Madagaskar*, Munich 1997, Langen-Müller, p. 249.

24. Centre de Documentation Juivre Contemporaire, Paris: Statement of Dieter Wisliceny at Pressburg, 18 November 1946.

25. Letter from Reinhard Heydrich to Foreign Minister Ribbentrop of 24 June 1940 respecting Jewish emigration (copy PolXII136).

26. Peter Longerich: *Politik der Vernichtung – Eine Gesamtdarstellung der nationalistischen Judenverfolgung*, Munich, 1998, Piper, 273f.

27. Walter Hagen (alias Wilhelm Höttl): *Die Geheime Front: Organisationen, Personen und Aktionen des deutschen Geheimdienstes*, Linz/Vienna, 1950, Nibelungern, p.27.

28. Schellenberg, *Memoiren*, pp 36.

29. Werner Best: *Reinhard Heydrich* in: Siegfried Matlock, *Dänemark in Hitlers Hand*, Husum, 1988: Husum Druck und Verlag, p. 160ff.

30. Interview with Lina Heydrich in *Jasmin*, 4/1969, p. 70ff.

31. Schellenberg, p. 35.

32. Quoted in Helmut Krausnick, *Hitlers Einsatzgruppen, Die Truppe des Weltanschauungskriegs 1938–1942*, Frankfurt/Main, 1985, Fischer, p. 138.

33. Wildt, *Generation des Unbedingten*, p. 557.

34. Quoted from Peter Longerich: *Der ungeschriebene Befehl: Hitler und der Weg zur Endlösung*, Munich, 2001, Piper, p. 191.

35. Gisevius, p. 240.

36. Wildt, p. 464.

37. Andrej Angrick: *Besatzungspolitik und Massenmord, Die Einsatzgruppe D in der südlichen Sowjetunion 1941–1943*, Hamburg, 2003, Hamburger Edition, p. 181.

38. Statement by former member of Field Hospital 173, Franz H., on 26 May 1965, quoted in Angrick, p. 184.

39. Kersten, p. 260.

40. Angrick, p. 411.

41. Angrick, p. 411.

42. Aronson, p. 214.

43. Aronson, p. 214.

44. Angrick, p. 413.

45. Angrick, p. 91.

46. Angrick, p. 181, footnote 179.

47. Angrick, p. 181.

48. Angrick, p. 248f.

49. Statement by Albrecht Zöllner of 26 April 1962, sheet 960, quoted in Angrick, p. 248, footnote 97.

50. Lutz Hachmeister, *Der Gegnerforscher – Die Karriere des SS-Führers Franz Alfred Six*, Munich, 1998, Beck, p. 285.

51. Hachmeister, p. 290.

52. Hachmeister, p. 289.

53. Hachmeister, p. 238.
54. Hachmeister, p. 217.
55. Hachmeister, p. 43.
56. Hachmeister, p. 116.
57. Hachmeister, p. 215.
58. Hachmeister, p. 170.
59. Wildt, p. 367, footnote 244.
60. Hachmeister, p. 149.
61. Hachmeister, p. 218.
62. Hachmeister, p. 220.
63. Hachmeister, p. 231f.
64. Hachmeister, p. 290f.
65. Hachmeister, p. 267.
66. Hachmeister, p. 291f.
67. Hachmeister, p. 234.
68. Wildt, p. 321.
69. Ronald Rathert, *Verbrechen und Verschwörung: Arthur Nebe, Der Kripochef des Dritten Reiches*, Vol. 17, Münster, 2001: LIT, p. 192f.
70. Rathert, p. 65.
71. Gisevius, p. 288.
72. Rathert, p. 77.
73. Bundesarchiv, Koblenz, ZSg 134/115, Judgment p. 6f.
74. Gisevius, p. 243.
75. Gisevius, p. 243.
76. *Spiegel* series: *Das Spiel ist aus – Arthur Nebe. Glanz und Elend der deutschen Kriminalpolizei*: 2 February 1950 edition.
77. Ralf Ogorrek: *Die Einsatzgruppen und die Genesis der Endlösung.* Berlin, 1996, Metropol, p. 114.
78. Angrick, *Besatzungspolitik*, p. 370.
79. ZStl439 R-Z 18a/60, Vol. 1, statement by Dr Albert Widmann, 11 January 1960.
80. *Spiegel* series, *Nebe*: 16 March 1950 edition.
81. Rathert, p. 136.
82. *Spiegel* series, *Nebe*, 13 April 1950 edition.
83. *Spiegel* series, *Nebe*, 9 February 1950 edition.
84. Peter Klein: *Die Einsatzgruppen in der besetzten Sowjetunion 1941–42, Die Tätigkeits-und Lageberichte des Chefs der Sicherheitspolizei und des SD*, Berlin, 1997, Edition Hentrich, p. 317ff.
85. Longerich, (1) *Der ungeschriebene Befehl*, p. 101.
86. Longerich, (2) *Politik der Vernichtung*, p. 353.
87. Longerich, (2), p. 353.
88. Longerich, (2), p. 378.
89. Longerich, (2) p. 378.

90. Quoted in Helge Grabitz, *NS-Prozesse, Psychoprogramme der Beteiligten*, Heidelberg 1985: C. F. Müller Juristischer Verlag, p. 31.

91. Christian Gerlach: *Kalkulierte Mode- Deustche Wirtschafts-und Vernichtungspolitik in Weissrussland 1941–44*. Hamburg, 1999, Hamburger Edition, p. 588f.

92. Angrick, p. 174ff.

93. Angrick, p. 179.

94. *Hamburger Institut für Sozialforschung, Ausstellungskatalog Verbrechen der Wehrmacht – Dimensionen des Vernichtungskrieges, 1941–44*, Hamburg, p. 60. Copy of a letter from Generaloberst von Brauchitsch, C-in-C Army, 28 April 1941.

95. As above at page 62, Heinrich Himmler with regard to Führer's special commission, 21 May 1941.

96. As above at p. 57, discussion notes of Rittmeister Schach von Wittenau, 6 March 1941.

97. As above at p. 63, Generaloberst Halder, Chief of Army General Staff, 11 June 1941.

98. As above at p. 75, Armee-Oberkommando 6, instructions regarding presence of soldiers at SD executions, 10 August 1941.

99. As above, p. 120, extracts from the memoirs of the German Jew Heinz Rosenberg.

100. As above, p. 163.

101. Angrick, p. 374. The description of the development of the gas lorries follows his account extensively.

102. Statement of Dr Theodor Leidig, 6 February 1959, Sheet 40, ZStL 439 AR-Z 18a/60 Vol. 1.

103. As above.

104. Ogorreck, p. 214.

105. Erich Raeder: *Mein Leben* (2 volumes) Tübingen, 1956/57, Fritz Schlichtenmeyer, Vol. 2: From 1935 to Spandau, p. 117.

106. *Prager Abend*, No. 132, 8 June 1942.

107. *Prager Abend*, No. 132, 8 June 1942.

108. Pilot Georg Schirmbock, quoted in Jochen Prien: *Geschichte des Jagdgeschwaders 77* (4 volumes), Hamburg, 1992–1995: Struve Druck, p. 704.

109. Prien, p. 710.

110. *Prager Abend*, No 132, 8 June 1942.

111. Pilot Georg Schirmbock, per Prien, p. 705.

112. Interview with Eberhard Jäckel, 8 April 2002.

113. Chief of Sicherheitspolizei and SD: letter to head of SS-Personnel Main Office, SS-Gruppenführer Schmitt dated 25 January 1942 with annexed letter from Goering dated 31 July 1941 containing instructions entitled *Endlösung der Judenfrage*, IMT XXVI, 710-PS.

114. Walter Stahlecker: 'Respecting draft plan for setting up provisional guidelines for the handling of Jews in the territory of the *Reichskommissariat Ostland*' (handwritten and corrected draft) 6 August 1941, Riga State Archive, 1026-1-3.
115. Wildt, p. 613.
116. Jochen von Lang: *Das Eichmann-Protokoll – Tonbandaufzeichnungen der israelischen Verhöre*, (Tape-recorded notes of the Israeli trials), Gütersloh, Bertelsmann, p. 69.
117. Lang, p. 69.
118. Letter by courier from Heydrich to Himmler dated 19 October 1941 respecting 'Movement of Jews from the Old Reich into the Litzmannstadt Ghetto'.
119. From: Peter Witte, Michael Wildt, Martina Voigt, Dieter Pohl, Peter Klein, Christian Gerlach, Christoph Dieckmann and Andrej Angrick, *Der Dienstkalendar Heinrich Himmlers 1941/1942*: Hamburg, 1999, Hans Christians, p. 246.
120. Goebbels, *Tagebücher*, diary entry for 13 December 1941: quoted in Christian Gerlach: *Krieg, Ernährung, Völkermord: Deutsche Vernichtungspolitik im Zweiten Weltkrieg*, Zurich, 2001: Pendo, p. 114.
121. Robert M. W. Kempner: *Eichmann und Komplizen*, Zurich, 1961, Europa Verlag, p. 72.
122. Witte *et al*, p. 293.

Chapter Four
1. *Der Neue Tag*, 20 November 1941.
2. Schellenberg, p. 225.
3. Gitta Sereny, *Albert Speer: Sein Ringen mit der Wahrheit*, Munich, 2001: Goldmann, p. 254.
4. Guido Knopp, *Hitlers Helfer* (2 volumes), Munich, 2000: C. Bertelsmann, Vol. 1, p. 168.
5. Fröhlich, Elke: *Die Tagebücher von Joseph Goebbels* (15 volumes, 1923–1945), Munich, 1994–2000, K. G. Saur.
6. Miroslav Kárny with Jaroslava Milotová and Margita Kárná: *Deutsche Politik im Protektorat Böhmen und Mähren unter Reinhard Heydrich, 1941–1942*, Berlin, 1997, Metropol, p. 103f.
7. As above, p. 105.
8. As above, p. 49.
9. As above, p. 205.
10. *Der Neue Tag*, 20 November 1941.
11. Secret speech of Heydrich, 2 October 1941 per Kárny (6) above, p. 115f.
12. Kárny, p. 116.
13. Kárny, p. 117.
14. Kárny, p. 118.
15. Kárny, p. 118.

16. Gustav von Schmoller: *Heydrich im Protektorat Böhmen und Mähren*, in: *Vierteljahrhefte für Zeitgeschichte, 27/1979*, pp. 626–645.

17. Kárny, p. 194.

18. Kárny, p. 202.

19. Cited in Kárny, p. 237.

20. Wilhelm Dennler, *Die böhmische Passion*, Freiburg, 1953: Dikreiter, Landesarchiv Schleswig-Holstein, Abt46Q1, No. 123.

21. Heydrich's letter regarding clamp-down on Swingkids, see www.bikonline.de <http://www.bikonline.de/>.

22. Document of 15 February 1942: Central State Archive, Prague (SUAP).

23. Walter Schellenberg, *Memoiren*, Cologne, 1956, p. 41.

24. Kersten, p. 125.

25. Kersten, p. 126

26. Schellenberg, p. 41.

27. Ulrich Popplow: *Reinhard Heydrich oder die Aufordnung durch den Sport* in: *Olympisches Feuer, Zeitschrift der deutschen Olympischen Gesellschaft*, Vol. 8, 1963, p. 14f.

28. Letter from Ernst Hoffmann, 26 January 1965 (copy), p.2, IfZ, Munich.

29. Popplow, p. 15.

30. *Völkischer Beobachter*, 3 December 1941.

31. Hans Joachim Teichler: *Internationale Sportpolitik in Dritten Reich*, Schorndorf, 1991, p. 344ff.

32. Popplow, p. 16.

33. Popplow, p. 15.

34. Interview with Edouard Husson.

35. Robert M. W. Kempner *Eichmann und Komplizen*, Zurich, 1961, Europa Verlag, p. 113.

36. Browning, p. 102ff.

37. Browning, p. 106.

38. Browning, p. 111.

39. Quoted in Mark Roseman: *Die Wannseekonferenz, Wie die NS-Bürokratie den Holocaust organisierte*. Munich, 2002, Propylaen, p. 126

40. Kurt Pätzold und Erika Schwarz: *Tagesordnung: Judenmord. Die Wannseekonferenz am 20 Januar 1942*, Berlin, 1992, Metropol, p. 105f.

41. Pätzold/Schwarz, p. 174.

42. Quoted in Roseman, p. 142.

43. As above, p. 142.

44. Walter Bargatzky: *Hotel Majestic, Ein Deutscher im besetzten Frankreich*, Freiburg, 1987, Herder, p. 103f.

45. Goebbels, diary entry 27 March 1942 respecting events against Jews in the Lublin District, quoted in Longerich, p. 504.

46. Calic, p. 523f.

47. Interview with Charles Sydnor.

48. Lina Heydrich, p.100f.
49. Letter from Lina Heydrichs to Herr Schneiders (Holland), 12 January 1962: NIOD NL, Sig.69/A a 2/3.
50. Kárny, p. 278.

Chapter Five
1. The description of the assassination is based on Miroslav Ivanov: *Das Attentat auf Heydrich*, Augsburg, 2000, Bechtermünz, p. 229f.
2. Hellmut G. Haasis: *Tod in Prag, das Attentat auf Reinhard Heydrich*, Reinbek, 2002, Rowohlt, p. 101f.
3. Interview with Alois Vincenc Honek.
4. Günther Deschner, 'Reinhard Heydrich, Technokrat der Sicherheit', p. 290, in: Roland Smelseer and Rainer Zitelmann: *Die braune Elite, 22 biographische Skizzen*, Darmstadt, 1990, Wissenschaftlich Buchgesellschaft.
5. Haasis, p. 56.
6. Kersten, p. 121.
7. Lina Heydrich, p. 119.
8. Haasis, p. 111.
9. Deschner, p. 102.
10. Lina Heydrich, p. 47.
11. Haasis, p. 24.
12. Haasis, p. 112.
13. Kárny *et al: Deutsche Politik im Protektorat Böhmen und Mähren*, Doc. 77.
14. Deschner, p. 109.
15. Himmler's speech to SS-Gruppenführer at Posen, 4 October 1943.
16. Lina Heydrich, p. 48.
17. From Himmler's speech at Heydrich's funeral in: RSHA: *Meine Ehre heisst Treue, Reinhard Heydrich*.
18. Author's researches.
19. Kersten, p. 117.
20. Henry Picker: *Hitlers Tischgesprche im Führerhauptquartier, 1941–1942*, Bonn 1951, Athenaeum, p. 97.
21. Haasis, p. 116.
22. As (17).
23. Kersten, quoted in: Ulrich Popplow: *Reinhard Heydrich oder die Aufordnung durch den Sport*, in *Olympisches Feuer, Zeitschrift der Deutschen Olympischen Gesellschaft*, Vol. 8, August 1963, p. 20.
24. Adolf Hitler's speech at Heydrich's funeral, as per (17).
25. Jaroslav Cvancara: *Nekomu zivot, nekomu smrt. Ceskoslovensky odboj a nacisticka okupacni moc 1941–1943*, Prague, 1997, Laguna/Proxima, p. 112ff.
26. Picker, p. 246.
27. Protocol, Karl Hermann Frank, 28 May 1942 quoted in: Kárny *et al*, at (13) above.

28. As above, p. 280.
29. As above, p. 285.
30. Picker, p. 176f.
31. Lidice, community publication, 1998, p. 38.
32. Lidice, community publication, 1998, p. 39.
33. Events in the church based on Haasis, p. 145ff.
34. Haasis, p. 152.
35. Brochure: *National Memorial for the Heroes of the Heydrichiade: Place of Reconciliation,* Prague, 2002, p. 7ff.
36. Interview with Hana Vorel.
37. Uwe Naumann: *Lidice, ein böhmisches Dorf.* Frankfurt/Main, 1983, Röderberg, p. 77.
38. Gotz Aly: Macht, Geist, Wahn: *Kontinuiatt deutschen Denkens,* Berlin, 1997, p. 189.

Chapter Six
1. Lina Heydrich, p. 118.
2. Lina Heydrich, p. 123.
3. Lina Heydrich, p. 126.
4. Führer-HQ, 20 April 1943, also see Lina Heydrich, p. 110ff.
5. *Beweisführung Berufsenstscheidung Entnazifierungs-Berufungsausschuss Land Schleswig-Holstein, Gesch-Zeich. VIII/6/Ia, Kiel, 12 January 1951.*
6. Author's interview with Helena Vovsova, Prague.
7. Author's interview with Helena Vovsova.
8. Author's interview with Helena Vovsova.
9. Author's interview with Helena Vovsova.
10. Walter Grunwald, Letter to Heinz Golz, Chairman of Theresienstadt Committee, Algaras, 14 August 1949.
11. Walter Grunwald, Letter to Heinz Golz, 14 August 1949.
12. Author's interview with Helena Vovsova.
13. Lina Heydrich, p. 128.
14. Lina Heydrich, p. 124.
15. Milan Platovsky *Survive and Live, Memoirs of a Czech in Chile,* Olympia, Prague, 1999.
16. Service Report on Fritz Brandstädter, Lina Heydrich file, If2M.
17. Letter from Heinrich Himmler to Lina Heydrich, 7 August 1943 in Lina Heydrich, p. 72f.
18. Lina Heydrich, p. 135.
19. Hans-Georg Wiedemann: 'Peter Thomas Heydrichs Erinnerungen an seinen Onkel Reinhard Heydrich', unpublished manuscript, 2002, p. 12.
20. Wiedemann, p. 12.
21. Wiedemann, p. 12.
22. Wiedemann, p. 12.

23. Letter from Lina Heydrich to her parents on Fehmarn, 6 February 1945, Lina Heydrich file, If2M.

24. Letter from Lina Heydrich to her parents, 6 February 1945, Lina Heydrich file, If2M.

25. Lina Heydrich, p. 135f.

26. Author's interview with Helena Vovsova.

27. Author's interview with Helena Vovsova.

28. Lina Heydrich, p. 140.

29. *Entnazifierungsbogen*: file Lina Heydrich, If2M.

30. English version (19 January 1949) of verdict against Lina Heydrich of 19 October 1948, People's Special Court, Prague, XIV Div. XIII, Lina Heydrich file, If2M.

31. Lina Heydrich, p. 145.

32. *Hauptentnazifierungsausschuss für den Landeskreis Oldenburg in Holstein, Berufungsentscheidung vom 12 Januar 1951, Geschäftszeichen VIII/6/Ia*: file Lina Heydrich If2M.

33. Copy deposition, witness Rita Griebel, file Lina Heydrich If2M.

34. *Hauptentnazifierungsausschuss für den Landeskreis Oldenburg in Holstein, Berufungsentscheidung vom 12 Januar 1951, Geschäftszeichen VIII/6/Ia*: file Lina Heydrich If2M.

35. *Hauptentnazifierungsausschuss für den Landeskreis Oldenburg in Holstein, Berufungsentscheidung vom 12 Januar 1951, Geschäftszeichen VIII/6/Ia*: file Lina Heydrich If2M.

36. Decision of *Landessozialgerichts*, 20 June 1958, p.4, *Landesarchiv Schleswig-Holstein, Abt. 794 Schleswig No 2 – Urteil 1952.*

37. Opinon of Michael Freund, 5 May 1956, p.3: as (36).

38. Dr Schönleitner, BmfA, to the *Landessozialgericht*, 5 July 1955: as (36).

39. Landessozialgericht Schleswig, lfile L4W1014/1015/54, 27 June 1958, basis for judgment, pp. 23–25, as (36).

40. Landessozialgericht Schleswig, lfile L4W1014/1015/54, 27 June 1958, basis for judgment, pp. 23–25, as (36).

41. Landessozialgericht Schleswig, lfile L4W1014/1015/54, 27 June 1958, basis for judgment, pp. 23–25, as (36).

42. Author's interview with Karl-Wilhelm Klahn.

43. Letter from Lina Heydrich to Mr Schneiders (Holland) dated 12 January 1962: NIOD NL Sig 69/A a 2/3.

44. *De Nieuwe Dag*, (Supplement *Plus*), 21 August 1965.

45. Lina Heydrich, interview for *Jasmin*, April 1969, p. 70ff.

46. *The New York Times*, 7 February 1979.

47. Lina Heydrich, p. 161.

48. Author's telephone conversation with Heider Heydrich.

49. Author's interview with Arno Ausborn.

50. *Fehmarnisches Tageblatt*, 16 August 1985.
51. Author's interview with Laurenz Demps.
52. Author's research.
53. H. H. Norden: *SS-Obergruppenführer Heydrich – An Exemplary Life*: Neo-Nazi web-site www.nazi-laucknsdapao.com <http://www.nazi-laucknsdapao.com/>.
54. Website as (53).
55. See speech by Elie Wiesel to the Bundestag, Berlin, 27 January 2000.
56. Witness statement by Hans Frank, IMT, Nuremberg.
57. Lina Heydrich, p. 97.
58. Witness statement by Ernst Kaltenbrunner, IMT Nuremberg.
59. Cross-examination Otto Ohlendorf, IMT Nuremberg.
60. Instruction on Streckenbach file, Gos Arxiv Rossiskoj Federacii (GARF), Moscow.
61. Author's interview with Jörg Friedrich.
62. Author's interview with Michael Wildt, 20 March 2002.
63. Hannah Arendt: *Eichmann in Jerusalem, ein Bericht von der Banalitt des Bösen*, Munich, 1965, Piper, p. 52.
64. Hans Safrian: *Eichmann und seine Gehilfen*, Frankfurt/Main, 1997, Fischer.
65. *Das Parlament*, nos 6–7, 2–9 February 2001, p. 13.
66. Wiedemann, pp. 19 and 24.
67. Wiedemann, pp. 19 and 24
68. Letter from Hans-Georg Wiedemann to the author, 23 November 2002.
69. Gitta Sereny: *Das deutsche Trauma, eine heilende Wunde*. Munich, 2002: C. Bertelsmann, p. 406.
70. Author's interview with Marte Beyer.
71. *De Nieuwe Dag*, (Supplement *Plus*), 21 August 1965.
72. Author's interview with Marte Beyer.
73. Letter dated 27 January 2002 from Heider Heydrich to the author.
74. Author's telephone interview with Reinhard Beyer Heydrich.
75. Author's telephone enquiry.
76. Tuwiah Friedman: *Three SS-leaders Responsible for Carrying Out the Final Solution of the Jewish Question in Europe were: Heydrich – Eichmann – Müller: A Documentary Collection of SS and Gestapo Documents on the Extermination of the European Jews, 1939–1945*: Haifa 1993, Makhon 1e-dokumentatsyah be-Yi'sra'el.

Appendix A

Chronology of Genocide

1933
22 March. The first concentration camp for opponents of the National Socialist regime and Jews is established at Dachau.

1935
15 September. The Nuremberg Laws relegate Jews to be second-class citizens.

1938
26 August. Following the annexation of Austria to the Reich, the SS begins a programme to compel Jewish emigration.

9 November. After the assassination of a German diplomat in Paris by a Jew, the Nazis murder ninety-one Jews and destroy synagogues and private property throughout Germany, this event being known as Reichskristallnacht ('The Night of Broken Windows in the Reich').

1939
24 January. Founding of the 'Reich Centre for Jewish Emigration' by Heydrich.

30 January. In a Reichstag speech, Adolf Hitler warns that 'the Jewish race in Europe will be destroyed' in the event of another World War.

1 September. The German invasion of Poland causes the outbreak of World War II. By May 1940, SS-Einsatzgruppen have murdered sixty thousand Poles and Jews in the conquered territory.

21 September. Heydrich forces all Polish Jews to live in city ghettoes.

27 September. The Gestapo and SS Security Service (SD) are combined into the Reichssicherheitshauptamt (RSHA).

October. Hitler approves the euthanasia of mentally disadvantaged persons, of whom seventy thousand are killed by 1941. The first mobile gas chambers are tried out.

12 October. Germany annexes areas of western Poland and sets up in the remaining territory not under Soviet jurisdiction a *General-Gouvernement* (GG) into which Jews, Poles and gypsies are to be deported.

18 October. It is proposed that Jews from Austria and Bohemia should set up a 'reservation' for themselves at Nisko on the San river, but this RSHA plan falls through.

23 November. All Jews in the GG are required to wear on their clothing a yellow six-pointed star with the word 'Jude' at its centre.

1940

February. Deportations of Jews from the Old Reich into the GG begin at Stettin.

24 March. Hermann Goering orders a temporary stop to Jewish deportations to Poland because the ghettoes are overfull.

27 April. Heinrich Himmler orders the building of a concentration camp at Auschwitz.

15 August. Adolf Eichmann of the RSHA investigates the feasibility of a plan to ship out all European Jews to Madagascar. This plan is abandoned as unworkable for lack of transport in early 1942.

12 October. Creation of the Warsaw Ghetto, which is sealed off on 15 November.

1941

1 March. Himmler visits Auschwitz and orders the building of a large camp at Birkenau.

26 March. Heydrich tells Goering of his plans for 'the Solution of the Jewish Question'.

20 May. An RSHA instruction mentions the 'imminent Final Solution'.

22 June. Following the German attack on the Soviet Union, *Einsatzkommandos* under Heydrich's orders commence mass executions of Jews. From August 1941, women and children are also included in the shootings. In the summer and autumn the massacres claim hundreds of thousands of people, more than 160,000 persons in Bessarabia alone.

2 July. Heydrich gives detailed orders for the murder of Jews and communist functionaries in the USSR.

15 July. Himmler introduces his *Generalplan Ost* which envisages German settlement in Slav areas to the cost of the indigenous populations.

31 July. Goering orders Heydrich to prepare 'the Total Solution of the Jewish Question in areas of German Influence'.

1 September. The wearing of the Yellow Star is required by Jews in the German Reich.

3 September. Successful trials are held at Auschwitz in which nine hundred Russian prisoners are killed using Zyklon B gas.

29/30 September. In a ravine at Babi Yar, a German Einsatzkommando shoots dead more than thirty-three thousand Kiev Jews.

12 October. 'Bloody Sunday at Stanislau' in the former Polish province of Eastern Galicia, twelve thousand Jews are shot dead.

13 October. Himmler orders SS-Polizeiführer Odilo Globocnik to set up a death camp in the GG, and on 1 November work on the camp at Belzec is begun.

15 October. The great 'drive' to the East begins with the deportation of twenty thousand Jews from Reich home territory. Another thirty-five thousand follow in November.

23 October. All Jews in the territories under German control are banned from leaving.

25 October. Eichmann approves the deployment of mobile gas chambers for mass-murders in the East. From November, these vehicles are at Minsk.

29/30 November. Fourteen thousand local Jews, and a thousand recently arrived by train from Berlin are murdered at Riga by shooting.

8 December. At Chelmo death camp in Poland, mobile gas chambers are used for the first time for the disposal of 152,000 Jews and gypsies.

12 December. After the declaration of war on the United States, Hitler demands the 'extermination of Jewry'. General-Gouverneur Hans Frank speaks on 16 December of the planned killing of 3.5 million Jews in the GG.

1942

20 January. At the Wannsee Conference in Berlin, Heydrich obtains agreement from the State Secretaries for his plans for 'The Final Solution' by the murder of up to eleven million European Jews.

20 February. According to official figures, since June 1941 2.5 million of 3.9 million Soviet prisoners of war have died of hunger, disease and hypothermia.

6 March. Eichmann reports the third wave of deportations (fifty-five thousand 'Reichsjuden'). Eleven days later the first deportation train arrives at the Belzec death camp.

1 May. Heydrich approves retrospectively the murder of a hundred thousand Jews in the Warthegau.

Beginning of May. After Heydrich's visit, the anti-Jewish 'actions' in White Russia are stepped up: by August, fifty-five thousand are murdered and another twenty-six thousand German Jews in the concentration camp at Minsk.

4–15 May. Eleven thousand Jews deported to Lodz in the previous autumn are gassed to death. Tens of thousands of Polish Jews die in the gas chambers at Belzec and Sobibor.

5 May. For the first time, all Jews arriving at Auschwitz-Birkenau by rail transport from eastern Upper Silesia are gassed to death immediately.

10 June. In reprisal for the assassination of Heydrich, the SS razes the village of Lidice to the ground, shoots all the men and deports the women and children.

4 July. Beginning of the selection process of Jews upon arrival on the ramp at Birkenau. This heralds the industrial mass-murder in gas chambers which by 1944 takes the lives of 1.1 million persons.

July to October. The machinery in the death camps is now running full out: at Treblinka 280,000 Jews die, at Sobibor 250,000, at Belzec over 100,000. The genocide is code-named *Aktion Reinhard* to honour of the memory of Reinhard Heydrich.

17 July. Himmler watches a gassing at Birkenau and orders the extermination of all Jews in the GG by the year's end. By then it will be 1.2 million.

28 October. For the first time Jews are deported from the 'assembly camp' Theresienstadt in Bohemia to Auschwitz and gassed to death there.

29 October. Himmler reports to Hitler that during the offensive against 'partisan bands' a total of 362,000 Jews were executed between August and November.

1943

January. A new wave of murders begins with the extermination of ten thousand ghetto inhabitants at Lemberg.

19 April. Statistician Richard Korherr reports that the number of Jews in the expanded Reich territory had 'reduced by about 3.1 million people' between 1933 and 1943.

16 May. After fighting lasting four weeks, the SS puts down the Jewish resistance in the Warsaw ghetto. The fifty-six thousand survivors are put to death at Treblinka.

21 June. Himmler orders the clearing of the ghettoes in the Baltic States and White Russia; their inhabitants are taken to death camps.

6 October. In a speech to SS men at Posen, Himmler describes the 'destruction' of the Jews as a proud duty of the National Socialist State.

19 October. *Aktion Reinhard*, responsible for killing off two million people since 1942, is formally wound down. By the end of November, the camps at Belzec, Sobibor and Treblinka have been shut down.

3 November. The remaining Jews in the Lublin area are liquidated during *Aktion Erntefest* (Harvest Festival).

1944

27 April. The deporation of 380,000 Hungarian Jews commences. Of these, about 250,000 are gassed at Auschwitz.

23 July. The Red Army liberates the first death camp, at Maidanek in Poland.

October. *Aktion 1005* ordered by Himmler, the disinterment and cremation of hundreds of thousands of corpses in order to conceal traces of the genocide, is concluded.

2 November. Himmler orders an end to the gassings in the concentration camps, but shootings continue.

1945

27 January. Soviet troops reach the death camp at Auschwitz-Birkenau, where they find seven thousand survivors. Sixty-six thousand had been evacuated beforehand in 'death marches'.

30 April. The US Army liberates Dachau. Hitler commits suicide in Berlin.

Appendix B

Biographical Notes

Adolf Hitler (1889–1945)

Of Austrian birth, but later naturalised German, from at least age sixteen was a follower of Schonerer and Lueger, Austrian nationalists whose doctrine was based on anti-semitism. Hitler, a music-lover and neo-pagan, was very impressed by Germanic myth, and Wagner's interpretations of it in operatic form. Fought in World War I on Western Front, was decorated with the Iron Cross, First and Second Class. Rabidly anti-Jewish, in 1921 he became head of the NSDAP, 1933 led NSDAP to power in Germany through democratic elections. On the death of President Hindenburg on 2 August 1934 Hitler combined the offices of Reichs Chancellor and Reichs President in personal union and deemed himself 'Führer and Reichs Chancellor'. The enabling legislation was unconstitutional, and accordingly everything Hitler did subsequently by virtue of this composite office was also unconstitutional. The Third Reich was an absolute dictatorship. Hitler was probably able to achieve this because others were convinced of his occult powers. Himmler believed that Hitler was in contact with another world which manipulated him (Kersten, *Himmler*): Hess stated in a national radio broadcast in 1934 that 'Higher forces act through Hitler in fulfilment of Destiny' (Konrad Heiden, The *Führer*, London, 1944), and his only friend of late childhood, August Kubizek, stated that he had seen how Hitler was taken over by 'a second Ego' in 1905 (Kubizek: *The Young Hitler I Knew*, Greenhill Books, 2006). Hitler was responsible for starting World War II by ignoring British and French ultimata to withdraw German troops from Poland in September 1939. Although no conclusive document exists, it is certain that Hitler ordered the murder of the Jews since it is impossible that either Himmler, Goering or Heydrich could have been running a secret independent programme of which Hitler was ignorant. Hitler valued Heydrich as his most efficient executioner and dubbed him 'The Man with the Iron Heart'.

Heinrich Himmler (1900–1945)

1929–1945 Reichsführer-SS, head of German police, created SS and subordinated police to it. 1931 accepted Heydrich into SS organisation as surveillance officer. 1934 destroyed power of SA under Ernst Röhm: planned 'germanisation of East' and set up system of death camps to achieve aims of Nazi racial ideologies. 1943 Reichs Interior Minister. April 1945 deprived of all offices by Hitler for negotiating with Allies: captured by British after capitulation: suicide by cyanide pill.

Hermann Goering (1893–1946)

Reichsmarschall. World War I fighter pilot, commanded JG Richthofen. Hitler's Deputy Leader. 1922 joined NSDAP: February 1923 appointed to command SA, participated in failed Hitler Beerhall putsch in Munich, fled abroad, 1926 returned to Germany, 1928–1948 Reichsminister, 1932–1945 President of Reichstag, 1933–1945 Minister-president of Prussia, 1933 Reichs Minister for Aviation 1935–1945 Luftwaffe commander-in-chief, 1940 Reichsmarschall. Lost favour with Hitler after failure in Battle of Britain. Heydrich received from Goering in Hitler's name formal instructions for the deportation and extermination of Jews. April 1945 arrested by SS at Berchtesgaden for treason, released early May and captured by US forces: 1946 tried at Nuremberg, condemned to death, cheated hangman by taking poison.

Joseph Goebbels (1897–1945)

From 1926 Hitler's chief propagandist. 1929 NSDAP Gauleiter for Berlin, head of Reich NSDAP Propaganda Office. 1933–1945 Reich Minister for Propaganda, a tireless agitator against Jews and opponents of the regime. 1944 Reichs Plenipotentiary for Total War, 30 April 1945 Reichs Chancellor by Hitler's Last Will and Testament: 2 May 1945 suicide in Berlin bunker.

Martin Bormann (1900–1945?)

Reichsleiter, head of NSDAP. 1924 convicted of political slaying. 1933 Under Rudolf Hess rose to be NSDAP financial administrator: May 1941, after Hess defected to Britain, became 'grey eminence' of Third Reich, always at Hitler's side and his 'agenda manager', so that access to Hitler was generally channelled through Bormann: recommended Heydrich as Reichs-Protektor in Czechoslovakia with direct access to Hitler in order to weaken position of Bormann's rival Himmler. 30 April 1945 executor of Hitler's Last Will and Testament, probably killed a few days later after escaping from Berlin bunker.

Heinrich Müller (1900–1945?)

Head of Gestapo. Originally an opponent of Nazism but admirer of Stalin's terror methods: 1933 transferred by Heydrich from Munich Kripo into Nazi police system: 1939 joined NSDAP, head of RSHA Amt IV (Gestapo): immediate superior of Eichmann (q.v.), to whom he passed down orders for the liquidation of Jews, concentration camp inmates and Russian PoWs: last heard of, Berlin May 1945.

Adolf Eichmann (1906–1962)

RSHA spokesman and administrator for Jewish Affairs. Rose through Austrian SS: 1934 responsible for 'Jewish Question' at SHA: organised emigration schemes for Jews at centres in Vienna, Prague and Berlin: from 1939 head of department RSHA IVB (deportations): 1940–1941 feasibility study, forced resettlement of Jews on Madagascar: January 1942 secretary to Wannsee Conference, administered deportation policy: after war fled to Argentina: 1960 kidnapped by Israeli agents at Buenos Aires: 1961 tried in Israel: 1962 executed.

Werner Best (1903–1989)

Heydrich's representative. 1931 joined SS: theoretician and administrator: 1935–1940 collaborated in expansion of SD and Gestapo: 1940 Heydrich fell out with him at RSHA over his fastidiousness: 1942–1945 Reichs Plenipotentiary for Denmark: 1947 sentenced to death in Denmark: 1951 reprieved and deported: spared by German justice.

Karl Hermann Frank (1898–1946)

Heydrich's representative in Prague. Sudeten German, NSDAP politician: 1939 after occupation of Czechoslovakia Chief of Police and Secretary of State under Reichs-Protektor Konstantin von Neurath and Heydrich: although not in favour of harsh reprisals after assassination of Heydrich shared guilt for massacres at Lidice and Lezaky: not appointed as successor to Heydrich: 1946 executed at Prague.

Bruno Streckenbach (1902–1977)

SS-Führer: Freikorps street-fighter: 1930 joined NSDAP, SS and SA: 1933–1939 head of Hamburg, Gestapo: headed massacres by Einsatzgruppen and police in Poland: 1941 Chief of Personnel, RSHA: 1942 took over as head of RSHA after demise of Heydrich, but replaced by Kaltenbrunner, 1943: later at front with Waffen-SS: commander 8th SS Div. Florian Geyer, Soviet PoW: 1956 released: never arrested in Germany.

Otto Ohlendorf (1907–1951)

SS-Einsatzkommando leader. 1936 joined SS and SD: 1939 head of RSHA Amt III (Inland Espionage): valued by Heydrich for his loyalty and fanaticism: 1941/1942 as head of Einsatzgruppe D responsible for murder of ninety thousand Jews and other 'enemies of the Reich' in USSR: 1946 at his trial did not deny the allegations but said he had had no option because it had been ordered by Hitler: 1951 executed at Landsberg.

Walter Schellenberg (1910–1952)

Head of espionage, RSHA: 1934 as young lawyer joined SD: active in Czechoslovakia and Holland: 1941 head of SD Foreign Espionage: favoured use of SS-Einsatzkommandos in East: 1942 broke up Admiral Canaris' Abwehr and absorbed it into RSHA: escaped severe penalty after war for his work saving concentration-camp Jews in 1945.

Rudolf Hoess (1900–1947)

Commandant of Auschwitz: Right-wing extremist WWI veteran: 1924 convicted of political slaying: 1933 SS-guard at Dachau and Sachsenhausen concentration camps: discussions with Himmler and Heydrich on transportation and methods of killing: twice Commandant, Auschwitz death camp (1940–1943, 1944–1945): at his trial accepted guilt for deaths of three million Jews: hanged at Auschwitz.

Franz Alfred Six (1909–1975)

1932 joined SA: 1935 joined Heydrich's security services as expert on journalism: led 'scientific research into opponents of regime': 1939 head of RSHA Amt VII: 1940 volunteered Waffen-SS: 1941 head of Vorkommando Moskau, whose members executed over a hundred civilians at Smolensk: 1948 received twenty years' imprisonment at Einsatzgruppen war-crimes trials, 1952 released: lived out remainder of his life quietly in Federal Republic.

Arthur Nebe (1894–1945)

Recognised criminologist in Weimar Republic: 1931 joined NSDAP and SS: 1936 head of Reichskriminalpolizeiamt under Heydrich: 1939 head of RSHA Amt V: 1940–1941 designed carbon-monoxide gas chambers, probably in charge T-4 operation in Germany which killed seventy thousand mentally disadvantaged persons: 1941 as head of Einsatzkommando D in Russia, responsible for thousands of murders: responsible for killing of fifty RAF escapers from Stalag Luft III prisoner-of-war camp: at some time before early 1944 joined circle of conspirators around Hans Oster and Ludwig Beck: in hiding after failure of 20-July plot: betrayed and arrested early 1945: executed by SS for treason, 3 March 1945.

Herbert Backe (1896–1947)

'Food Dictator' of the Third Reich: Russian-German, hated Slavs as much as Jews. 1922 SA-member, later SS: 1933 State Secretary, from 1942 *de facto* Minister for Farming: planned the wartime food supply for the Reich at the expense of starvation for millions in the East: committed suicide while in Allied custody. A radical personality lacking human emotions, he became Heydrich's friend and collaborator.

Bibliography

Amort, Cestmir. *Heydrichiáda*. Prague, 1965: Nase Vojsko-SPB.

Arad, Yitzhak, Shmuel Krakowski and Shmuel Spector. *The Einsatzgruppen Reports. Selections from the Dispatches of the Nazi Death Squads' Campaign Against the Jews, July 1941– January 1943*. New York, 1989: Holocaust Library.

Aronson, Shlomo. *Reinhard Heydrich und die Frühgeschichte von Gestapo und SD*. Stuttgart, 1971: DVA.

Arzt, Heinz. *Mörder in Uniform. Nazi-Verbrecherorganisationen*. Rastatt, 1987: Moewig.

Berschel, Holger. *Bürokratie und Terror. Das Judenreferat der Gestapo Düsseldorf 1935–1945*. Essen, 2001: Klartext.

Best, Werner. 'Reinhard Heydrich'. In: Matlock, Siegfried. *Dänemark in Hitlers Hand. Der Bericht des Reichsbevollmachtigten Werner Best*. Husum, 1988: Husum Verlag, p. 160ff.

Birn, Ruth Bettina. *Die Höheren SS- und Polizeiführer. Himmlers Vertreter im Reich und in den besetzten Gebieten*. Düsseldorf, 1986: Droste.

Browder, George C. *Hitler's Enforcers. The Gestapo and the SS Security Service in the Nazi Revolution*. New York/Oxford, 1996: Oxford University Press.

Burgess, Alan. *Seven Men at Daybreak*. London, 1960: Evans Bros.

Calic, Edouard. *Heydrich – l'homme clef du IIIe Reich*. Paris, 1982: Opera Mundi.

Crankshaw, Edward. *Gestapo. Instrument of Tyranny*. London, 1956: Putnam. Reprinted London, 2002: Greenhill.

Cvancara, Jaroslav. *Akce atentat*. Prague, 1991: Magnet-Press.

Cvancara, Jaroslav. *Nekomu zivot, nekomu smrt. Ceskoslovensky odboj a nacisticka oku-pacní moc 1941–1943.* Prague, 1997: Laguna/Proxima.

Delarue, Jacques. *Histoire de la Gestapo.* Paris, 1962. [English edition: *The History of the Gestapo.* London, 1964: Macdonald.]

Dennler, Wilhelm. *Die böhmische Passion.* Freiburg, 1953: Dikreiter.

Deschner, Günther. *Reinhard Heydrich. Statthalter der totalen Macht.* Esslingen, 1999: Bechtle.

—— 'Reinhard Heydrich – Technokrat der Sicherheit'. In: Smelser, Ronald and Rainer Zitelmann. *Die braune Elite. 22 biographische Skizzen.* Darmstadt, 1990: Wissenschaftliche Buchgesellschaft.

Diewald-Kerkmann, Gisela. *Politische Denunziation im NS-Regime oder Die kleine Macht der 'Volksgenossen'.* Bonn, 1995: JHW Dietz Nachfolger.

Friedman, Tuwiah. *Drei verantwortliche SS-Führer für die Durchführung der Endlösung der Judenfrage in Europa waren: Heydrich – Eichmann – Müller: Eine dokumentarische Sammlung von SS- und Gestapo-Dokumenten über die Vernichtung der Juden Europas 1939–1945.* Haifa, 1993: Makhon le-dokumentatsyah be-Yi'sra'el.

—— *Himmlers Teufels-General: SS- und Polizeiführer Globocnik in Lublin und ein Bericht über die Judenvernichtung im General-Gouvernement Polen, 1941–1944.* Haifa, 1994: Makhon le-dokumentatsyah be-Yi'sra'el.

Gellately, Robert. *The Gestapo and German Society. Enforcing Racial Policy 1933–1945.* Oxford, 1991: Clarendon.

Georg, Enno. *Die wirtschaftlichen Unternehmungen der SS.* Stuttgart, 1963: DVA.

Graber, G.S. *The Life and Times of Reinhard Heydrich.* New York, 1980: David McKay. [London, 1981: Hale].

Haasis, Hellmut G. *Tod in Prag. Das Aattentat auf Reinhard Heydrich.* Reinbek, 2002: Rowohlt.

Hamsik, Dusan, and Jiri Prazak. *Bomba pro Heydricha.* Prague, 1964: Mláda fronta.

Hoffmann, Peter. *Die Sicherheit des Diktators. Hitlers Leibwachen, Schutzmaßnahmen, Residenzen, Hauptquartiere.* Munich 1975: Piper [English edition: *Hitler's Personal Security.* London, 1979: Macmillan Press].

Höhne, Heinz. *Der Orden unter dem Totenkopf. Die Geschichte der SS.* Augsburg, 2000: Weltbild. [English edition: *The Order of the Death's Head.* London, 1969: Secker and Warburg.]

Honzik, M. *Za Heydrichem otaznik (Fragezeichen hinter Heydrich).* Prague, 1989: Prace.

Ivanov, Miroslav. *Das Attentat auf Heydrich.* Augsburg, 2000: Bechtermünz.

Jäckel, Eberhard. 'From Barbarossa to Wannsee: The Role of Reinhard Heydrich'. In Shmuel Almog. *The Holocaust: History and Memory – Essays*

Presented in Honor of Israel Gutman. Jerusalem, 2001: Yad Vashem Publications.

Johnson, Eric. *The Nazi Terror. Gestapo, Jews and Ordinary Germans*. London, 1999: John Murray.

Kalibová, Miroslava. *Lidice*. Lidice, 1998: Kokos.

Kárny, Miroslav with Jaroslava Milotová and Margita Kárná. *Deutsche Politik im 'Protektorat Böhmen und Mähren' unter Reinhard Heydrich 1941–1942*. Berlin, 1997: Metropol.

Kershaw, Ian. *Hitler 1889–1936: Hubris*. London, 1999: Allen Lane, The Penguin Press.

—— *Hitler, 1936–1945: Nemesis*. London, 2000: Allen Lane, The Penguin Press.

Kersten, Felix. *Totenkopf und Treue. Heinrich Himmler ohne Uniform. Aus den Tagebuchblättern des finnischen Medizinalrats*. Hamburg, 1952: Hamburg. [English edition: *The Kersten Memoirs, 1940–1945*. London, 1956: Hutchinson.]

Klein, Peter. *Die Einsatzgruppen in der besetzten Sowjetunion 1941/42. Die Tätigkeits- und Lageberichte des Chefs der Sicherheitspolizei und des SD*. Berlin, 1997: Edition Hentrich.

Knopp, Guido. *Die SS. Eine Warnung der Geschichte*. Munich, 2002: C. Bertelsmann.

Knopp, Guido and Jörg Müllner. 'Heydrichs Herrschaft'. In: Knopp, G. *Die SS. Eine Warnung der Geschichte*. Munich, 2002: C. Bertelsmann.

Koch, Peter-Ferdinand. *Die Geldgeschäfte der SS. Wie deutsche Banken den schwarzen Terror finanzierten*. Reinbek, 2002: Rowohlt.

Krausnick, Helmut. *Hitlers Einsatzgruppen. Die Truppe des Weltanschauungskriegs 1938–1942*. Frankfurt a.M., 1985: Fischer.

Lang, Jochen von. *Die Gestapo. Instrument des Terrors*. Munich, 1993: Heyne.

Lenk, Rudolf. *L'attentat – das Attentat. Prague/Prag le/am 27 Mai 1942*. Hamburg, 1997: Verlag Dr. Kovan (Studien zur Zeitgeschichte, vol. 12).

Lozowick, Yaacov. *Hitlers Bürokraten. Eichmann, seine willigen Vollstrecker und die Banalität des Bösen*. Zurich, 2000: Pendo.

MacDonald, Callum. *The Killing of SS Obergruppenführer Reinhard Heydrich. 27 May 1942*. London: Macmillan 1990.

MacDonald, Callum and Jan Kaplan. *Prague in the Shadow of the Swastika. A History of the German Occupation 1939–1945*. Vienna, 2001: Facultas.

Nanach, Jens. *Heydrichs Elite. Das Führerkorps der Sicherheitspolizei und des SD, 1936–1945*. Paderborn/Munich, 1998: Schöningh.

Naumann, Uwe. *Lidice. Ein böhmisches Dorf.* Frankfurt a.M., 1983: Röderberg.

Norden, Peter. *Salon Kitty. Ein Report.* Munich/Bergisch Gladbaach, 1976: Gustav Lübbe Verlag.

Ogorrek, Ralf. *Die Einsatzgruppen und die 'Genesis der Endlösung'.* Berlin, 1996: Metropol.

Paillard, Georges and Claude Rougerie. *Reinhard Heydrich, protecteur de Bohême et Moravie: le violoniste de la mort.* Paris, 1973: Librairie Arthène.

Pätzold, Kurt. 'Reinhard Heydrich'. In: Pätzold/Schwarz. *Tagesordnung: Judenmord, Die Wannsee-Konferenz am 20. Januar 1942.* Berlin, 1992: Metropol.

Paul, Gerhard and Karl-Michael Mallmann. *Die Gestapo: Mythos und Realität.* Darmstadt, 1996: Primus.

——— *Die Gestapoim Zweiten Weltkreig: 'Heimatfront' und besetztes Europa.* Darmstadt, 2000: Primus.

Peuschel, Harald. *Die Männer um Hitler. Braune Biographien.* Düsseldorf 1982: Droste.

Ramme, Alwin. *Der Sicherheitsdienst der SS. Zu seiner Funktion im faschistischen Machtapparat und im Besatzungsregime des sogenannten Generalgouvernements Polen.* Berlin, 1970: Deutscher Militärverlag.

Reitlinger, Gerald. *The SS: Alibi of a Nation, 1922–1945.* London, 1956: William Heinemann.

Rhodes, Richard. *Masters of Death. The SS-Einsatzgruppen and the Invention of the Holocaust.* New York, 2002: Alfred A. Knopf.

Russell, Stuart and Jost W. Schneider. *Heinrich Himmlers Burg. Das weltanschauliche Zentrum der SS. Bildchronik der SS-Schule Haus Wewelsburgs 1934–1945.* Essen, 1989: Heitz & Höffkes.

Safrian, Hans. *Eichmann und seine Gehilfen.* Frankfurt a.M., 1997: Fischer.

Sakkara, Michele. *L'uomo dal cuore di ferro (Reinhard Heydrich).* Rome, 1993: BEST.

Schneider, Wolfgang. *Die Waffen-SS.* Reinbek, 1998: Rowohlt.

Sigmund, Anna Maria. *Die Frauen der Nazis II.* Vienna, 2000: Überreuter.

Smelser, Roland and Enrico Syring. *Die SS: Elite unter dem Totenkopf. 30 Lebenläufe.* Paderborn, 2000: Ferdinand Schöningh.

Ströbinger, Rudolf. *Das Attentat von Prag. Richard Heydrich. Statthalter Hitlers. Seine Herrschaft und die Hintergründe seines Todes.* Bergisch Gladbach, 1976: Bastei-Lübbe.

Sydnor, Charles W. 'Reinhard Heydrich. Der ideale National-sozialist' in: Smelser, Roland and Enrico Syring. *Die SS. Elite unter dem Totenkopf. 30 Lebenläufe.* Paderborn, 2000.

Sydnor, Charles W. 'Executive Instinct. Reinhard Heydrich and the Planning for the Final Solution'. In: Berenbaum, Michael and Abraham Peck. *The Holocaust and History. The Known, the Unknown, the Disputed and the Reexamined.* Bloomington, 1998: Indiana University Press.

Tuchel, Johannes and Reinold Schattenfroh. *Zentrale des Terrors. Prinz-Albrecht-Straße 8: Hauptquartier der Gestapo.* Berlin, 1987: Siedler.

Wagner, Patrick. *Hitlers Kriminalisten. Die deutsche Kriminalpolizei und der Nationalsozialismus.* Munich, 2002: C.H. Beck.

Whiting, Charles. *Heydrich. Henchman of Death.* Barnsley, Yorks., 1999: Leo Cooper.

Wiener, Jan G. *The Assassination of Heydrich.* New York, 1969: Grossman.

Wildt, Michael. 'Der Hamburger Gestapochef Bruno Streckenbach. Eine nationalsozialistische Karriere'. In: Bajohr, Frank and Joachim Szodrzynski. *Hamburg, in der NS-Zeit.* Hamburg, 1995: Ergebnisse Verlag.

—— *Die Judenpolitik des SD 1935–1938.* Munich, 1995: Schriftenreihe der Vierteljahrszeitschrift für Zeitgeschichte (vol. 71).

—— *Generation des Unbedingten. Das Führungskorps des Reichssicherheitshauptamts.* Hamburg, 2002: Hamburger Edition.

—— *Nachrichtendienst, politische Elite und Mordeinheit. Der Sicherheitsdienst des Reichsführers SS.* Hamburg, 2003: Hamburger Edition.

Wykes, Alan. *Heydrich.* New York, 1973: Ballantine Books.

Documents

Key to sources:
BABL=Bundesarchiv Berlin-Lichterfelde, Abt. III
IMT=International Military Tribunal (Nuremberg War Crimes Tribunals)
NARA=United States National Archives and Records Administration

Auswärtiges Amt, Referat DIIIG. Foreign Office speech notes of Under-Secretary of State Luther for the (later postponed) Conference Regarding the Jews of 8 December 1941.

IMT stenographic partial transcript, Conference on the Jewish Question, chaired by Feldmarschall Goering at the Reich Aviation Office, 12 November 1938 (IMT Document 1816-PS).

Report on RSHA: here Amt III (SD) and Amt IV (Gestapo): (English original at NARA Record Group 319, Box 1, Folder XE 013764).

Reichsführer SS/SS Personal Hauptamt: PA No. H222A. Personal File, Heydrich, Reinhard, SS No. 10120 (BABL) with the following documents: Extract from Career (after death).

Head of Sicherheitspolizei and SD: Letter to Head of SS-Personalhauptamt (SS Main Personnel Office), SS-Gruppenführer Schmitt dated 25 January 1942 with attachment, Goering's letter of 31 July 1941 entitled *Endlösung der Judenfrage* ('Final Solution of the Jewish Question')(BABL).

NSDAP Gau-Leitung Halle-Merseburg: Letter to Gregor Strasser dated 6 June 1932 regarding Heydrich's alleged Jewish ancestry with extract from *Hugo Reimanns Musik Lexicon*, 1916. (BABL)

NS-Auskunft (Gehrke): Letter to Reichsorganisationsabteilung dated 22 June 1932 containing an 'Opinion on the Racial Origins of former Oberleutnant zur See Reinhard Heydrich' and an *Ahnenliste* (genealogy).

Reichsführer-SS file note to NSDAP-Gauleitung Hamburg, dated 5 October 1931, regarding Heydrich's Party membership.

Deutsches Kriminalpolizeiblatt (German Criminal Police Gazette) of 28 May 1942 and 2 June 1942: Hue and Cry following Murder Attempt on Heydrich.

Hauptamt Sicherheitspolizei (Documents from Instytut Pameici Norodwej (Institute of National Remembrance), Warsaw, Microfilm No. 362, signature 1-9): Activity Report on the *Einsatzgruppen* in Poland (Operation *Tannenberg*) of 6, 7, 14, 16 and 17 September 1939.

Heydrich, Reinhard. (From 1934 under heading 'Der Chef der Sicherheitspolizei und des SD'):

Letter to Commissioner Kurt Daluege, 5 March 1933.

Urgent telegram dated 9 November 1938 containing orders to all State Police (Stapo) centres and stations: *Massnahmen gegen Juden in der heutigen Nacht* ('Measures against Jews Tonight') (IMT document 3051-PS).

Express mail dated 11 November 1938 to Ministerpräsident Goering: *Aktion gegen die Juden* (Operation against the Jews) (IMT document 3058-PS).

Express mail dated 30 January 1939 to Foreign Minister von Ribbentrop: *Die Reichszentrale für jüdische Auswanderung* (The Reich Centre for Jewish Emigration).

Advice regarding his temporary absence from Berlin, 1 September 1939.

Express mail dated 21 September 1939 to the heads of all Sicherheitspolizei *Einsatzgruppen*: *Judenfrage im besetzten Gebiet* ('The Jewish Question in the Occupied Territories') (Copy) Israeli Police document No. 775.

Letter dated 21 January 1940 to Daleuge regarding the work session of 20 January 1940.

Letter dated 24 June 1940 to Foreign Minister von Ribbentrop on Jewish emigration (Copy Pol XII 136).

Letter dated 14 October 1940 to Foreign Office Under-Secretary of State Luther on expulsion of Jews from Baden.

Letter of 31 December 1940 to Schmitt, Head of SS-Personnel Office regarding affiliation of Malsen-Ponickau, Schmitt's reply of 22 February 1941: also letter to Schmitt dated 11 February 1941 on problems of promotion.

Under letter heading 'Reichsminister of the Interior': Letter dated 21 November 1941 to Foreign Minister von Ribbentrop: *Kennzeichnung der Juden* (Outward Identification of Jews).

Express mail dated 19 October 1941 to Reichsführer-SS Himmler: *Einweisung von Juden aus dem Altreich in das Ghetto Litzmannstadt* (Installation of Jews from the Old Reich into the Litzmannstadt Ghetto).

Letter dated 8 January 1942 to Foreign Office Under-Secretary of State Luther regarding the postponement of the (later) Wannsee Conference.

Report No. 9 dated 27 February 1942 (extracts) regarding the activities of *Einsatzgruppen* in the USSR (IMT document 3876-PS corresponding to document in evidence US-808).

Heydrich, Lina: Letter dated 15 June 1942 to SS-Führer Richard Hildebrandt.

Ohlendorf, Otto: Affidavit regarding massacres by *Einsatzgruppen* (IMT document 2620-PS).

SS-RSHA:

List of Participants and Agenda for the Conference on the Jewish Question, Berlin, 30 January 1940 (Wilhelmstrasse) (Israeli Police document No. 468).

Notes from the Conference of 10 October 1941 *Uber die Lösung von Judenfragen* (Regarding the Solution of Jewish Questions)(Israeli Police Document No. 1193).

This is a revised bibliography. The original version can be seen in *Heydrich: Das Gesicht des Bösen*, Mario R. Dederichs. Piper Verlag GmbH, Munich, 2005.

Index

Adenauer, Konrad, 181
Amen, John Harlan, 179–80
Anspach, Paul, 132
Arendt, Hannah, 184
Aronson, Shlomo, 15, 33, 35, 43, 56
assassination of RH, *see under* Heydrich,
    Reinhard
Ausborn, Arno, 175–6
Auschwitz death camp, 115, 134, 138, 159,
    164, 178, 185
Auschwitz II, 115
Austria, 82, 88

Baatz, Bernhard, 183
Babi Yar, 108, 110–11, 113, 158
Bach-Zelewski, Erich von dem, 151
Bacher, 155
Bad Godesberg, 70
Bad Kreuznach, 131, 139
Bad Wiessee, 72
Bad Wittekind, 28
Balti, 116
Baltic States, 90, 108
Balzac, Honoré de, 102
Baranowice, 109–10
Barcelona, 36

Barth, Karl, 187
Basletta, Giulio, 133
Bavarian Interior Ministry, 51
Bayreuth, 26
Bayrische Volkspartei, 63
Beck, Ludwig, 103, 105
Beethoven, Ludwig van, 150
Behrends, Hermann, 40
Belzec death camp, 118, 134, 138
Benes, Eduard, 158
Benn, Gottfried, 187
Belgium, 132
Berlin: Document Centre (Bundesarchiv,
    Lichterfeld), 12; Himmler and RH
    move to, 62; Prinz-Albrecht-Strasse, 66,
    69, 70–1, 76–7, 129; Reichstag fire, 60;
    RH's funeral, 148–50; RH's grave,
    176–7; 'Salon Kitty', 129–30; torchlight
    procession in 1933, 57; Werneuchen
    aerodrome, 116; *see also* Wannsee
    Conference
Best, Werner, 92, 99–100, 146, 165, 169,
    182
Beucke, Heinrich, 34–5
Beutel, Lothar, 104
Beyer, Marte, *see* Heydrich, Marte

Bialystok, 109–10
Biansk, 134
Biberstein, Ernst, 181
Birnbaum, Johanna, *see* Heidrich, Johanna
Blobel, Paul, 111, 138, 181
Blomberg, Werner von, 81
Boden, Margarete, *see* Himmler, Margarete
Bohemia and Moravia, *see* Czechoslovakia
Böhme, Horst, 151, 152
Bormann, Martin, 123, 127
Brandstädtler, Fritz, 165
Brandt, Karl, 145
Brauchitsch, Walther von, 111–12
Braune, Werner, 181
Brecht, Bertolt, 158
Breitscheid, Rudolf, 49
Brissaud, André, 43
Browning, Christopher R., 134, 137
Buchenwald concentration camp, 62, 178
Bülow, Hans von, 24
Burckhardt, Carl Jacob, 73–4, 76–7
Burgess, Alan, 16

Canaris, Erika, 35
Canaris, Wilhelm, 35–6, 38, 133
Chelmno death camp, 115
Ciano, Galeazzo, 130
Communists, Communism: and first con-
    centration camps, 60–2; and
    Einsatzgruppen, 108; and Jews, in *Mein
    Kampf*, 38; occupy Halle, 30–2; as oppo-
    nents of the NSDAP, 46; Reichstag fire,
    60; RH in street fighting with, 48; RH
    on 'eastern Jews', 93; RH uses Müller's
    expertise in, 63–5; siege of Halle, 32–3;
    'swing fans' sent to, 128–9; *see also* KPD
concentration camps: control of Dachau
    passed to SS, 61; after the *Anschluss*, 82;
    International Red Cross inspection,
    73–4; and *Schutzhaft*, 15, 61
Cracow, 93, 119
Crankshaw, Edward, 43
Curda, Karel, 152, 154

Czechoslovakia: assassination of RH,
    141–4; death of RH's killers, 152–5; exe-
    cution of Elias, 151; Government-in-
    Exile, 123, 124, 143, 158; reprisals for
    death of RH, 151–2, 155–8; RH crowns
    himself in Prague, 121–2; RH declares
    state of emergency, 125; RH's speech
    stiffens resistance, 126–7; trial of Elias,
    123

Dachau concentration camp, 61–2, 72
Dalnik, 108
Daluege, Kurt, 60, 71, 77, 150, 170
Daniels, Herbert E., 130
DDR, 181
death camps: Aktion Reinhard, 159; clear-
    ing of traces of graves, 138–9; execu-
    tion of commandants, 181; in opera-
    tion before Wannsee Conference, 134;
    replace Einsatzgruppen, 15; *see also*
    Auschwitz; Belzec; Chelmno;
    Maidanek; Sobibor; Treblinka
Demps, Laurenz, 176
Descher, 169
Deschner, Günther, 43, 146
Deumling, Joachim, 183
Deuxième Bureau (French intelligence), 53
Dick, Walter, 143–4
Diels, Rudolf, 63, 67
Dietrich, Sepp, 70
DNVP (Deutsch-Nationale Volkspartei), 57
Dönitz, Karl, 177
Dniepropetrovsk, 108
Dresden: Conservatory, 24, 45, 56; SD, 70
Düsseldorf, 82–3

Eckart, Dieter, 33
Eckart, Karl Graf du Moulin, 53
Eberstein, Elise Baroness von, 23, 45
Eberstein, Friedrich Karl Freiherr von, 33,
    37–8, 40, 45, 70
Edrich, Viktoria, 52
Ehrensberger, 155

Eichberger, Josef, 24
Eichmann, Adolf: appointed head of Amt
    IV D4 (B4), 91; on atmosphere at
    Wannsee Conference, 135; at Dachau,
    61; and Madagascar solution, 92; pre-
    pares agenda for Wannsee, 134–5; on
    RH relaxing after Wannsee, 137; at
    Vienna Emigration Centre, 88; told by
    RH of the Final Solution, 118; trial in
    Jerusalem, 184–5
Eicke, Theodor, 61–2, 72, 77
Einsatzgruppen: actions in USSR, 98, 134;
    addressed by RH, 93; division of labour
    with Wehrmacht, 111–13; formation of
    by RH, 90; and Führer-Order to shoot
    Jews, 94; leaders, 93; massacres, 108–11;
    in Poland, 15, 100, 134; operate mobile
    gassing chambers, 115; post-war trials,
    95–6, 97; replaced by fixed concentra-
    tion camps, 15; RH continually updated
    with reports, 108; RSHA's involvement
    with ignored at Nuremberg, 179; in
    Russia, 102, 105; trial of Ohlendorf,
    179–80; trial of Streckenbach, 182
Elias, Alois, 123–4, 127, 151
Epp, Franz Ritter von, 59–60
euthanasia programme, 104–5
Eutin, 39

Federal Republic of Germany, 172, 174,
    181–2
Fehmarn Island, 40, 51, 161, 169, 172,
    173–4, 176, 187
Fenelon, Rob, 177
Fest, Joachim, 83
Flachowsky, Karin, 56
Fraenkel, Heinz, 46, 48
Frank, Hans, 119, 133, 179
Frank, Karl Hermann, 150, 151, 161, 170
Frass, Georg, 132
freemasons, 30, 46, 74, 76, 99, 100
Freikorps, 30–3, 35, 47
Freund, Michael, 16, 172

Frick, Wilhelm, 56
Friedman, Tuviah, 189
Friedrich, Jörg, 183
Fritsch, Werner von, 81–2
Fromm, Bella, 73
Fromm, Erich, 146

Gabcik, Jozef, 141–3, 153
gassing: exhaust gassing in stable chambers,
    106, 114; mobile gassing chambers,
    114–15, 138; Zyklon B used at
    Auschwitz, 115, 134
Gebhardt, Karl, 144
General-Gouvernement, 90
Gercke, Achim, 54–5
Gereke, Günther, 35
Gestapo (Geheime Staatspolizei): arrest of
    Kopecky, 155–8; declared an 'illegal
    organisation' at Nuremberg, 179; in
    Düsseldorf, 82–3; Goering and, 62; the
    Fritsch affair, 81–2; Himmler replaces
    Diels, 67; lead actions on
    Reichskristallnacht, 86–7; kill RH's
    killers, 153–4; Müller's role in, 63–6; in
    Prague, 125; subsumed into RSHA, 15;
    see also RSHA
Gildisch, Kurt, 71–2
Gisevius, Hans Bernd, 67, 103–4
Gleiwitz, 89
Globocnik, Odilo, 118, 158
Goebbels: anti-Weimar sentiment, 49; on
    genocide, 138; praises RH's work in the
    Protectorate, 127–8; relations with
    Hitler, 48; RH's knowledge of dal-
    liances, 79; on RH's political acumen,
    123; RH's regard for, 86–7
Goerdeler, Carl Friedrich, 103
Goering, Hermann: cedes control of
    Prussian political police to Himmler,
    62; as conduit to Hitler, 122; and dam-
    age on Reichskristallnacht, 87–8; in first
    Hitler Cabinet, 56; at Nuremberg War
    Crimes Trial, 72, 179; orders RH to

present plan for Final Solution, 118; relations with Hitler, 48; RH's knowledge of morphine habit, 79–80; RH submits draft for 'Solution of Jewish Question', 117–18; unable to silence Klausener, 71

Goering, Ilsa, 73

Goldhagen, Daniel, 185

Gollwitzer, Helmut, 187

Gorazd, Bishop of Prague, 153, 154–5

Gmund, 48

GPU (Soviet intelligence), 53, 62

Great Britain: and assassination of RH, 141, 143, 151, 173; and dropping of Madagascar plan, 92; Hitler orders killing of POWs, 107; RH's copying of 'C' moniker, 52

Greater German Freedom Movement, 47

Griebel, Rita, 171

Grodno, 108

Grünel, Maria, 71

Grunwald, Walter, 164

Grynszpan, Herschel, 86

Haasis, Hellmut G., 145–6

Hacha, Emil, 121, 124, 151

Halder, Generaloberst Franz, 112

Halle, 21; communist siege, 32–3; Conservatory, 25–7, 30, 41, 44, 139; occupied by communist insurgents, 30–2; Royal Reform High School, 28, 30, 33

Hamburg, 128–9; Institute for Social Research, 111, 183

Händel, Georg Friedrich, 21, 33

Hanseatic Yachting School, 39

Hansen, Gottfried, 42

Heiden, Erhard, 47

Heidrich, Johanna (née Birnbaum), 56

Heidrich, Johann Gottfried, 56

Heindorf, Maria, see Heydrich, Maria

Heindorf, Wolfgang, 44

Henlein, Konrad, 127

Held, Heinrich, 59

Hess, Rudolf, 177

Hey, Julius, 25

Heydrich, Bruno: concert in memory of, 139; curriculum vitae, 24–6; debts, 56; and Halle Conservatory, 25–7; heart attack, 45; loyalty to Kaiser, 28; neutral towards Jews, 38; RH's veneration for, 27–8; and 'Süss' entry, 37, 54; sings at RH's marriage, 51; as a Wagnerian, 22, 23, 25, 26, 27

Heydrich, Carl Julius Reinhold, 37, 38

Heydrich, Elisabeth (née Krantz), 22–3, 44–5, 75

Heydrich, Ernestine Wilhelmine (née Lindner), 37, 54

Heydrich, Gertrud (née Werther), 44, 166

Heydrich, Heider, 168, 169, 170, 187, 188

Heydrich, Klaus, 72, 147, 161–2, 168

Heydrich, Lina: applies for pension, 16–17; awarded pension, 172–3; death, 176; declines Hitler's offer of Jungfern-Breschan, 162; defends RH, 174–5; denazification, 169–71, 174; on effect of Jewish policy, 167; first meets RH at Kiel, 40–1; and Karel Kaspar, 147, 168; knowledge of RH's infidelity, 77; life at Jungfern-Breschan, 139, 166–8; marriage to RH, 51–2; personality, 163, 164; remarries, 174; return to Fehmarn, 169; and RH's introduction to Himmler, 45; on RH's isolation, 79; RH's last words to, 161; RH's marriage proposal, 41; on RH's personality, 145; on RH's relationship with the Church, 75–6; on RH's relationship with Nebe, 104; on RH's street fighting, 48; RH telephones for pistol, 59; use of slave labour in Jungfern-Breschan, 163–4, 171; her version of Reichskristallnacht, 85–6

Heydrich, Maria (Maria Heindorf), 22, 44

Heydrich, Marte (Marte Beyer), 168, 169, 187–8

Heydrich, Peter Thomas, 165–6, 186–7, 189
Heydrich, Reinhard
  ancestry
    Bruno Heydrich and 'Süss' entry, 37,
    54; entry on RH's file card, 13; Gercke's
    swift settling of the debate, 54–5; hires
    private genealogist, 55; used by his
    superiors, 55, 68
  assassination and aftermath
    as 'blood sacrifice', 14; curse of King
    Wenceslaus, 121–2, 147; death, 144;
    death mask, 174; Gabcik and Kubis's
    attack, 141–2; grave in Berlin, 176–7;
    infection to RH's wound in Bulovka hos-
    pital, 143–4; last words, 161; and Lina
    Heydrich's pension, 172–3; memorial
    on hairpin bend, 150; Nebe at death-
    watch, 107, 148; significance of, 17;
    State Funeral, 147–50
  childhood and youth
    birth, 22; choice of name, 22; at Halle
    Royal Reform High School, 28, 30, 33;
    inflammation of the brain, 22–3;
    obtains *Abitur*, 33; serves with Halle
    Technische Nothilfe, 32–3
  and the Church: leaves, 170; Lisa
    Heydrich and his anti-Catholicism,
    74–5; and mourning after RH's death,
    148; orders killing of Klausener, 71–2;
    Nazi declaration of faith, 13
  and Himmler
    conference with Held, 59; first meeting
    with, 45–6; impresses, 45, 50; irreplace-
    ability of RH to, 18, 49, 67; RH forbids
    Himmler to use 'du', 79; RH's subordi-
    nation to, 55, 68–9, 77, 123; visit
    Einsatzgruppen in Grodno, 108
  and the Jews: as chief architect of the
    Holocaust, 117; demands alternative to
    shooting, 113–14; on 'more perfect
    ways' of killing, 137–8; on need for ter-
    ritorial Final Solution, 92; ordered by
    Goering to present plan for Final
    Solution, 118; his orders on
    Reichskristallnacht, 88; orders shooting
    of Jews, 93, 94; on Paris synagogue
    attacks, 133; recommends creation of
    Reich Centre for Jewish Emigration, 88;
    recommends wearing of badge, 88; the-
    ory of freemasons as 'instruments of
    revenge', 76; watches film of mass
    shooting, 113–14
  and Lina Heydrich: first meeting at Kiel,
    40–1; last words to, 161; marriage, 51;
    marriage proposal, 41
  military career
    as air-gunner in Poland, 116; as an avia-
    tor, 18; banned from flying by
    Himmler, 117; discharged from
    Reichsmarine, 43–4, 79; enters
    Reichsmarine, 33; Freikorps, 30–3; joins
    signals officer branch, 36; with North
    Sea fleet at Wilhelmshaven, 35; officer
    training at Mürwik Naval College, 34;
    solo flights over Holland, Moldavia and
    Norway in Me 109, 116–17
  and the NSDAP
    ambition to be 'First Man of German
    Reich', 139; endorses their racial theo-
    ries, 17, 125–6; the Church as threat to,
    75; influence on RH of early Freikorps
    experience, 33; joins in 1931, 45; RH as
    ideal Nazi, 18, 177; RH's youthful
    nationalism, 39–40; on SS as 'assault
    troop' of the party, 69
  personal relations: with Canaris, 133;
    Daluege refuses to receive RH, 60; with
    Goebbels, 86–7; with Müller, 63–5; with
    Nebe, 104; with Six, 99–100
  personality
    appearance, 11–12, 73; arrogance, 23,
    42; attention to detail, 128; brutality,
    16–18; bullied, 34–5; as a childhood
    outsider, 23; coldness, 67, 78, 83; death
    wish, 145; as described to pension tri-
    bunal, 16–17; dual personality, 19, 35,
    77; energy, 18; harshness, 146; instinct
    for people, 50, 79; lack of friends,

78–9; memory, 79; music, 19, 22–8, 35; observation of rules of sport, 133; recklessness, 140, 145, 150; smokes and drinks after Wannsee Conference, 137; voice, 28, 34
police and SS career
affectation of 'C' moniker, 53; card-index system, 13, 51, 52, 53, 70, 79; his concept of a centralised police force, 62, 74; considers introducing his Prague methods into France, 139; creation of RSHA, 15, 90; eavesdropping and 'Salon Kitty', 129–30; escapes posthumous condemnation at Nuremberg, 178–9; execution of Hamburg 'swing fans', 128–9; forms SD, 50–1; forms Einsatzgruppen, 90; the Fritsch affair, 81–2; at Gestapo HQ during the 'Night of the Long Knives', 70–1; head of Gestapo office, 63; head of International Criminal Police Commission, 83; Heinz Heydrich receives RH's files, 166; joins SS as Untersturmführer, 48; named as 'Chief of the SD at Reichsführer-SS', 52; promoted to SS-Gruppenführer, 73; promoted to SS-Sturmbannführer, 50–1; RH's own file card, 12–14; RH's knowledge of leaders' secrets, 79–80; street fighting with Communists, 48; takes over running of Prussian political police, 62
as Reichs-Protektor (Bohemia and Moravia)
compares Czechs to Jews, 125; considers racial problem in the Protectorate, 126–7; crowns himself in Prague, 121–2; and the fate of Elias, 123–4, 127; without bodyguard, 140
sports
awards, 14; fencing, 18, 28, 36, 78, 130–3, 139; flying as a 'sporting' challenge, 115; long-distance running, 36–7; pistol shooting, 36; riding, 18, 28, 36–7,

130, 163; sailing, 28, 36–7, 39; swimming, 28, 36, 130–1; victor of Reich Full Pack March, 130; wins Reich Sport Badge, 123
and women: eavesdropped in 'Salon Kitty', 130; escapades in Berlin, 77–8; as 'irresistable' to, 36; scandal at Kiel, 42
Heydrich, Reinhard (Beyer), 188–9
Heydrich, Siegfried Heinz, 22, 44–5, 56, 165–6
Heydrich, Silke, 139, 168, 169, 187
Hildebrandt, Richard, 51
Himmler, Gebhard, 46
Himmler, Heinrich: as admirer of Hitler, 47–8; as admirer of RH, 122–3; bans RH from flying, 117; comments on Tuchatshevski case, 65; as conduit to Hitler, 122; and depth of Aryan origins, 54; distrusts structure within RSHA, 95; entrusts Globocnik with expansion of death camps, 118; at funeral of Klaus Heydrich, 162; and germanising of Warthegau, 90; first meeting with RH, 45–6; heads Prussian political police, 62; Hitler discusses destruction of Jews with, 119; impressed by RH, 45, 50; irreplaceability of RH to, 18, 49, 67; life sketch, 46–7; on medieval witchcraft trials, 100; nominated Reichsführer-SS, 47; opens Dachau, 61; orders detention of Hamburg 'swing fans', 128; promotes RH to SS-Sturmbannführer, 50–1; his racial brutality, 147; rejects genocide as Bolshevist, 92; at RH's funeral, 147, 149; RH subordinate in his presence, 55, 68; rules on mobile gas lorries, 115; seizure of power in Munich, 59–60; splits power between RH and Wolff, 77; stomach cramps, 80; tours SD on Zuccalistrasse with Röhm, 53; visits Einsatzgruppen in Grodno with RH, 108; visits Lina Heydrich at Jungfern-Breschan, 167–8; visits RH in Bulovka

hospital, 144–5; warns Lina Heydrich over public utterances, 165; witnesses mass shooting, 106

Himmler, Margarete (*née* Boden)

Hindenburg, Paul von, 56–7

Hiss, Mathilde, *see* Osten, Mathilde von

Hitler, Adolf: and the *Anschluss,* 82; anti-Weimar sentiment, 49; arrest and death of Röhm, 72–3; condolences sent to Klaus Heydrich's funeral, 162; curbs Goering's power, 62; and decision for genocide, 134; discusses destruction of Jews with Himmler, 119; effect on, of RH's death, 147; exploits Himmler's devotion, 47–8; first Cabinet, 56–7; Führer-Order to shoot Jews, 94; and Madagascar plan, 91; *Mein Kampf,* 38, 48; and the 'Night of the Long Knives', 69–73; offers Jungfern-Breschan to Lina Heydrich, 162; orders killing of POWs, 107; orders reprisals for RH's death, 150–2; power struggle with Strasser, 49; 'prophecy' of destruction of Jewish race in Europe, 88, 119; rages against RH's recklessness, 150; refuses RH the execution of Elias, 127; on Reichskristallnacht, 86–7; resists RH's insinuations against Raeder, 115; and RH's draft for 'Solution of Jewish Question', 117; at RH's funeral, 149–50; and the 'seizure of power', 56–7; on usefulness of RH's non-Aryan origins, 55; *see also* July 20 1944 plot

Hoffmann, Ernst, 55, 130

Holland, 116

Hollbaum, Walter, 144

Honek, Alois Vincenc, 143–4

Honiok, Franz, 89

Höppner, Rolf-Heinz, 118

Horninger, 50

Hoess, Rudolf, 61, 65

Höttl, Wilhelm, 92

Hunger, Lisa, 169

Husson, Edouard, 133

International Criminal Police Commission, 83

International Red Cross, 73–4

Italy: fascism in, 95

Jäckel, Eberhard, 16, 86, 117

Jacob, Berthold, 80–1

Jeckeln, Fritz, 118

Jehovah's Witnesses, 164

Jerusalem, 136, 184–5

Jews: Austrian, 135; Babi Yar, 110–11; and Bolshevism, 93; 'and Bruno Heydrich, 37–8, 54; Czech, 125, 135; and Einsatzgruppen massacres, 108–15; emigration becomes 'evacuation', 135–7; executions at Kishinyov, 94; expansion of death camps, 118; in fencing, 133; first shootings at Dachau, 61; freemasons as 'instruments of', 76; helped by Heinz Heydrich, 166; Hitler orders Final Solution, 118–19; in 'international science', 99; Lina Heydrich on effect of policy on, 167; Lina Heydrich on RH's relation to, 175; in Luxemburg, 135; *Mein Kampf,* 38; as opponents of the NSDAP, 46; German, 86, 100, 118, 135, 138; Reichskristallnacht, 85–8; Polish, 90; slave labour at Jungfern-Breschan, 163–4; the 'stab in the back' of 1918, 30, 33; wearing of badges, 88; 'World Jewry' conference, 101

John, Karl, 166

Jordan, Rudolf, 53–4

July 20 1944 plot against Hitler, 66, 102–3, 105, 107–8, 174

Kaltenbrunner, Ernst, 66, 107, 179

Kamenez-Podolsk, 108

Kapp, Wolfgang, 32

Kaspar, Karel, 147, 168

Kaufmann, Karl, 51

Kaunas, 118

Keitel, Wilhelm, 90

Kempner, Robert, 79

Kersten, Felix, 55, 67, 78, 80, 130, 145
Kiel, 33, 35, 36, 40, 131; *Landesgericht*, 109
Kishinyov, 94, 111
Kladno, 151–2
Klahn, Karl-Wilhelm, 174
Klausener, Erich, 71–2
Kleikamp, Gustav, 36, 40–1
Klein, Johannes, 18, 142
Klein, Lotte, 18–19
Klüver, Oberstleutnant von, 31
Kopecky, Cyril, 155–8
Kopkow, Horst, 64
KPD (German Communist Party), 48, 50, 64, 83
Krantz, Elisabeth, *see* Heydrich, Elisabeth
Krantz, Georg Eugen, 22, 24, 25
Krantz, Hans, 44
Krantz, Kurt, 44
Kripo, 66, 101
KTI (Criminal Technical Unit), 104, 106
Kubis, Jan, 141–3, 153
Kurhesse, 87

Lammers, Hans, 162
Landsberg War Crimes Tribunal, 95–6, 97, 98, 101–2
Lauck, Gerhard, 178
Lebram, Hans Heinrich, 34, 36, 38
Leipzig, 49
Leuben, 24
Lezaky, 152
Lichner, Maria Rosine, 56
Lichtenstein, Abraham, 38
Lidice, 151–2, 158
Lindner, Ernestine Wilhelmine, *see* Heydrich, Ernestine Wilhelmine
Lippert, Michael, 72
Lithuania, 108
Lochhausen, 52
Lodz, 118, 135, 152
Losert, Josef, 132
Lublin, 100, 118
Lubny, 113

Luckner, Felix Graf von, 29, 34
Ludendorff, Erich, 40
Lüdicke, Julius Hermann, 23
Ludwig, Wilhelm, 175
Lucius, Major, 30, 32
Luftwafffe, 116–17
Lüng, Pidder, 49
Luther, Martin, 91
Lütjenbrode, 40–1, 50
Luxemburg, 135

McCloy, John, 181
Madagascar, 91
Madeira, 36
Maercker, Georg, 31–2
Maidanek death camp, 118, 134
Maly Trostinez death camp, 134
Malz, Heinrich, 183
Mann, Heinrich, 158
Mann, Thomas, 61, 155–6
Manninen, Lina, *see* Heydrich, Lina
Manninen, Mauno, 174
Manstein, Erich von, 113
Manvell, Roger, 46, 48
Maser, Werner, 175
Massmann, Wilhelm, 171
Mattner, Walter, 111
Mauthausen concentration camp, 82, 155
Mehlhorn, Herbert, 53, 89
Meinicke-Pusch, Waldemar, 173
Meisinger, Josef, 81
Mengele, Josef, 159
Mennecke, Dr Fritz, 83
MI6, 53
Minsk, 83, 106, 108, 113, 118
Mogilov, 106, 111, 115
Mohr, Werner, 39, 45
Moldavia, 96, 108, 116
Moravec, Emanuel, 153
Moringen youth concentration camp, 129
Mossad, 184
Müller, Heinrich: brutality, 103; as Communist expert, 62; involvement in

Polish border incident, 89; orders on Reichskristallnacht, 87; relations with RH, 63–5; RH plays Nebe against, 104
Mundschütz, Martin, 96
Munich: Beerhall putsch, 38, 47, 86; Das Braune Haus, 50–1, 54, 59
Mürwik Naval College, 34, 39
Musmanno, Michael, 98
Mussolini, Benito, 91

Naude, Horst, 78
Naujocks, Alfred, 89
Naumann, Erich, 181
Nebe, Arthur: appointed Einsatzgruppen head, 93; death, 181; and exhaust gassing experiments, 106, 114; head of Kripo, 101, 103–4; and killing of British POWs, 107; July 20 bomb plot, 102–3, 105, 107–8, 181; recruits for 'Salon Kitty', 129; relationship with RH, 104; at RH's deathwatch, 107, 148; weeds personnel from the Gestapo, 66
Neu-Babelsberg, 71
Neuengamme concentration camp, 83
Neurath, Konstantin Freiherr von, 122, 123, 163
'Night of the Long Knives', 69–73
Novgorod, 109
Norden, H. H., 177–8
Norway, 116
Noske, Gustav, 31
NSDAP: as alternative in Weimar Republic, 38–9; Himmler joins, 47; Ohlendorf joins, 94; RH joins in 1931, 45; struggle between Hitler and Strasser, 49
Nuremberg War Crimes Trials, 17, 62, 72, 178–81

Oberg, Carl, 53
Oberstein, Friedrich Carl von, 28
Odessa, 108
Ohlendorf, Otto: appointed Einsatzgruppen head, 93; blames Führer-Order, 97; cross-examination at

Nuremberg, 179–80; as head of Inland-SD, 95; massacre at Simferopol, 113; sentenced to death, 181; studies fascism in Italy, 95; trial, 95–6, 97; tries to resign from SD, 95
Opalka, Adolf, 153
Oppenheim, Alfred, 82–3
Oppenheim, Martha, 83
Opus pro smrtihlava, 11
Osten, Hans von, 176
Osten, Jürgen von, 40, 41, 169
Osten, Klaus von, 176
Osten, Lina von, see Heydrich, Lina
Osten, Mathilde von, 41, 169
Oster, Hans, 103
Ott, Adolf, 181

Paillard, Georges, 43
Papen, Franz von, 56–7
Paris, 133, 137
Patzan, Panitzer von, 129
Petrek, Vladimir, 153, 154–5
Plötzensee, 102
Pohl, Dieter, 158
Pohl, Oswald, 77, 133
Poland: 'border incident' and invasion, 89–90; Einsatzgruppen in, 15, 100
Prague, 121–3, 125, 127, 135, 141–5, 148, 150; People's Special Court, 170; Schloss Jungfern-Breschan, 139, 161–4, 166, 168, 171
Prast, Otto-Ernst, 117
Pretsch, 93
Priem, Arnulf, 178
Protivin, 155

Rademacher, Franz, 91
Raeder, Erich, 42, 43, 115
Rasch, Otto, 180
Rath, Ernst von, 86
Rau, Johannes, 185–6
Raubal, Geli, 79
Ravensbrück concentration camp, 62, 152
Rendsburg Kolonial Frauenschule, 42, 43

Reich Centre for Jewish Emigration, 88
Reichenau, Generalfeldmarschall Walter von, 112
Reichskristallnacht, 85–8, 101
Reichsmarine, 33–7, 39–45
Ribbentrop, Joachim von, 80
Ricardi, Hans-Günter, 61
Riemann, Hugo, 37, 54
Riga, 108, 118, 158
Röhm, Ernst, 45, 53, 59, 70, 72–3, 79
Rosenberg, Alfred, 133
Rottach-Egern, 168
Rougerie, Claude, 43
Rovno, 108
RSHA (Reichssicherheitshauptamt): Amt II, 65; Amt III, 65; Amt IV, 65; Amt IV B4 (D4), 91, 134, 184; Amt IV D2, 183; Amt V, 102, 103; Amt VII, 98, 99; and Einsatzgruppen, 15; formation of, 15, 90, 99; Himmler distrusts structure within, 95; and Interior Ministry, 136; issue invitations to Wannsee Conference, 119; not mentioned at Nuremberg War Crimes Trial, 179; post-war careers of officials, 183–4; subsumes the Gestapo and SD, 15
Rumania, 111

SA (Sturmabteilung): intelligence service as rival to SD, 53; and the 'Night of the Long Knives', 69–73; plays no further role, 73; SS subsumed within, 47
Sachs, Willy, 170, 172
Sachsenhausen concentration camp, 62, 89
Safrian, Hans, 185
Sakkara, Michele, 174
Schäfer, Emanuel, 89
Scharfe, Gustav, 24
Schellenberg, Walter, 63, 77–9, 82, 92, 122, 129–30, 139
Schillung, Gertrud, 168
Schirmböck, Georg, 117
Schleicher, Elisabeth von, 71
Schleicher, Kurt von, 71

Schleswig-Holstein, 172
Schmid, Wilhelm, 72
Schmid, Willi, 72
Schmidt, Dr Johannes, 53, 71
Schmidt, Otto, 81–2
Schmitt, Paul, 72
Schulz, Karl, 183
Schulz-Dornburg, Richard, 25
Schutzhaft, 15, 61, 90
SD (Sicherheitsdienst): and the *Anschluss*, 82; average age of leaders, 74; declared an 'illegal organisation' at Nuremberg, 179; as the elite of the elite, 53, 93; formation of, in 1931, 49, 50–1; independence from SS within SA, 53; involvement in Tuchatshevski case, 64–5; kidnap Berthold Jacob, 80–1; murders in White Russia, 113; Ohlendorf joins, 95; and Polish border incident, 89; recruitment, 52–3; 'Reports for the Reich', 80; RH characterises work of, 83; RH named as 'Chief of the SD at Reichsführer-SS', 52; run Chelmno death camp, 115; Six in charge of *Gegnerforschung*, 99; as sole organ of NSDAP intelligence, 63; subsumed into RSHA, 15; *see also* RSHA
Seetzen, Heinz, 117
Sereny, Gitta, 187
Simferopol, 113
Sierk, Douglas Detlef, 158
Sipo (Sicherheitspolizei): and grouping of Jews into ghettoes, 91; Heydrich appointed chief, 74; murders in White Russia, 113; and unwritten orders for Final Solution, 118; within RSHA, 90
Six, Franz: appointed Einsatzgruppen head, 93; imprisoned after war, 181; as leader of Vorkommando Moskau, 98, 100–1; maltreated by RH, 99–100; surprise at terror in USSR, 97–8; trial, 101–2
Sladek, 156
Smolensk, 98, 101
Sobibor death camp, 118

Sommer, Paul, 133
SPD (German Socialist Party), 48–9
Speer, Albert, 122, 140, 148, 165
SS (Schutzstaffel): control Dachau, 61; declared an 'illegal organisation' at Nuremberg, 179; as growth of, as guard unit within SA, 47; Himmler on need for racial hardness, 147; murders in Poland early in war, 90; relation to SD, 52–3; RH on role of, 69; search for Nachrichtenmann leads to RH, 45; Totenkopfverband units, 61; victory over SA, 73
Stahlecker, Walther, 118, 180–1
Stahlhelm, 40, 57
Stalag Luft III, 107
Stalin, Josef, 62
Stavanger, 116
Stein, Milan Platovsky, 164
Strasser, Gregor, 47, 49, 53–4, 70–1
Strauch, Eduard, 181
Streckenbach, Bruno, 93, 182
Stuckart, Wilhelm, 136
Sudetenland, 88
Süss, Ehregott, 37
Süss, Ernestine Wilhelmine, *see* Heydrich, Ernestine Wilhelmine
Süss, Gustav Robert, 37, 54
Süss, Marie Rosine (*née* Stegedly), 37
Svarc, Jaroslav, 153
Sydnor, Charles W., 17–18, 43, 49, 139

Tabor, 156
Theresienstadt concentration camp, 125, 163–4
Thomsen, Harro, 183
Thule Gesellschaft, 33
Todt, Fritz, 150
Treblinka death camp, 115, 118, 185
Trotha, Adolf von, 39
Tuchatshevski, Mikhail, 64–5

Uckermark youth concentration camp, 129
Udet, Ernst, 116–17

Ukraine, 96, 108–11, 113
United States of America: Madagascar, and hostages against, 91
USSR: Einsatzgruppen in, 15, 102, 105–6, 108–11

Valcik, Josef, 141–2, 153
Vanek, Ladislav, 158
Versailles, Treaty of, 33–4, 39, 88
Vienna Emigration Centre, 88
Vilna, 108
Vitebsk, 108
Völkischer Schutz-und Trutzebund, 33
Volkspartei, 94
Vorel, Hana, 155–8
Vovsova, Helena, 102–3, 168

Wagner, Adolf, 70
Wagner, Cosima, 26
Wagner, Richard: Bruno Heydrich's taste for, 22, 23, 25–7; inspiration of *Tristan und Isolde* for RH's name, 22; marriage, 25; music at RH's funeral, 149
Wagnitz, Herbert, 168
Waldtrudering, 45, 48
Wannsee Conference: confirms genocide in writing, 15, 135; euphemisms at, 136–7; and Holocaust denial, 177–8; Luther as advocate of Madagascar solution, 91; as official policy, 137; RH as chief talker at, 134; State Secretaries invited to, 119
Warthegau, 90
Wehner, Dr Bernhard, 105
Wehrmacht: absence of, from Wannsee Conference, 134; appalled by SS brutality, 90; arrest Anspach, 132; atmosphere at, 135–6; Canaris speaks out on behalf of, 133; support Einsatzgruppen killings, 108, 111–13
Weimar Republic, 38–9, 49, 53, 65
Wenceslaus, King, 121, 125, 147
Werther, Gertrud, *see* Heydrich, Gertrud
Wessel, Horst, 177
Wiasma, 134

INDEX

Widmann, Dr Albert, 104, 106
Wiedemann, Hans-Georg, 187
Wiepert, Peter, 40
Wiesel, Elie, 178
Wildt, Michael, 91, 183
Wilhelm II, Kaiser, 28, 30
Wilhelmshaven, 35, 40
Wischnewski, Ingo, 189
Wischnewski, Silke, *see* Heydrich, Silke

Wohlhynien, 90
Wolff, Frieda, 168
Wolff, Karl, 77, 168
Wüllner, Franz, 24
Wünsdorf, 37

Zapp, Paul, 111
Zenetti, Leopold von, 170
Zirpins, Walter, 183